For Bob –
With all good wishes,
James I. Robertson, Jr.

9.30.06

THE STONEWALL BRIGADE

THE
STONEWALL
BRIGADE

JAMES I. ROBERTSON, JR.

LOUISIANA STATE UNIVERSITY PRESS
Baton Rouge

|||||||||||||||||||||||||||||||||||||||||||||||||||||||||||||||||||||||||||||||||||||||||||||||||||||||||||||||||||||

FOREWORD

Civil War battles are popularly recounted as one army pitting its strength against another at a given place and time. Basically this is true, but detailed studies of military operations indicate that an army seldom functioned as an entity. In a sense, an army was a loose confederation of strong component parts, each with its own duties, positions—and independence. Orders for battle were usually issued to divisions, but the basic attacking units were not divisions as a whole. Rather, they were the three or more brigades composing each division. When an assault took place, the division normally attacked in columns of brigades, each 150 to 300 yards behind the other.[1]

---

1. The division was the basic unit in the organization and administration of the army in the field. Its size precluded its participation in battle as a unified command.

A brigade was in effect a modern task force, quite capable of working independently of other units. Its freedom of movement and action came from its composition. Before 1860 the accepted definition of a brigade was "two or more regiments of infantry or cavalry, or both, under the command of a brigadier-general." [2] In Civil War practice, however, such a combination rarely if ever existed. [3] Normally an infantry brigade consisted of four or five regiments (from the same state, in the case of the South) supported by a battery of four to six artillery pieces. Each brigade had a distinctive and independent position in the column, with the infantry trudging four abreast in front followed by lines of artillery, supply wagons, and ambulances. When camp was pitched, each brigade was assigned its own site. A brigade staff generally consisted of an assistant adjutant general, quartermaster, commissary officer, ordnance officer, surgeon, and such aides-de-camp as the brigadier deemed necessary. This composition gave the brigade, even on the command level, an air of independence.

In short, therefore, the brigade was the fundamental fighting unit of the army.

One of the most famous brigades in American history—and certainly the most renowned in Confederate military history—initially was known as Virginia's First Brigade. In time it officially and popularly was called the Stonewall Brigade. It and its first commander, Thomas J. Jackson, received their nicknames simultaneously at the baptism at First Manassas. Cherished by its namesake, and serving with him until his death, the brigade achieved a reputation almost without parallel for agility, gallantry, and pugnacity. The best-known American novelist who fought for the Confederacy, John Esten Cooke, was so certain the brigade had no equal that he once wrote of it:

Army Regulations, Adopted for the Use of the Army of the Confederate States (Atlanta, 1861), 59. See also Department of the Army, *American Military History, 1607–1953* (Washington, 1956), 234.

2. William Gilham, *Manual of Instruction for the Volunteers and Militia of the Confederate States* (Richmond, 1862), xvi.

3. One manual of arms stated that cavalry and infantry were not even to march together "unless the proximity of the enemy makes it necessary." *Army Regulations,* 85.

The Old Stonewall Brigade! What a host of thoughts, memories and emotions do these words excite! How like a call to the charge sounds the simple mention of the famous band! These veterans have fought and bled and conquered on so many battlefields, that memory grows weary almost of recalling their glories . . . The soul of their leader seemed to have entered every breast—and "Stonewall's Band" became the terror of the enemy. To meet the enemy, was to conquer him, it might almost be said, so obstinately did the eagles of victory continue to perch upon the old battleflag. The laws of the human body seemed to have been reversed for these men. They marched, and fought, and triumphed, like war machines which felt no need of rest, or food, or sleep.[4]

Cooke's praise, while somewhat extravagant, expressed the affection felt for the brigade throughout the South, a feeling that to some extent still exists. Whether called "Stonewall's Band," "Jackson's Foot Cavalry," "The Men of Manassas," or the Stonewall Brigade, this organization made an impact on history few units can match. It has been likened to the Macedonian Phalanx of Alexander, the Tenth Legion of Caesar, the Paladines of Charlemagne, the Ironsides of Cromwell, and the Old Guard of Napoleon.[5] Douglas Southall Freeman termed it the Southern Cromwell's "Model Brigade." [6]

They were rough fighters, these men of Stonewall Jackson. Eventually they came to the conviction that they could defeat any given number of Yankees at any time—a conviction amply justified by their war record. They achieved a reputation for invincibility accepted by North and South alike. Confederate troops seemed to grow in confidence if they knew the Stonewall Brigade was charging in an assault with them. Federal soldiers came to feel that the brigade possessed some superhuman power, a quality which they attributed to the unpredictable and mysterious Jackson. A New York prisoner once asked a staff officer of Jackson's: "What sort of man is your Stonewall Jackson anyway? Are his soldiers made of gutta-percha, or do they run on wheels?" [7]

---

4. John Esten Cooke, *Stonewall Jackson and the Old Stonewall Brigade*, edited by Richard Harwell (Charlottesville, 1954), 16–17.
5. *Southern Historical Society Papers*, XL (1915), 158.
6. Douglas Southall Freeman, *Lee's Lieutenants: A Study in Command* (New York, 1942–44), II, 4, 97.
7. Henry Kyd Douglas, *I Rode with Stonewall* (Chapel Hill, 1940), 135.

The dazzling reputation achieved by the brigade stood in marked contrast to the simplicity of its origins. All members were from around the Valley of Virginia. Most were of Scotch-Irish, German, Swedish, or English descent, nurtured in the rustic surroundings of small hillside farms, raised in the wholesome outdoors of an invigorating climate, and by nature hardy, robust, and fun-loving. Little class distinction was to be found among these folk. One veteran of the brigade estimated that not more than one out of thirty of the members owned slaves.[8] Yet they were strongly Virginian in their sentiments; moreover, they were exceedingly clannish in their associations. Partly as a result of their devotion to locale, friends, and family, members of this organization, unlike those of most Civil War units, attached little significance to the regiment to which they belonged. Their pride lay more in their membership in the Stonewall Brigade.

The battle flags of the brigade fluttered amid the smoke of thirty-nine engagements. Its original muster rolls list a total of 2,600 men, and it is reasonable to assume that more than 5,000 served in the unit during the course of the war. Yet at Appomattox only 210 men remained—none above the rank of captain. That Jackson's special affection for the brigade may have been more hazardous than beneficial is suggested by the comment of one of the survivors: "Whenever there was extra hard duty to be performed, General Jackson always sent his old brigade to the post of duty for fear the other brigades under his command would think and say he favored his old command." [9]

The brigade was characterized by a combination of Jackson's iron-cored discipline and a feeling of confidence derived from success. It fought savagely and devotedly, marched long and hard, and only once during the war ever disappointed a commander. On the other hand, it discarded tents and knapsacks, preferring the open bivouacs and the bare necessities in order to lighten its burden on marches. The men served under commanders they did not like, even having the audacity to threaten the murder of one if the

8. Dr. Hunter McGuire, in *Confederate Veteran*, VII (1899), 506.
9. John O. Casler, *Four Years in the Stonewall Brigade* (Guthrie, Okla., 1893), 66. Hereinafter cited as Casler, *Stonewall Brigade*.

Yankees did not oblige them in the next battle. If ordered to cook three days' rations prior to a campaign, they did so willingly—then promptly ate the food rather than carry it with them into action. For experience soon taught these men that they could always secure abundant supplies from the Yankees who were forced to flee before them.

When all was lost at Appomattox, the survivors of the brigade returned home and lived their last days in fond recollection of their war record. Their positions as survivors of the Men of Manassas seemed to place them a little higher than the other fragments of an army known for gallantry. That they gloried in their status during the war is evidenced by a familiar verse:

> And men will tell their children,
> Tho' all other memories fade,
> How they fought with *Stonewall Jackson*
> In the old "Stonewall Brigade." [10]

Here for the first time is the full story of the Stonewall Brigade, recounted insofar as possible by the members themselves. No effort has been made to conceal the brigade's shortcomings or to overlook its military sins. A confidence gained on many battlefields as a result of hard-won victories gave the unit a cockiness that, to say the least, sometimes hampered its discipline. Moreover, it had its share of cowards, deserters, and stragglers. It was an exceptional brigade, but by no means a perfect one. Yet its weaknesses, when viewed against its achievements, are so negligible that it does stand out as the model brigade which Douglas Freeman termed it.

---

10. From John Esten Cooke, "The Song of the Rebel," *Southern Illustrated News,* I (1863), 5.

|||||||||||||||||||||||||||||||||||||||||||||||||||||||||||||||||||||||||||||||||||||||||||||||||||||||||||

ACKNOWLEDGMENTS

No historian labors alone. Many persons contribute in varying degrees to the preparation of any historical work; this one was no exception. I am particularly indebted to Dr. Bell I. Wiley of Emory University, who gave generously of his time, encouragement, and counsel, not only in the development of this study but also in the more demanding chore of molding a graduate recruit into a successful doctoral candidate. Drs. Walter B. Posey, James Z. Rabun, and J. Harvey Young, professors and colleagues at Emory, each read the study; each in his own inimitable fashion suggested a number of valuable revisions. To Richard Harwell, now librarian at Bowdoin College, go sincere thanks for many references to unknown material and for other favors cheerfully rendered.

Scores of persons in the Valley of Virginia placed their homes and Civil War documents at my disposal. I would be remiss if I did not single out the following for special acknowledgment: Mr. and Mrs. Lee Miller and Lewis N. Barton of Winchester, the late John W. Wayland and Mrs. Harriet Childs of Harrisonburg, Major Henry F. Seals of Staunton, the late W. Hugh McAllister and Joseph Carpenter of Covington, Colonel William Couper of Lexington, Mrs. Richard B. Lee of Roanoke, Misses Ellen and Margaret Bosang of Pulaski, plus the many newspaper editors throughout the Valley who helped immeasurably in the tedious search for that most elusive of Civil War sources: Confederate letters, diaries, and reminiscences.

Profound thanks go also to Misses India Thomas and Eleanor Brockenbrough of the Confederate Museum, William M. E. Rachal of the Virginia Historical Society, Ray D. Smith of Chicago, Illinois, Edmund Lee Jones of Wheeling, West Virginia, and to the ever-courteous staffs of the Library of Congress, National Archives, Virginia State Library, Duke University Library, Alderman Library of the University of Virginia, Southern Historical Collection of the University of North Carolina Library, and Candler Library of Emory University.

I shall ever be grateful to the United Daughters of the Confederacy for granting this study the Mrs. Simon Baruch University Award.

It is both customary and fitting that married historians confer the last words of gratitude upon their wives. They form a rear-rank echelon marked by lack of attention and, if they type, continually sore fingers. Should this devoted regiment ever be organized, my wife Libba will qualify for colonel. She has weathered a six-year campaign with patience more than worthy of this sacrificial sect. And she assuredly was the most devoted camp follower that the Stonewall Brigade ever possessed.

JAMES I. ROBERTSON, JR.

McLean, Virginia
November 1962

CONTENTS

Foreword, v
Acknowledgments, xi

I   Citizen Soldiers, 3
II   The Stones of the Wall, 10
III   Baptism into Battle, 23
IV   Immortality at Manassas, 35
V   The Test of Patriotism, 51
VI   The First Taste of Defeat, 64
VII   Hide-and-Seek in the Valley, 79
VIII   Jackson's Foot Cavalry, 91
IX   "Fighting Is Becoming Quite Fashionable", 104
X   Service on the Peninsula, 114
XI   "Into the Jaws of Death", 125
XII   Groveton and Another Manassas, 138
XIII   The Maryland Invasion, 153
XIV   Life in Winter Quarters, 169
XV   Chancellorsville Heartache, 182
XVI   "The Whole Campaign Was a Blunder", 194
XVII   Slaughter at Spotsylvania, 209
XVIII   The Bitter End, 227
XIX   Epilogue, 242

Appendix, 248
Sources, 253
Index, 263

THE STONEWALL BRIGADE

II

CHAPTER I

CITIZEN SOLDIERS

Flames leaped skyward and the flash of explosions broke the darkness of a warm spring night. Above the crackle of burning wood could be heard the shouts of frantic men as they rushed with torches from one building to another, igniting new fires that sent the sweet smell of blazing pine drifting into the hills overlooking Harpers Ferry, Virginia. Down one of the hills raced the force which motivated that destruction: two companies of Virginia militia, though civilian dress and a variety of weapons gave them the appearance of a mob.

The date was April 18, 1861. The Virginians were trying to prevent the destruction of the U.S. Arsenal at Harpers Ferry by its garrison of forty-five Federal soldiers. Hardly had the handful of bluecoats crossed the Potomac River to the safety of Maryland when the Virginians dashed into the village and began extinguishing the less serious of the fires. Several thousand muskets were confiscated by men who had every intention of using them in the days ahead. While efforts were made to put out the flames, the commander of the militia, Colonel James W. Allen, proudly proclaimed the Federal arsenal to be thenceforth the property of the Commonwealth of Virginia.

With the expulsion of Federal troops from the town where John Brown's scheme of emancipation had collapsed in failure, civil war came forcibly to Virginia. However, the wheels of secession in the Old Dominion already had begun turning. On April 15 Governor John Letcher received a telegram from Secretary of War Simon Cameron asking that three regiments of infantry be sent to quell a Southern Confederacy that had flexed its muscles three days before at Fort Sumter. Letcher bluntly refused. "You have chosen to inaugurate civil war," he wired Cameron, "and having done so we will meet you in a spirit as determined as the Administration has exhibited toward the South." [1]

Scores of residents throughout the state echoed Letcher's sentiments. Many who had been moderates or had exerted calmness in the debates over secession "were now furiously indignant at the insult to Virginia," Mrs. Cornelia McDonald wrote. Upon arriving at Winchester, she added, "every person I met was full of joy; those who a week ago were so violently opposed to secession had completely turned round, and were as ardent and exultant as any one." [2]

On April 17 the secession convention, meeting in secret session, severed Virginia from the Union by a vote of 81 to 51. The governor purposely kept the action quiet until state troops could occupy Harpers Ferry.

Control of the Ferry was absolutely necessary. It was the northern gateway to the Valley of Virginia, a thin strip of land extending three hundred miles to the Tennessee border. This quiet area of rolling hills was not important simply because it was the grain-producing basin of the state. Geographically, it split Virginia into

1. Beverly B. Munford, *Virginia's Attitude toward Slavery and Secession* (Richmond, 1909), 282.
2. Cornelia A. McDonald, *A Diary with Reminiscences of the War and Refugee Life in the Shenandoah Valley, 1860–1865* (Nashville, 1934), 14–15.

two unequal parts; occupation of the Valley by Federal forces would isolate the smaller northwestern sector from the rest of the state. True, Union sentiment in western Virginia was strong, but Richmond felt that the district could be kept in check through pressure from the Valley.

To turn the key in the lock of that northern gateway, Governor Letcher called on militia companies throughout the Valley to form and to occupy Harpers Ferry with all possible haste. At Staunton, merchants locked their shops, took down their shotguns from the mantels, and struck out with William S. H. Baylor's "West Augusta Guards." On their arrival at Lexington they found companies that had been disbanded since John Brown's raid congregating for the march northward. It was the same at Strasburg, Winchester, Charlestown, and Martinsburg, as well as at dozens of county seats and country villages.

Being the closest, the Charlestown and Winchester companies reached the Ferry first. Their arrival on the evening of April 18 occasioned the evacuation and partial destruction of the arsenal. On the following morning the Staunton contingent arrived by train. The journey had not been without incident. One of the militiamen found it necessary to hold a cocked pistol at the engineer's head to make him complete the trip.[3]

With the April 22 announcement by Governor Letcher of Virginia's secession, and his accompanying call for troops, a "gathering of the clans" took place around Harpers Ferry. "Men began to gather towards that point from all parts of the state," Mrs. Cornelia McDonald recalled. "Men of all grades and pursuits; farmers from their ploughs, boys from their schools came in companies which in sport they had formed for drilling, students from the colleges, all were making to the point of expected conflict."[4] A resident of Berkeley County wrote his brother in Ohio: "Hardly one family around here, but some one, two, or three, of its members have gone to defend the rights of the south; we may be over run, but may not be easily subdued." And he added prophetically: "I tell you

---

3. R. U. Johnson and C. C. Buel (eds.), *Battles and Leaders of the Civil War* (New York, 1884–87), I, 111–18. Hereinafter cited as *Battles and Leaders*.
4. McDonald, *Diary*, 16.

now, brother, the first blood that the northern troops shed on Virginia soil will be the beginning of a contest such as was never seen this side of the Atlantic." [5]

Spirits were high among the Valley men who assembled at Harpers Ferry. "I have never seen such an outpouring of popular feeling in behalf of the South," one captain wrote to his newspaper. "We are in the midst of a great revolution; our people are united as one man, and are determined to maintain their rights at every sacrifice." [6]

Even though the various companies had not been organized and had no over-all commander, the men worked hard at soldiering. They listened patiently and emulated awkwardly the manner of marching and the manual of arms as taught to them by appointed drillmasters and aged militia officers. Soon the rough edges began to disappear. Captain Baylor reported of his company: "The men work willingly, eat heartily, and sleep as soundly on the ground, as a prince in a palace. They are ready for a fight, and I believe are eager to show their courage in driving back any invading force." [7] The same could have been said of most of the other companies.

Naturally, such eagerness was bound to produce false alarms, and these in turn exposed the cowards. One night soon after the occupation of Harpers Ferry, the long roll broke the stillness. A soldier turned over and shouted to his companion to grab his gun and hurry. The companion suddenly professed illness; he did not think himself capable of moving. "Well, hand me your gun," the first man said, "and I will try to handle your place too."

"Here it is," the companion moaned, "but don't you disgrace that gun." [8]

A week of chaos and disorganization gave proof of the need for an experienced commander. A man was needed who would brook no foolishness and at the same time instill the rudiments of military training into youths who possessed more martial enthusiasm than experience. Accordingly, General Robert E. Lee, commanding all

5. J. W. Thatcher to Samuel Thatcher, in *Annals of Iowa*, Ser. 3, XII (1915–21), 367.
6. Staunton *Vindicator*, April 26, 1861.　　7. *Ibid.*
8. *The Land We Love*, III (1867), 342.

Virginia forces, on April 27 ordered a relatively unknown officer to take charge of the troops at Harpers Ferry. Little enthusiasm greeted his arrival; little was merited. The Confederate colonel who rode unannounced into camp on the twenty-ninth was of medium stature and careless dress. Below a high forehead were blue eyes that seemed always sleepy, a sharp nose, thin and pallid lips, and a full brown beard badly in need of a comb. His conversation was crisp to the point of curtness, and his high-pitched drawl often shocked those on whom his dominating personality had made a marked impression. One recruit likened him to "a crouching lion"; yet the colonel was all too well known to Virginia Military Institute cadets serving in the ranks. They referred to him as "Tom Fool" because he was, by almost unanimous agreement, the most enigmatic and unpredictable professor in the history of the military academy. A favorite couplet among cadets had been:

> Great Lord! At what a wonder!
> Major Jackson—Hell and thunder! [9]

No man knew at the time that the members of the brigade and this officer, Thomas J. Jackson, were beginning an association in name and campaigns that would live long after their deaths.

In view of the inexhaustible studies dealing with Thomas Jonathan Jackson, it would be superfluous to recount here in detail his life and military career. Born in what is now West Virginia in 1824, this Cromwellian Confederate idol was a colorless graduate of West Point, inconspicuous in the Mexican War and well-nigh forgotten with the coming of peace. After resigning from the army in 1852, Jackson became a professor of military science at the Virginia Military Institute, located in the sleepy hamlet of Lexington, which lies midway in the famous Shenandoah Valley where Jackson won immortality. At VMI Jackson quickly gained a reputation for being a stickler for discipline. His many eccentricities and his quiet nature did not endear him to the cadets, who looked on him with contempt—but reacted to him with respect.

---

9. C. M. Barton to Joseph Barton, September 28, 1855, letter in possession of Lewis Barton, Winchester, Va. See also Randolph Barton, *Recollections: 1861–1865* (Baltimore, 1913), 7.

His career as professor was stormy, for he would tolerate nothing short of expulsion for any serious breach of military conduct. Little wonder that on at least two occasions cadets challenged him to duels. One of the cadets who wished to kill him later became a most devoted subordinate—and one of the last commanders of the brigade.

At the secession of Virginia, Jackson promptly volunteered his military services. He was given a colonel's stars and ordered to Richmond to train new Virginia recruits.

On the Sunday that Jackson and members of the Corps of Cadets who were to assist him prepared to leave, a farewell ceremony was planned in Lexington. The schedule called for the corps to march out promptly at noon after a fifteen-minute prayer from Jackson's pastor, Dr. William S. White. The minister finished his prayer in ten, but Jackson would not begin the march until noon, and he sat immobile upon his horse, deaf to the impatience of corps and spectators, until the courthouse bell tolled the hour.[10]

Jackson remained at Richmond only a few days before he was transferred to Harpers Ferry and put in command of one of the most heterogeneous armies ever assembled. The force was officially known as "The Army of the Shenandoah"; however, it consisted of forty-five hundred undisciplined Virginians who were armed with everything from hunting knives to shotguns and who were attired in motley clothing ranging from gaudy militia uniforms to home-spun shirts and coonskin hats. And, as Jackson learned, the men were as independent in spirit as they were in appearance.

He quickly effected a military reformation. Militia officers were either sent home or put into the ranks. Companies were reorganized and combined into regiments. Camps were assigned in orderly fash-ion, and at least twelve miles of fortifications were constructed. Guards working on twenty-four-hour shifts picketed the whole area. And Jackson scrutinized men reporting for sick call so closely that soldiers with minor ailments became reluctant to seek the surgeon's help.

New units that arrived at the training camp expecting to have

10. Elizabeth R. P. Allan, A March Past, edited by Janet A. Bryan (Richmond, 1938), 119.

a pleasant picnic were abruptly jolted by the stern commander. A newly organized Charlestown company came strolling into Harpers Ferry with two wagons straining under the weight of luxuries and accessories. Jackson ordered the wagons and their contents returned to Charlestown—an action that prompted one member of the company to grumble of him: "He considered a gum cloth, a blanket, a tooth brush and forty rounds of cartridges as the full equipment of a gentleman soldier." [11]

At the same time and with much more intensity, Jackson began a rigorous program to transform the raw recruits into soldiers. Reveille sounded promptly at 5 A.M., and for the next seventeen hours the men went through a severe routine that included at least seven hours of marching.[12] That weather did not in any degree alter the schedule was attested by one officer who told in his diary of marching twenty-four miles one day in a storm of hail and rain.[13] Many of the men doubtless shared the sentiment of the soldier who wrote that the long marches were performed "with no ostensible purpose than to prove our metal and endurance." [14]

Yet therein lies part of the secret of Jackson's success. No one, especially the men who served under him, ever denied that Jackson was a severe disciplinarian. He hounded and pounded the Valley recruits until they acquired the rudiments of soldiering as much to spite him as to please him. Like the VMI cadets, the men of his Virginia brigade initially exhibited little affection for their commander. But as the days passed, the new soldiers came to see and appreciate the value of Jackson's training. Within a year these men would be recognized as one of the most elite units in Confederate service—a reputation every man in the brigade attributed readily to the enigmatic colonel who organized and trained them.

11. David Humphreys, *Heroes and Spies of the Civil War* (New York, 1903), 195–96.
12. Jackson's Order Book, April 29–May 30, 1861, Confederate Museum, Richmond, Va.
13. Diary of Capt. J. Q. A. Nadenbousch, 2nd Regiment, in M. H. and A. H. Gardiner, *Chronicles of Old Berkeley* (Durham, 1938), 155. See also Staunton *Vindicator*, May 24, 1861.
14. George Baylor, *Bull Run to Bull Run: Or, Four Years in the Army of Northern Virginia* (Richmond, 1900), 19.

|!|I|!|I|!|I|!|I|!|I|!|I|!|I|!|I|!|I|!|I|!|I|!|I|!|I|!|I|!|I|!|I|!|I|!|I|!|I|!|I|!|I|!|I|!|I|!|I|!|I|!|I|!|I|!|I|!|I|!|I|

CHAPTER II

THE STONES OF THE WALL

Noble state pride and love of home" impelled the Valley men to arms in 1861.[1] A section intensely unionist a year earlier could not by sentiment watch its state join the Confederacy and not go with her. Thus, when the Old Dominion "had taken her stand with her Southern sisters," a future Stonewall Brigade member wrote dramatically, "I felt it my duty to lay down the plow and pruning-hook and take up the sword and the battle-axe." [2]

Out of the Valley came hundreds of men to answer their state's call. From them were formed five regiments and a battery of artillery which were designated as the First Brigade, Virginia Volun-

---

1. James McMurran, 4th Regiment, in Ben LaBree (ed.), *Camp Fires of the Confederacy* (Louisville, 1898), 278–79.
2. Baylor, *Bull Run to Bull Run*, 18.

teers. Within the regiments were forty-nine companies, each with a letter and distinctive nickname. The Second and Thirty-third Regiments originated in the lower (northern) end of the Valley, in the area around Harrisonburg, Winchester, and Charlestown. The Fourth Regiment came from the upper (southern) end of the Valley, and included companies from Pulaski, Marion, Bristol, Wytheville, and as far down the Valley as Lexington. The Staunton and Augusta County area, midway in the Valley, provided the nucleus for the Fifth Regiment, the largest unit in the brigade. The smallest regiment, the Twenty-seventh, was composed of men from the Lexington area and the counties to the west. (Actually, the Twenty-seventh was more a battalion than a regiment, since it lacked a full complement of ten companies.) Associated with the Stonewall Brigade until the latter part of 1862 was the Rockbridge Artillery. This Lexington battery was commanded initially by an Episcopal rector, William Nelson Pendleton, who later became chief of Lee's artillery.

Soon after the formation of Virginia's First Brigade, some wit among its members conceived nicknames for each of the regiments. The Second was called "The Innocent Second" because it refrained from pillaging. "The Harmless Fourth" received that name for its good behavior in camp, and "The Fighting Fifth" earned its name for reason of an opposite quality. A large element of Irishmen was partly responsible for the sobriquet "The Fighting Twenty-seventh," though in time it justified its name by an extraordinary casualty rate in battle. When the newest regiment in the brigade became the first to be plagued with "graybacks," it was promptly dubbed "The Lousy Thirty-third." [3]

As was the case with most Confederate units, the Stonewall Brigade experienced great changes in its personnel during the course of the war. Its original muster consisted of 2,611 men. Eleven months later, at the battle of Kernstown, battle casualties, illness, and resignations had depleted the ranks to 1,418 effectives. By the end of the Second Manassas Campaign, the brigade was down to 635 men; yet enlistments and men returning from sick leaves

3. Casler, *Stonewall Brigade*, 103–104.

brought the number up to 1,200 by the end of 1862. Although replacements continued to trickle in until the end of the war, they were never enough to offset tremendous casualties incurred at Chancellorsville, Gettysburg, and Spotsylvania. Barely 200 men remained after Jackson's slashing flank attack on General Joseph Hooker at Chancellorsville. So many members were captured at Spotsylvania that the Stonewall Brigade was consolidated with the remnants of three other brigades and served out the war in relative obscurity. At Appomattox 210 officers and men surrendered.[4]

Apparently only in the spring of 1862, when Jackson was moving from one victory to another in the brigade's own native region, did the unit's ranks swell to full strength of 3,000 men. Brigade returns for May 3, 1862, list 3,681 present for duty. This evidently was the highest number of men it ever possessed at one time. After the victorious but costly Valley Campaign, the five regiments began to decline in strength; every battle further depleted their rolls. That this unit surrendered with as many members as it had when it was shattered at Spotsylvania illustrates a marked degree of faith in the Stonewall Brigade on the part of the Valley men who served in it.

In contrast to what many Federal soldiers believed, the men of this unit were neither supermen nor geniuses. They ranged in age from schoolboys to grandfathers. An examination of signatures on pay rolls shows comparatively few X's by which illiterates made their marks. The members of the Stonewall Brigade pursued a variety of occupations and professions. For the most part, they were of the humble beginnings that characterized the Valley folk. If there was anything unusual about this brigade, it was the large number of descendants of non-English foreign-born in its ranks.

The Valley regiments had considerably more German descendants than did most units of comparable size recruited in the Tidewater. Company A of the Fifth Virginia, organized at Winchester and known as the "Marion Rifles," was composed almost entirely

---

4. LaBree (ed.), *Camp Fires of the Confederacy*, 284; *Southern Historical Society Papers*, XV (1887), 6, 44, 84, 88, 90, 93, 458, 464, XXI (1893), 57, 237; G. F. R. Henderson, *Stonewall Jackson and the American Civil War* (New York, 1905), I, 146.

of Americanized Germans, or "Old Germans," as they were generally called. This unit was also considered the boy company of the Stonewall Brigade. Of its original eighty-seven members, only five were over the age of twenty-one. When Louis J. Fletcher, aged eighteen, became its captain in late 1861, he was nicknamed "Jackson's pet" and the "Boy Captain of the Stonewall Brigade." [5]

Many men of Irish and Scotch-Irish stock were to be found in the brigade. The "Emerald Guards," Company E, Thirty-third Virginia, was made up entirely of Irishmen from the New Market area. In its ranks were men with such names as Conner, Fitzgerald, Green, McCarthy, and Mulligan. Its first captain, Marion Sibert, was shot through both legs at First Manassas. Because of the fondness of its members for liquor and brawling, this company was the "problem child" of the Stonewall Brigade. On at least one occasion Jackson wrote Richmond of its disorganized and unmanageable ways.[6]

The Scotch-Irish were represented in every company of the brigade, which may explain in part why most of the regimental chaplains were Presbyterians. Thompson McAllister was first captain of Company A, Twenty-seventh Virginia (later Carpenter's battery). Two of the captains of the Rockbridge Artillery were John McCausland and William McLaughlin. Dr. Hunter McGuire left the ranks of the Second Virginia to become Jackson's personal physician.

Many of the Valley residents were only two or three generations removed from European immigrants. That is why, in reading down a list of the first company commanders in the Stonewall Brigade, one feels almost as if he were reading the roster of a boatload of non-British immigrants. It is perhaps ironic that grandsons of men who journeyed to America's shores to share in its freedom and prosperity would join in a war against the Union. But most of these

5. Unidentified newspaper clipping, Records of the 5th Virginia Infantry, Virginia Archives. See also Ella Lonn, *Foreigners in the Confederacy* (Chapel Hill, 1940), 2, 16.
6. U.S. War Department (comp.), *War of the Rebellion: A Compilation of the Official Records of the Union and Confederate Armies* (Washington, 1880–1901), Ser. I, Vol. V, 977. Hereinafter cited as *Official Records*; unless otherwise stated, all references will be to Ser. I. See also *Confederate Veteran*, XIV (1906), 477.

humble folk, isolated by two mountain ranges, had come to look upon Virginia, not the United States, as their nation.

Negro slaves were as rare in the Valley brigade as they were in the Valley. So far as could be ascertained, no colored men served as soldiers in the five regiments. Even Negro body servants apparently were few in number. Jackson's cook and valet, Jim Lewis, served that commander faithfully to his death. Two Negroes by the name of "Pete" and "Israel" cooked for members of the Rockbridge Artillery at various periods of the war.[7] A private in the Fourth Virginia wrote late in 1862 of hiring "John's Jim" to do his cooking for the coming year.[8] But for these examples, no mention of Negroes was found in diaries, letters, or reminiscences of Stonewall Brigade members.

Relatively speaking, the Valley brigade was a young unit. Three-fifths of its members were between the ages of eighteen and twenty-five. While the most common age appears to have been nineteen, a large majority of the men were in their early twenties. The ages of twenty-three and twenty-four rank second and third in frequency. There was a considerable sprinkling of all ages up to thirty; the number decreases markedly for those between thirty-three and thirty-seven, then steadily declines.

As might be expected, most of the younger members of the brigade were drummer boys, whose ages ranged from sixteen to nineteen, with one exception. Private David Scantlon, Company C, Fourth Virginia, was drummer boy for his company, yet he was fifty-seven years old and old enough to be father of most of the members of the "Pulaski Guards."[9] A few of the brigade privates were seventeen and under. From all indications, the youngest

7. Edward A. Moore, *The Story of a Cannoneer under Stonewall Jackson* (New York, 1907), 66. Hereinafter cited as Edward A. Moore, *Cannoneer*. L. Minor Blackford (ed.), *Mine Eyes Have Seen the Glory* (Cambridge, 1954), 203.
8. Jim P. Charlton to Oliver Charlton, November 20, 1862, Jim P. Charlton Letters, in possession of Mrs. Richard B. Lee, Roanoke, Va.
9. At the height of the battle of First Manassas, Scantlon was ordered by Colonel James Preston to "beat the rally" so that the regiment could be reformed. Scantlon promptly did so, after turning his back to the sound of battle. When asked the reason for such an action, the old drummer replied, "Do you suppose I wanted the Yankees to shoot a hole thru my new brass drum?" Richmond *Times-Dispatch*, November 27, 1904.

original member of the Stonewall Brigade was Albert L. Moore, Company A, Second Virginia. He was listed as a fifteen-year-old student in April, 1861. On the other extreme, the oldest man in the unit was John Wright, aged sixty, and listed as a laborer at the time of his enlistment in Company B, Second Regiment.

The Valley soldiers varied as much in occupation as in age. Farmers were the most numerous, which was natural in that rich grain and apple-producing area. Thirty-five extant company muster rolls reveal the following distribution of occupations:

Farmers	811
Laborers	477
Carpenters	217
Students	142
Clerks	137
Merchants	107
Tanners and shoemakers	102
Blacksmiths	75
Masons	70
Painters	61
Machinists	57
Teachers	45
Lawyers	41
Tailors	40
Carriage-makers	33
Cabinet-makers	31
Millers	30
Printers	26
Doctors	22
Boatmen	20
Wheelwrights	16
Railroad employees	11
Butchers	11
Drivers	9
Constables	8
Civil Engineers	8
Gunsmiths	6

Bakers	6
Silversmiths	5
Distillers	5
Gentlemen	4
Weavers	2
Dentists	2
Postmaster	1
Minister	1

The occupational background of Company G, Second Virginia, seems to have been typical of the Stonewall Brigade as a whole. The men of this company, known as the "Botts Greys" from their first captain, Lawson Botts, came mostly from the Charlestown area. Of its 92 members, 35 were farmers, 17 were students, 15 were professional men, 11 were clerks, 7 were artisans, and 7 were merchants.[10]

The brigade had several unusual units, among which was Company I, Fourth Virginia, the "Liberty Hall Volunteers." Of its 69 members, 57 were students at Washington College. At least one-fourth of them were studying for the ministry. The company was organized by James J. White, professor of languages at the college. Average age of the members was twenty. The officers themselves were little more than youths. Although Captain White was thirty-two, his two lieutenants were twenty-one and eighteen. Of the five men serving as sergeants, two were twenty-one, two were nineteen, and one was eighteen. Perhaps because of its youth, the company suffered unusually heavy losses, its casualties aggregating 203 among the 161 men who served in the company during the war.[11]

Another exceptional company was the West Augusta Guards of the Fifth Regiment. Composed almost entirely of Staunton

---

10. John Yates Beall, hanged in New York in 1865 for piracy and espionage, began his army career in this company. See *Confederate Veteran*, VII (1899), 66–69.

11. This imbalance of figures is due to the fact that many men, wounded in one battle, were killed in another; many were wounded several times. Broken down, the company's casualties were: 26 killed in action, 42 died of disease, 16 died of other causes, 43 captured, and 76 wounded. Richmond *Times-Dispatch*, June 21, 1910; *Confederate Veteran*, XXXIX (1931), 13.

citizens, this unit had only two farmers; the rest were merchants, clerks, or students. Undoubtedly the most flamboyant company in the brigade was the gaudily-attired Company F, Fourth Regiment, the "Grayson Daredevils." Ninety-four of its 97 members were farmers. There was also a doctor, a blacksmith, and a student. The members prided themselves for their marksmanship. According to one source, when 135 answered the initial call for the 100-man company, the captain got rid of the 35 excess applicants by staging a shooting match. Each applicant had to fire at a target while on a dead run, and those who missed the farthest were lopped from the roll.[12]

One of the best components of the Stonewall Brigade and, indeed, one of the most celebrated batteries in the whole Confederate Army was the Rockbridge Artillery, mustered into service at Harpers Ferry. Jackson found it necessary to restrict its membership, lest its numbers swell out of proportion to the other units. On its first roll were 28 college graduates, 25 theological students, and 7 men who held masters' degrees from the University of Virginia.[13] In the course of the war, 45 of its members received officers' commissions. Although it lost 145 men (exclusive of those elevated to officer status), at Appomattox it surrendered 93 gunners—more than it possessed when it first entered Confederate service.

Within the ranks of the Valley brigade were a number of men who distinguished themselves in both war and peace. Eight eventually attained the rank of general. William S. H. Baylor, Elisha Franklin Paxton, James A. Walker, and William Terry rose through the ranks to command of the brigade. The Reverend Mr. Pendleton obtained the wreathed stars of a brigadier when he assumed command of Lee's artillery. Pendleton's son-in-law, Edwin G. Lee, was forced by tuberculosis to resign as colonel of the Thirty-third Virginia. In 1864, however, he came out of semi-retirement,

---

12. F. G. DeFontaine, *Army Letters of Personnae, 1861–1865* (Columbia, 1897), 82–83. For an imaginative sketch of one of the "Daredevils," see Benson J. Lossing, *Lossing's Pictorial Field Book of the Great Civil War* (Philadelphia, 1886–89), Pt. 8, p. 590.
13. *Confederate Veteran*, XVII (1909), 340, XXVI (1928), 49. Slightly higher figures are given in Mary Anna Jackson, *Memoirs of "Stonewall" Jackson* (Louisville, 1895), 160. Hereinafter cited as Mrs. Jackson, *Memoirs*.

was appointed a general, and took charge of organizing the Valley forces against General Philip Sheridan's invasion.

Huge (six feet, four inches tall) John Echols was commanding the Twenty-seventh Virginia at Kernstown when he was severely wounded. After recuperating he was promoted to general and commanded a brigade that saw action in southwestern Virginia. John McCausland, one of the first officers of the Rockbridge Artillery, served later as colonel of the Thirty-sixth Virginia. At the end of the war he was a brigadier general of cavalry.[14]

Controversial John R. Jones of the Thirty-third Regiment also received a brigadier's commission—but not without a struggle. In the April, 1862, elections he ran for both major and lieutenant colonel, and received a double defeat. He nevertheless commanded Jackson's division at Sharpsburg and won tacit praise from his superior. Why he abruptly left the army early in 1863 is not certain. The accepted story was that he was suffering from an ulcerated leg. However, one brigade member wrote that he was quietly cashiered "for getting behind a tree at the battle of Fredericksburg." [15]

Two very capable colonels barely missed promotion. By the spring of 1862, James W. Allen had so distinguished himself as commander of the Second Regiment that he was recommended for brigadier. Before the orders could be delivered, he was killed at Gaines' Mill.[16] Abram Spengler rose rapidly from captain of the "Hardy Grays" in the Thirty-third Regiment to colonel in Lee's army. According to one source, a brigadier's commission that had already been prepared for him was lost in the confusion of Richmond's fall.[17]

Henry Kyd Douglas, R. W. Hunter, Wells J. Hawks, James H. Waters, Dr. Hunter McGuire, Robert Lewis Dabney, R. K. Meade,

---

14. Before the war McCausland served with Jackson on the VMI faculty. For an account of his colorful career, see *Confederate Veteran*, XXV (1927), 88.

15. John O. Casler to Randolph Barton, April 9, 1906, Records of the 33rd Virginia Regiment, Virginia Archives.

16. Charles D. Walker, *Memorial, Virginia Military Institute* (Philadelphia, 1875), 21–25. Hereinafter cited as Walker, *VMI Memorial*. Allen's wife was a niece of General William N. Pendleton.

17. John W. Wayland, *A History of Shenandoah County, Virginia* (Strasburg, Va., 1927), 644.

James Power Smith, and A. Sandie Pendleton all left the ranks of the Stonewall Brigade to serve on Jackson's staff. Thirteen of the company captains won promotion to regimental command by gallantry.[18] Of this number, eleven were graduates of the Virginia Military Institute. Over one hundred men, connected with the academy as students, professors, or alumni, served in Jackson's army. As a result, many of the companies early in the war were called on to provide drillmasters for units stationed near Richmond and Harpers Ferry. Two companies thus utilized were James Walker's Pulaski Guards (Company C, Fourth Virginia) and the "Continental Morgan Guards" (Company K, Fifth Virginia), captained by John Avis and George W. Kurtz.[19] The latter unit was most conspicuous in the early months of the war because of its buff and blue uniforms—exact replicas of the uniforms worn by George Washington's Revolutionary army.

Several noted families were also represented in the brigade. Robert E. Lee, Jr., served as a private in the Rockbridge Artillery. His cousin, William Fitzhugh Lee, lieutenant colonel in the Thirty-third Virginia, died from wounds received at First Manassas. Colonel Raleigh T. Colston of the Second Virginia was the grandson of John Marshall and himself a skilled lawyer. Two sons of Union admiral David D. Porter served in the Rockbridge Artillery.[20] So also did the father of the Confederacy's best-known female spy, Belle Boyd.

Three members of the brigade achieved postwar fame in the field of medicine. Dr. Hunter McGuire became president of the American Medical Association. Dr. William Hay, who was transferred from the brigade to Staunton in 1862 to take charge of a Confederate military hospital, carried into private practice his reputation as one of the "expert operating surgeons in service." [21] Dr. Samuel

---

18. John W. Rowan, J. Q. A. Nadenbousch, Raleigh T. Colston, Lawson Botts, James A. Walker, William Terry, W. S. H. Baylor, Charles A. Ronald, R. D. Gardner, J. H. S. Funk, James K. Edmondson, H. J. Williams, and Daniel M. Shriver.
19. It was at the Winchester home of Captain Kurtz that Jackson posed for the famous "Winchester Photograph."
20. W. G. Bean (ed.), "A House Divided: The Civil War Letters of a Virginia Family," *Virginia Magazine of History and Biography*, LIX (1951), 397.
21. *Confederate Veteran*, XXXIV (1926), 9.

Rush Sayers enlisted as a private in the "Wythe Grays" of the Twenty-seventh Virginia and soon became surgeon of the regiment. After the war he continued his practice in Wytheville and became internationally known as a diagnostician.

Prominent clergymen were always conspicuous in Jackson's army. With the exception of General Pendleton, most of them were of Jackson's Calvinistic tenets. Dr. Robert L. Dabney left Hampden-Sydney College to become chaplain of the Twenty-seventh Virginia. Dabney soon was promoted to Jackson's headquarters and served for a short period as chief of staff. He patiently endured the laughs and catcalls of the men of the Stonewall Brigade, who found him a hilarious sight attired in a Prince Albert coat and beaver hat. Yet they all came to love him. Andrew Grigsby, a caustic commander of the Twenth-seventh Virginia, once snorted, "Our parson is not afraid of Yankee bullets, and I tell you he preaches like hell!" [22]

Dabney's tenure with Jackson was short. The minister who made the most lasting impression upon the troops was Abner Crump Hopkins, "The Fighting Chaplain" of the Second Virginia. He was as fiery in his soldiering as he was in his preaching. On several occasions during the war he put away his Bible, grabbed a musket, and joined the regiment in assaulting Federal positions. He distinguished himself for gallantry in the battle of Mine Run, fought late in November, 1863. Hopkins was also largely responsible for the religious revivals that swept through the brigade's camps in the winters of 1862–63 and 1863–64. At war's end he buried his belligerence and for twenty-three years served as director of the Union Theological Seminary in Richmond.

Many members of the Stonewall Brigade became prominent after the war in law and politics. Sam Letcher, brother of Virginia's governor, commanded the "Montgomery Fencibles" of the Fourth Virginia, and afterwards became a well-known figure in state politics. Frederick W. M. Holliday, forced by ill health to resign as colonel of the Thirty-third Virginia, served in the Second Session of the Confederate Congress. He was elected governor of the state in 1878. His lieutenant governor was James A. Walker, next to the

22. Thomas C. Johnson, *The Life and Letters of Robert Lewis Dabney* (Richmond, 1903), 264. Hereinafter cited as Thomas C. Johnson, *Robert Lewis Dabney*.

last man to command the brigade. The last commander, William Terry, served two terms in Congress.

The Valley brigade's most distinguished alumnus in Washington politics was John Warwick Daniel, who enlisted in the "Allegheny Rifles" of the Twenty-seventh Virginia. In 1864, while serving as a major, he was so crippled in the fighting in the Wilderness Campaign that he spent the remainder of his life on crutches. After a two-year term in the House of Representatives, Daniel served for twenty-three years in the United States Senate, where he was known among his colleagues as "The Lame Lion." [23]

Two members of the First Brigade became outstanding jurists. Captain John H. Fulton of the "Wythe Grays," Fourth Virginia, served in the Virginia House of Delegates during Reconstruction, and later had a long tenure as circuit judge for the upper Valley. After his discharge from the Rockbridge Artillery, D. Gardiner Tyler was twice elected to Congress, then spent twenty-four years as judge of the Fourteenth Judicial District. A compatriot in arms, Launcelot Minor, declined a judicial post and for years was chief attorney for the Missouri Pacific Railroad.

One characteristic of the Stonewall Brigade deserves special mention. To a large extent this unit was a family affair, or, as one historian has termed it, a "cousinwealth." [24] So many families contributed such a large number of sons, cousins, and other close relatives that the muster rolls at times read like genealogical tables.

For example, Company C, Fifth Virginia, contained eighteen members of the same Bell family. In the course of the war six were killed in action and five died of disease.[25] David W. Barton of Winchester gave six sons to the brigade. Two were wounded and two were killed, one almost within sight of his home. Three brothers and a cousin belonging to the Sexton family served in Company D, Fourth Virginia. All died in battle or prison. Four sons and a nephew of Pulaski County's John Caddall served in the Fourth Regiment. Only three came home in 1865. David Timberlake of Frederick County likewise sent four sons into the army. All served

23. See *Southern Historical Society Papers*, XLI (1916), 88–112.
24. W. G. Bean, *Stonewall's Man: Sandie Pendleton* (Chapel Hill, 1959), 42.
25. *Confederate Veteran*, XXI (1913), 86, XXIII (1915), 57.

in Company G, Second Regiment. Three were invalided for life. Four Carpenter boys served in the battery named after the oldest brother, Captain Joseph Carpenter. He was killed at Slaughter Mountain. His brother John succeeded to the command of the battery and lost an arm in 1864. A third was permanently maimed by a wound in the lungs, and the fourth brother lost a leg in the closing months of the war.[26]

Although the Stonewall Brigade included many individuals who rose to prominence both on the battlefield and in the postwar years, most of the members were men whose records in war were more outstanding than their contributions to peace. From the thrill of first engagements to the seriousness and maturity that stem from long and intimate association with death, these men gave their every effort to a cause perhaps doomed from its inception. Most learned to endure patiently and with good humor bare feet, tattered clothes, empty stomachs, and dirty bodies. Some were able to steel themselves to tragedy of every sort. Yet others never recovered from the loss of relatives and friends within their ranks.

Sadness mixed with valor, perseverance mixed with humor— such was the saga of the Stonewall Brigade.

---

26. Edward A. Moore, *Cannoneer*, 155–56.

CHAPTER III

BAPTISM INTO BATTLE

What was the almost magical hold that Stonewall Jackson came to have on this brigade? Why did it endure the rigid discipline, the long marches, hurl itself into battle with almost suicidal force, suffer hardships in excess of, and more consistently than, a majority of Confederate units, when the man for whom it sacrificed seldom spoke, rarely smiled, and usually rewarded its efforts with a quick nod of his head or a barely discernible sparkle in his eye? What was the unseen magnetism between Jackson and what became the Stonewall Brigade?

No one knows the full answer. If this mysterious force could be revealed, there for all to see would be the key to greatness for such figures as Alexander the Great, Caesar, Charlemagne, Napoleon, Lee—and "Tom Fool" Jackson. One can only speculate as to the nature of that indefinable something that motivated the brigade to the pinnacles of military glory.

Certainly the men loved Jackson for his earnestness. They fought hard for him because he fought to win. A tie or semi-victory was never enough. Victory must be total and conclusive. The brigade quickly came to share this conviction with their commander, and their devotion to him increased as he guided them from one success to another. His bravery, strength, and resoluteness, coupled with the fame to which he led them, gave the men a pride that surpassed that of all other units in a Confederate army noted for valor. At the same time, Jackson the general never placed himself above his men. He shared their interests and goals, felt their happinesses and sorrows, and treated them not as subordinates but as comrades in arms. In time his soldiers overlooked his silence, gruffness, and punctilious devotion to duty. They came to see his other side—his courtesy, kindness, and patience. Jackson became known for doing simple things for his men, things of little tangible value in themselves but indicative of such thoughtfulness and benevolence as to endear him forever to the recipients. As one biographer has stated: "A general with an eye for the welfare of his men was apt to become immensely popular." [1] And Jackson's popularity in the Civil War ranked second only to that of the Confederate demigod Robert E. Lee.

A mutual confidence between commander and commanded is one of the secrets of the success enjoyed by Jackson and his Stonewall Brigade. The men were so devoted to him that they would attempt the impossible if he requested it. "I do not think," a captain in the Fifth Regiment wrote his father in 1862, "that any man can take General Jackson's place in the confidence and love of his troops . . . I have learned to look up to him with implicit confidence, and to approach him with perfect freedom, being always assured of a kind and attentive hearing." [2]

---

1. Frank E. Vandiver, *Mighty Stonewall* (New York, 1957), 168.
2. William S. White, *Sketches of the Life of Captain Hugh A. White, of the Stonewall Brigade* (Columbia, S.C., 1864), 61. Hereinafter cited as William S. White, *Hugh White*. For a similar opinion, see John S. Robson, *How A One-legged Rebel Lives* (Richmond, 1876), 46.

Jackson's men cheered him whenever they saw him, even on the secret marches for which he became famous. Where the brigade was concerned, Jackson often found it necessary to conceal himself, lest their shouts divulge their presence to the Federals. When a loud yell emanated from some sector in Jackson's camp, men would say admiringly, "That's Jackson or a rabbit!" [3]

In the first days of the war many of the brigade members smiled openly at the piety of their commander. Most of them had never seen a man so dedicated to his God, and the spectacle of prayers and silent meditation by this warrior at all hours of the day and night had its humorous side. Yet just as Jackson's spirit of battle rubbed off on the men, so too did his faith. Soon the brigade was as noted for its worship as its fighting. Wherever it camped, chapel tents were among the first to be pitched, and at the frequent church services, Jackson himself acted as usher for his men.[4] His devout Christianity was perhaps the trait the men remembered most. As one aged veteran wrote years after the war: "I went in a minny Battle with Stonewall. I loved that man. A true Christian." [5]

The men applied to Jackson a variety of names, though they rarely called him "Stonewall." Their favorite appellation was "Old Jack." Those uninitiated into his faith spoke of him as "Old Blue Light." Some called him "Hickory" or "Square Box," the latter alluding to the unusual size of his feet.[6] Regardless of the name given him, Jackson was loved like a father. In turn, he was as proud of the men of his brigade as any parent is of his offspring. He was said to have remarked on one occasion: "My men sometimes fail to drive the enemy, but the enemy always fail to drive my men." On another occasion he told a member of his staff: "You cannot praise these men of my brigade too much; they have fought, marched and endured more than I ever thought they would."

---

3. Casler, *Stonewall Brigade*, 128–29. A more dramatized version of the phrase is given in John Esten Cooke, *Wearing of the Gray* (New York, 1867), 47.
4. John K. Hitchner, Rockbridge Artillery, in *Confederate Veteran*, XXXII (1924), 468.
5. J. G. Bailey, 2nd Regiment, to J. V. Bidgood, May 7, 1913, Confederate Records for 2nd Virginia Regiment, Virginia Archives.
6. *Confederate Veteran*, V (1897), 287; *Southern Historical Society Papers*, XXXVIII (1910), 270.

Mutual trust, admiration, and respect seemed to mold Old Jack and the Stonewall Brigade into an entity. The reverential attitude of the men toward Jackson proved a disadvantage to the commanders who succeeded him, for they all suffered initially from unconscious comparison with the "Mighty Stonewall."

However, such feelings came with time and cultivated affection. They were not evident in those spring days of 1861, when Harpers Ferry was the scene of fervid activity and grudging obedience. For a month Jackson literally pounded military training and discipline into the men. Those who could not endure the hard life were replaced by sturdier men selected from eager recruits who flocked daily to the camps. Those who remained were converted into soldiers. A few were unhappy with their lot, but the majority reacted with pride and good humor. When George Flagg of the Second Regiment was observed carrying two buckets of soapy water across a field, his comrades chided him for bearing slops. "Slops!" Flagg shouted back at them. "This is not slops. It is patriotism!" [7]

Although the troops generally heeded Jackson's orders, there were instances when old habits got the best of military discipline. When Jackson on one occasion discovered that some of the soldiers had large quantities of whisky stored in town, he ordered it poured down the gutters. Imbibers gathered quickly at the foot of the street and scooped it up. Jackson, very much exasperated, ordered the remainder cast over the bluffs into the Potomac. Again he was outwitted, for the soldiers simply went down along the river bank and caught the whisky in buckets as it rained down from above. [8]

Another popular story of misbehavior concerned a member of the Fifth Regiment who stole a skillet and had it in use when its owner spied it. The culprit was taken before his colonel. When asked to state his case, the accused said he knew it was his skillet: his mother had sent it to him in a letter. The colonel thereupon dismissed the charges with the comment: "A man who can deliver as ready a lie as that will make a good soldier." [9]

---

7. Douglas, *I Rode with Stonewall*, 6.
8. John N. Opie, *A Rebel Cavalryman with Lee, Jackson and Stuart* (Chicago, 1899), 19–20.
9. *Confederate Veteran*, II (1894), 90.

Some of the troops were deeply religious, like their commander, and most of them manifested much interest in spiritual concerns. One evangelist who visited Harpers Ferry wrote that he "could have sold more than $100 worth of books a month, if my assortment had been larger—especially if I could have had a good supply of testaments." [10] A correspondent in the brigade wrote his newspaper of the extreme piety of the men, and outlined the religious observances as worship each Sunday, prayer meeting once a week, and prayers every night.[11]

On May 23 General Joseph E. Johnston arrived to take command at Harpers Ferry. He found nine regiments and two battalions of infantry, plus four companies of artillery. His observations confirmed what had previously been reported by his inspector general, namely, that the troops were raw and inexperienced. Yet he must have agreed with that officer's further comment: "To make up, however, for this loose state of things, so striking to the professional eye, it must not be forgotten that a fierce spirit animates these rough-looking men; and if called upon, even now, to meet the enemy, I have no fear of the result of the battle." [12]

To Jackson's care were entrusted four of the regiments and the Rockbridge Artillery. On June 1 the regiments were officially designated as the Second, Fourth, Fifth, and Twenty-seventh, and a week later all were mustered into Confederate service. Jackson seemed pleased with the assignment, and soon after taking over the First Brigade, as it was now called, he wrote his wife: "I am very thankful to our Heavenly Father for having given me such a fine brigade." [13]

The men continued drilling and mastering the rudiments of war. Much action was expected, but little actually occurred. The Fifth Regiment participated in the neutralization of the Baltimore & Ohio Railroad, but no fighting was involved.[14] The Fourth Regiment was disturbed on several nights by local pranksters trying to

---

10. William W. Bennett, *A Narrative of the Great Revival Which Prevailed in the Southern Armies* (Philadelphia, 1877), 99. Hereinafter cited as Bennett, *Great Revival.*
11. Lexington *Gazette*, May 23, 1861.   12. *Official Records*, II, 471, 861–62.
13. Mrs. Jackson, *Memoirs*, 168.
14. See *Battles and Leaders*, I, 118–19, 122–23.

raid the camp. A few shots into the darkness sufficed to end these annoyances.[15] Several expeditions were sent out toward Martinsburg to locate General Robert Patterson's Federal army, known to be somewhere just across the Potomac in Maryland. No encounters resulted.

On Sunday morning, June 15, General Johnston received word that Patterson's army was marching southward toward Virginia. Without waiting for the permission of his superior, Johnston ordered Harpers Ferry evacuated. Most of the men, accompanied by families and friends in carriages, started down the winding road that led to Winchester (which Johnston considered of far more strategic importance than Harpers Ferry). Jackson and his brigade were dispatched to Bunker Hill to put themselves astride the Winchester–Martinsburg road and block Patterson's move.[16] The First Brigade, eager for action, marched briskly and seemed unaware of fatigue. "Though some of them were suffering from hunger," wrote Jackson, "this and other privations appeared to be forgotten and the march continued at the rate of about three miles an hour." By nightfall, however, men unaccustomed to such a pace began to drop along the roadside. Tired bodies and taut nerves played havoc with the force. When an infantryman's musket accidentally fired, the lead regiment delivered a wild volley and charged into the darkness. At 2 A.M., after what had seemed an eternity to the men, Jackson called a halt for the night.[17]

The brigade soon moved into an area four miles south of Martinsburg and, in deference to the farmer on whose land they had bivouacked, established what was called "Camp Stearns." For two weeks the men marched back and forth, daily expecting an encounter with Patterson. Jackson himself had stated publicly that should the Federals move against him, "I shall no longer stand on

15. James H. Langhorne, 4th Regiment, to his sister, May 31, 1861, James H. Langhorne Letters, Virginia Historical Society.
16. As the 2nd Virginia passed Johnston on the way northward, the commander is reputed to have said to a staff officer: "I would not give one company of regulars for the whole Regiment." Hunter McGuire and George L. Christian, *The Confederate Cause and Conduct in the War between the States* (Richmond, 1907), 207.
17. Mrs. Jackson, *Memoirs*, 162; D. B. Conrad, 2nd Regiment, in *Southern Historical Society Papers*, XIX (1891), 84–85.

controversy." [18] Time after time, the recruits leaped eagerly into position in response to an alarm. Upon learning that it was false, they would grumble and retire to camp with "a snail-like pace," as if hoping Patterson might suddenly pop up in the distance.[19]

Heightening the situation was the fact that most regiments had no tents and few uniforms and were thus exposed to the elements.[20] Until the last of June the brigade's only military activity was the crippling of the Baltimore & Ohio Railroad in and around the railroad shops at Martinsburg. In a week's time (June 19–26) over forty locomotives and three hundred cars were captured. In all, fourteen engines were hooked up to horses and drawn along the turnpike to Winchester. The rest of the equipment, including roundhouses, trestles, culverts, track, etc., was burned.[21]

Like his men, Jackson began to fidget impatiently for action. He was well pleased with the way his units had adapted to army life, but the inactivity was beginning to tell on everyone. A roving reporter for *Harper's Weekly* noted that Jackson's troops were "under very strict discipline, but seem discontented and not in very good condition." [22] At 7:30 A.M. on a sunny July 2 the boredom was broken. Colonel J. E. B. Stuart, reconnoitering near Williamsport, reported that Federal columns had started southward. Jackson's orders expressly directed him to retire to Winchester in the event of any Federal advance. Yet, at least to Jackson's thinking, uncertainty as to the exact size of the force seemed to dictate further investigation.[23]

Accordingly, the lethargic air of Jackson's camp gave way to sudden activity. Colonel Kenton Harper, an aged veteran of the War of 1812, assembled his Fifth Regiment for a northward scout. They were shortly joined by Jackson and Captain Pendleton's

---

18. *Official Records*, II, 814.
19. See James H. Langhorne to his mother, June 23, 1861, Langhorne Letters.
20. For example, see Regimental Returns, 4th Virginia, Companies B and C, June, 1861, War Records Group 109, National Archives.
21. W. M. McAllister, 27th Regiment, to his wife, June 26, 1861, Thompson McAllister Papers, Duke University Library. See also Edward Hungerford, *The Story of the Baltimore and Ohio Railroad, 1827–1897* (New York, 1928), II, 10–12.
22. *Harper's Weekly*, July 13, 1861.
23. Jackson's reasons for moving against Patterson are outlined in *Official Records*, II, 186.

Rockbridge Artillery, the latter being for the most part college youths from the Lexington area. In the meantime, those men in the Second, Fourth, and Twenty-seventh Regiments not posted on camp guard duty were busily engaged loading baggage wagons for a possible withdrawal. Satisfied that the camp was well organized, Jackson mounted his horse and jogged to the front of the Fifth Regiment. The wave of his hand signaled the start of the march.

Surfeited as they were with rumor, most of the troops paid scant attention to this new alarm; a few unconcealed grumblings even floated from the ranks about "another wild goose chase." Yet as the column moved toward Williamsport, Captain Pendleton became increasingly apprehensive over the safety of his battery. He finally sought and secured Jackson's permission to place three of his guns at a strategic location along the road; greatly relieved, he then continued the march with nothing more than "a common six-pounder." [24]

Marching in open and rolling country that was broken here and there by clumps of thin pines or heavy oaks, the small Confederate force reached a point four miles south of Williamsport at a little before 9 A.M. Back in the ranks the men were beginning to complain of the heat and dust. Between coughs they continued to mutter doubts as to the wisdom of the march. Then, as the head of the column moved over a rise, there for the first time the Virginians saw bluecoated troops—hundreds of them, with flags flying and bayonets glistening in the morning sun—drawn up in battle lines a half-mile down the road. Valley troops were so ignorant of war that they broke from the ranks and climbed atop fences and up into trees to get a better view.

A moment later the Virginians heard the unfamiliar whizzing of bullets passing by; and when Jackson ordered the companies off the road and into the woods to the right, so many men clambered over an old rotten fence that it broke under the weight, scattering soldiers in every direction. [25] Under Jackson's calm commands, the

---

24. Susan P. Lee (ed.), *Memoirs of William Nelson Pendleton* (Philadelphia, 1893), 146. Hereinafter cited as Lee (ed.), *Pendleton*.

25. Unidentified newspaper clipping, Jedediah Hotchkiss Papers, Library of Congress.

confusion quickly passed. Most of the companies took up positions at the edge of the woods looking out into an open field. Several squads detailed as sharpshooters scampered over and occupied a nearby farmhouse and barn. In the meantime, Pendleton wheeled his six-pounder off into the woods to cover the dusty lane.

Barely had Jackson made his dispositions when Federal troops began moving out into the field. Unknown at the time to the Confederates, these were elements of the First Wisconsin, Eleventh Pennsylvania, and Captain William McMullen's Independent Rangers. The Virginians remained quiet as blue skirmishers let go a spattering fire to feel out the positions of their foe. As the first wave of Federals got halfway across the field, firing blindly into the woods, the Confederates answered with a well-directed volley that caused the Yankee line to buckle temporarily in confusion.

Patterson's troops scurried to the cover of trees and ravines. For an hour firing was heavy and erratic as recruits on both sides demonstrated the need for further practice with muskets. From an elevated position behind his men, Jackson soon discerned Federal columns moving to turn both his flanks. Woefully outnumbered, the Virginia companies were ordered to fall back several hundred yards on the reserve elements. The Federal troops mistook the withdrawal for a retreat. They rushed forward to take advantage of the moment, while their cannon, now unlimbered, began to bark from behind them. A large body of bluecoated cavalry dashed down the road to flank Jackson's left—only to run almost down the barrel of Pendleton's six-pounder. "The Lord have mercy on their souls!" the pious Pendleton shouted. "Fire!" With a hearty "Amen, brother!" the gunners sent a solid shot into the midst of the Federals, who promptly scurried pell-mell in the opposite direction.

With his position now revealed, Pendleton turned his gun on the Federal battery posted on the crest across the road. In the brisk exchange the rector was able to disable one Union gun; but at the same time, he wrote later, "the balls whizzed by us with tremendous force and startling music." [26]

Convinced now of the great strength of the Federals, Jackson

---

26. Lee (ed.), *Pendleton*, 146; Judith W. McGuire, *Diary of a Refugee* (Richmond, 1889), 34.

ordered his command to fall back on Colonel Allen's Second and Colonel James Preston's Fourth Regiments, both of which had rushed forward from camp at his call. The appearance of the Second on the field thwarted a final Federal flanking attempt. The Fourth was not engaged, but concerned itself largely with protecting Pendleton's three unmanned guns until Jackson's troops reached them. Once his men were safely behind the battery, Jackson was more than willing to continue the contest. But Patterson had had enough. By 10:30 A.M. the last shot had been fired and what Johnston termed "the affair at Falling Waters" was over.

Patterson's expedition, a force of about 3,000 men under General George Cadwallader, suffered casualties of 10 dead and 50 captured (the latter snatched up by Stuart's patrolling troopers). Jackson's number of dead, out of 350 engaged, was the same, with a negligible number of wounded. So firm had been Jackson's stand that General Patterson estimated his force at 3,500 men.[27] Despite the relative smallness of the engagement, it vividly pointed out the need for more training and seasoning. For instance, when the first Federal shell exploded over Company I of the Fifth Regiment, one man dropped his gun and went racing down the road. An officer shouted at him and demanded to know why he was running. Without ever breaking his stride, the recruit hollered back, "Because I can't fly!"

Another member of the same company was grazed in the neck and fell moaning to the ground, frantically trying to stem a small trickle of blood. He begged someone to lift him to his feet; when a comrade obliged, the wounded man beat a hasty exit to the rear. And another soldier was so overjoyed at Jackson's order to retire that, in his haste to get through a growth of honeysuckle, he ripped his trouser leg—from crotch to ankle—completely off the rest of his trousers.[28]

General Johnston, hearing of Jackson's engagement on the night of July 2, quickly moved his Winchester forces northward in support. On the following morning he met Jackson's brigade at Darkesville. If Johnston was displeased at Jackson for provoking

27. *Official Records*, II, 157.
28. Opie, *Rebel Cavalryman*, 21–22, 189; Lee (ed.), *Pendleton*, 146.

a battle, he never mentioned it in official dispatches. For four days the Confederates waited expectantly for Patterson to come down and renew the struggle, but the Federal commander seemed content to remain at Martinsburg and let the Rebels come to him. Jackson was more than willing to do so. In a letter to his wife shortly after the Falling Waters scrap, he expressed his confidence by stating: "I want my brigade to feel that it can itself whip Patterson's whole army and I believe that we can do it." Little wonder that when Johnston finally ordered the whole army to return to Winchester, disappointment was apparent on every Virginian's face.[29]

For ten days the impatient troops camped around Winchester, "eager to give the abominable wretches a warm reception," one of them boasted.[30] The ladies of the town were kept busy rolling bandages and sewing uniforms. "Even tents," one of them commented, "were made by fingers that had scarcely ever used a needle before." [31]

On July 15 the First Virginia Brigade was swelled to a strength of 2,611 men with the addition of the recently organized Thirty-third Regiment. The brigade's full complement now existed: the Second Regiment from the Winchester–Charlestown area, the upper (southern) Valley's Fourth Regiment, the "battle-proven" Fifth from the Staunton community, the small Twenty-seventh Regiment from in and around Lexington, the Thirty-third Regiment, with its newly uniformed troops from New Market to Martinsburg, and Pendleton's battery of four pieces and unusually youthful gunners. All itched to have another go at Patterson's troops.

Then, at noon on July 18, each regimental commander received a simple communiqué from Jackson: Winchester was to be evacuated and the army was to proceed eastward across the Blue Ridge Mountains. None of the officers could understand it. It seemed to them that Johnston was handing over Winchester to the Federals and running for the hills that formed the eastern boundary of the

---

29. *Official Records*, II, 472–73; Henderson, *Stonewall Jackson*, I, 130.
30. John H. Graybill, *Diary of a Soldier of the Stonewall Brigade* (Woodstock, Va., n.d.), 3.
31. McDonald, *Diary*, 17.

Valley. The men in the ranks knew less than the colonels, but the galloping back and forth of couriers and staff officers convinced them that something was in the wind.

By 3 P.M. the whole army was in motion, down the dusty streets and eastward toward the brownish-green hills that rose majestically in the afternoon sun. Residents of Winchester lined the streets, cheering, singing, and shouting words of encouragement to loved ones and relatives. Regimental bands began to blare out lively choruses of "Dixie" and "The Bonnie Blue Flag." How proud a sight it was, wrote Mrs. Cornelia McDonald, to witness the departing army "in gallant array, with the Confederate banners waving, the bands playing, and the bayonets gleaming in the sun. . . . Many of the companies were made up of mere boys, but their earnest and joyous faces were fully as reassuring as the martial music was inspiriting." [32]

Others among the 1,700 residents of Winchester were not so moved. The sight of kin and close friends marching off to unknown battlefields gave rise to much weeping, heightened no doubt by the realization that Winchester was now void of all protective troops save hospitalized soldiers left behind by Johnston and equivalent in number to the town's population. The townspeople had no way of knowing the deprivations which would befall them in the course of the war. As Jackson's Valley base, and as a target for conquest by both sides, Winchester would be captured and recaptured more than seventy-five times. In one twenty-four-hour period alone it changed hands four times.[33]

---

32. *Ibid.*, 28, 51.
33. Frederic Morton, *The Story of Winchester in Virginia* (Strasburg, Va., 1925), 143–50, 193.

III

CHAPTER IV

IMMORTALITY AT MANASSAS

Uppermost in the puzzled minds of the troops who followed the winding road eastward from Winchester was their eventual destination. Were they en route to fight or were they simply moving to another spot to sit and wait out the war? Just outside of town Johnston halted the army and sent the answer to their question through the ranks. A Confederate army in the Centreville–Manassas Junction area had been attacked by heavy Federal forces. The Valley regiments were rushing to reinforce the army, and the likelihood was strong that there would be a fight. A wild cheer rolled down the columns as each regiment received the news. The First Brigade, in the van of Johnston's army, promptly resumed the march on a dead run. Yet the oppressive heat and the distance to be covered soon caused the men to slow down to the "route step" usually employed on marches.[1]

At sundown Jackson's men reached the Shenandoah River, suspended their clothes and cartridge belts from their musket barrels, and forded the breast-high stream. Wet soldiers continued marching briskly until sundown, when the four-abreast columns began ascending the steep, packed road that led through the mountains. The march up was long and hard; weariness began to tell on the army; straggling reached "fearful" stages. At midnight the lead regiments stumbled through Ashby's Gap and moved slowly down the hillside that leveled at the bottom into the plains of Manassas. By 2 A.M. the army could go no farther. Jackson ordered his regiments to bivouac halfway down the mountain slope. Men slumped down beside trees and boulders and quickly dropped off into an exhausted slumber. Jackson, making a final sentry inspection, discovered guards correctly at their posts—but sound asleep. He knew that the raw troops were completely fatigued and that an attack by Federals was highly improbable. With an uncharacteristic benevolence he allowed the guards to go to bed, while he himself acted as a solitary but vigilant guard throughout the remainder of the night.

At dawn the columns again were kicking up dust as they proceeded to the railroad depot at Piedmont. The trains had not arrived when the troops reached the railhead and fell out to the shade of nearby trees. In a few minutes the locomotives came into view and shortly wheezed to a stop. Men climbed aboard the freight cars and held on as the trains jerked into motion toward Manassas. At several stops along the way citizens crowded around the soldiers, bestowing food and encouragement on men in whose hands the destiny of Virginia had been placed.

It was late in the afternoon when the trains ground to a halt at Manassas. Men hurriedly formed ranks and marched off through broken country toward Beauregard's army, aligned in battle position near a lazy stream known as Bull Run. The Valley regiments

---

1. See *Southern Historical Society Papers*, IX (1881), 130. For allowing Johnston to escape unmolested from the Valley, Patterson shortly was sent into retirement and replaced tardily by General N. P. Banks.

passed fresh graves that gave evidence of the action of the eighteenth, then went into camp in a clump of pines just behind Blackburn's and Mitchell's Fords. The position of the Valley regiments was in support of General James Longstreet's brigade, which formed the extreme Confederate right.

The night passed in uneasiness and fearful expectation. Most of the men in the brigade held up well; a few did not. One member of the Thirty-third Regiment tried to exempt himself from further duty by shooting off his toe. His aim was poor and he blew off half his foot.[2] The sleep of a majority of the troops was broken at 4:30 A.M. on a Sunday that gave early promise of being sultry. The roar of cannon suddenly echoed from the left. Hastily the brigade formed into battle line to guard the two fords. There it remained for three hours until, just as the sun was beginning to climb over the trees, a courier galloped up to Jackson with urgent orders.

To the surprise of the men in the ranks, they were suddenly wheeled to the rear and double-quicked through woods and across fields. Toward 11 A.M. the panting and perspiring troops pulled up behind the crest of Henry House Hill, the anchor of the Confederate left. This ridge ran at right angles to Bull Run, its northern end overlooking the Stone Bridge. To the northwest lay Matthews Hill, and between the two ridges was a deep ravine through which meandered Young's Branch. The northern face of Henry House Hill was bare; its other three slopes were heavily wooded, making it easily defensible should Federals assault it from the north or northwest. Even as Jackson rode up to the crest to look over the lay of the land, Federals in strength could be seen pressing toward Matthews Hill, trying to envelop the meager defending force there of three Confederate brigades.

Jackson quickly sent word to General Bernard Bee, commanding in the sector, that he was on the field. He hoped the Confederates might hold out until he could deploy his own men. But the gray line on Matthews Hill was buckling; Jackson's orders to his five regimental colonels were crisper and more curt than usual. Two accompanying batteries—commanded by Captains John Imboden and Hugh M. Stanard—were placed in the center of the crest, with

2. Casler, *Stonewall Brigade*, 33.

the Fourth and Twenty-seventh Regiments stationed as support in their rear. The Fifth Regiment was posted on their right, a little detached from the main body in order to utilize the cover of a small clump of trees. To the left of the guns were the Second and Thirty-third Regiments, all of the latter and part of the former being sheltered in another grove. It was five hundred yards from Colonel Arthur Cummings' Thirty-third across the bare and level crest to the position of Colonel Harper's Fifth. The regiments were in two lines, each two ranks deep. Because the Fourth and Twenty-seventh overlapped each other behind the guns, their ranks appeared eight deep.

For two and a half hours the brigade lay hugging the ground behind the crest. Gravity and astonishment were written on every face as shells exploded over the men's heads and into their midst. The stream of wounded who crawled and limped over the hill and through their ranks told of the severity of the fight across the way and only added to the misery of the Virginians. One veteran later wrote of a soldier in Company C of the Fourth Regiment who, after every nearby explosion, earnestly beseeched: "Oh Lord! Have mercy upon me! Have mercy upon me!" A companion lying next to him seconded his every plea with "Me, too, Lord! Me, too, Lord!" [3]

Over on the left, fear was just as prevalent in the Thirty-third Regiment. One of the "characters" in the brigade was "Old Major" William Nelson, an elderly gentleman serving with Pendleton's artillery and known to the men for the half-civilian, half-military dress that he wore. During this bombardment, one soldier later wrote, a member of the Thirty-third suddenly screamed out, "Good Lord! What have I done that the devil should come after me?" Nearby troops looked apprehensively at the shouting man and saw him gazing with eyes full of fear toward the woods to the left. There rode Nelson, calm and unconcerned, a tremendous stovepipe hat atop his head.[4]

All the while the din of battle grew increasingly louder. Near 2 P.M. larger numbers of demoralized men poured through the ranks of the Virginia brigade and gave notice that the Confederate

3. J. B. Caddall, 4th Regiment, in Richmond *Times-Dispatch*, November 27, 1904.
4. Randolph Barton, 33rd Regiment, in *Confederate Veteran*, VIII (1900), 483.

line on Matthews Hill had broken. Those posted near where Jackson stood quietly saw General Bee ride up and confirm verbally to Jackson what they had surmised. Bee was covered with dirt and perspiration; his sword dangled loosely in his right hand. "General!" he shouted at Jackson. "They are beating us back!"

Jackson gazed calmly for a moment at the avalanche of blue pouring down the opposite hillside and replied, "Then, sir, we will give them the bayonet." [5] He then ordered the First Brigade up to a position just below the crest of the hill.

Bee yanked his horse around and galloped toward Henry House, around which his retreating men were swarming. The South Carolinian rose in his stirrups and, pointing his sword to the hilltop, cried, "Look! There is Jackson standing like a stone wall! Rally behind the Virginians!" [6] Fragments of the three brigades began to veer to the right and fall in behind Jackson's line.

In the meantime, Jackson had ordered his nervous men into a crouched position, poised for any command. The troops were heartened considerably when Pendleton's four-gun battery and five other cannon under Ephraim Alburtis jingled up to the top of the ridge and were quickly rolled into position. Yet at least one man in Jackson's brigade still felt some discomfort. When General P. G. T. Beauregard rode up to the base of Henry House Hill, Private Sam Wright of the Second Regiment was so happy to see the commander in the sector that he left ranks and walked jubilantly up to the General, who accepted his warm handshake. [7]

The noise had now become almost ear-shattering. Cannon firing on both sides, shells bursting, and the constant crack of musketry all were supplemented by cheering Federal soldiers now moving up

---

5. Henderson, *Stonewall Jackson*, I, 145.
6. A dispute has long existed as to whether Bee was referring to Jackson or Jackson's men "standing like a stone wall." The statement given in the text is the one commonly used. Different versions of the origin of the name "Stonewall" may be found in Douglas, *I Rode with Stonewall*, 10; *Confederate Veteran*, VIII (1900), 483; *Southern Historical Society Papers*, XIX (1891), 164–67; Barton, *Recollections*, 13; John Haskell, *The Haskell Memoirs*, edited by Gilbert E. Govan and James Livingood (New York, 1960), 22–23; Freeman, *Lee's Lieutenants*, I, 733–34; Vandiver, *Mighty Stonewall*, 161; Walker, *VMI Memorial*, 224; William Couper, *One Hundred Years at V. M. I.* (Richmond, 1939), II, 161–62.
7. Baylor, *Bull Run to Bull Run*, 21.

the hill amid swirling dust and smoke. Jackson's line became obscured by a yellow haze. The commander himself, wearing a blue
military coat with the shoulder straps of a U.S. colonel, rode up
and down the line. His eyes blazed from beneath a kepi that sloped
over his forehead. "Steady, men, steady!" he said to the nervous,
crouched troops. "All's well! All's well!" When a spent bullet struck
his left hand, breaking a finger, he brushed it off as a scratch and
wrapped the bleeding hand in a handkerchief. All the while he
kept his eyes to the front.[8]

The situation was perilous. Waves of bluecoats, invigorated by
the taste of victory, swarmed up the face of Henry House Hill. Two
Federal batteries, eleven guns under Captains J. B. Ricketts and
Charles Griffin, came halfway up the rise and quickly opened a
direct fire obliquely into Jackson's left, which recoiled in confusion.
At that moment cavalry under the command of the dashing Stuart
(who was guarding Jackson's western flank) raced down the hill
and tore into the exposed Federal right. Almost simultaneously
Colonel Arthur Cummings, who had been viewing the action from
atop the hill, returned to his Thirty-third Regiment; smiling grimly,
the Mexican War veteran shouted, "Boys, they are coming! Now
wait until they get close before you shoot." [9] But the combination
of close-range bombardment and the near approach of Federal
infantry was more than the Valley men could stand. Seeing Stuart's
horsemen galloping into action, the regiment leaped over the crest
and sent scattered shots through the dust in the direction of the
Federal lines. Cummings, visibly excited and without orders, bellowed, "Charge!" and with a roar the Thirty-third Regiment broke
from its position and dashed toward the two batteries barely discernible in the fog of battle.[10]

Griffin, on Ricketts' right, had fired only two rounds from his
Federal battery when a line of dust-covered infantry appeared in
the smoke to his right. The troops scaled a snake-rail fence and continued forward. They halted momentarily while an officer stepped

8. *Battles and Leaders*, I, 236.   9. Barton, *Recollections*, 11–12.
10. After the war Cummings explained his unauthorized assault by declaring that
his men were so nervous he was not sure he could even maintain his position. He felt
too that the men would do much better if they could get into action and not have
to stand further bombardment from an enemy they could not see. *Southern Historical
Society Papers*, XXXIV (1906), 369.

out and appeared to make a brief speech. The line then moved westward a few yards, suddenly swerved southward, and started for the guns. In the dust, smoke, and confusion, Federal gunners withheld their fire to ascertain if the troops were expected reinforcements. The hesitation was fatal. Seventy yards from the two batteries, the infantry—Jackson's Thirty-third Regiment—delivered a sweeping fire into the guns that sent men and horses crumpling to the ground. Ricketts himself fell seriously wounded. Of more overall importance, the shock of the Virginians' assault destroyed the morale and effectiveness of both batteries for the remainder of the battle. Griffin managed to drag off three of his guns, leaving the others behind to become the targets of conquest by both sides.

Joyfully the Thirty-third Regiment rushed for the cannon—only to run headlong into terrible fire from the New York Zouaves and the First Michigan, both of which had been stationed in support of the batteries. The force of the Federal fire sent the Virginians back up the hill in disorder. They collapsed against the Second Regiment, creating further confusion on the Confederate left. As order was being restored, an excited officer of the Thirty-third rushed up to Jackson. "General!" he exclaimed. "The day is going against us!"

"If you think so, sir," came the quiet admonition, "you had better not say anything about it." [11]

The Federals were not lacking in courage. Again they started up the steep slope of Henry House Hill. Artillery behind them tried to cover their advance with a blanket barrage. Jackson watched the oncoming lines for a few seconds, then turned to the officers of the Fourth and Twenty-seventh Regiments standing behind him and said, "Order the men to stand up. We'll charge them now and drive them to Washington." [12] Like a man "determined to conquer or die," the General looked up his line and shouted, "Reserve your fire until they come within fifty yards, then fire and give them the bayonet; and, when you charge, yell like furies!" [13]

The men along the crest braced themselves. Except for members

---

11. Henderson, *Stonewall Jackson*, I, 150.
12. J. Gray McAllister, *Sketch of Captain Thompson McAllister, Co. A, 27th Virginia Regiment* (Petersburg, 1896), 18.
13. Lexington *Gazette*, August 1, 1861; Henderson, *Stonewall Jackson*, I, 151.

of the Thirty-third Regiment, none had yet seen the Federals. The signal was given; men who had fidgeted and squirmed under an almost three-hour bombardment leaped over the hilltop—"glad of the chance," one of them wrote.[14] An unbroken line swelled across the open plain and delivered a murderous fire into the face of the unsuspecting Federals. The Union line fell apart. Before it could recover, "like wild men" the Second, Fourth, and Twenty-seventh Regiments charged down the hill by companies, leaning forward as if bucking a strong wind.[15] Above the crash of musketry and roar of cannon came that piercing cry forever after known as "the Rebel yell." [16]

The center of the Federal line melted away as Jackson's three regiments broke through and veered left and right. The Fifth Regiment rushed into action, adding extra momentum to the charge. All four regiments swept across the hillside and past the two silent batteries. Lieutenant Frank Paxton of the Fourth Regiment planted his regiment's colors beside the guns. In a matter of minutes the flag was pierced by no less than fourteen bullets.[17] Part of the Fifth Regiment then gathered about the batteries. A captain in the unit prior to the charge had promised a barrel of whisky to the first of his company to reach the guns. As the captain dashed up to the battery, there sitting on one of the cannon was Private Jim Frazier, smiling and shouting, "Don't forget that barrel, captain!" [18]

Colonel William Harman of the Fifth came up and found the wounded Ricketts, with whom he had served in the Mexican War, still lying beside his battery. Harman quickly had Ricketts borne to the rear in an ambulance of the Fifth Regiment.[19] Elsewhere

---

14. James N. Bosang, *Memoirs of a Pulaski Veteran of the Stonewall Brigade* [Radford, Va., 1912], 8.

15. John W. Daniel, 27th Regiment, in *Confederate Veteran*, XXXIX (1931), 358.

16. Daniel always insisted this was the first instance in the war when this famous yell was given. Richmond *Times-Dispatch*, November 27, 1904.

17. John G. Paxton (ed.), *Elisha Franklin Paxton: Memoir and Memorials* (New York, 1907), 12–13. Hereinafter cited as Paxton (ed.), *Memoir*. See also John L. Johnson, *The University Memorial* (Baltimore, 1871), 348.

18. LaBree (ed.), *Camp Fires of the Confederacy*, 322. The same story, with variations, appears in Opie, *Rebel Cavalryman*, 35–36, and in W. S. Dunlop, *Lee's Sharpshooters* (Little Rock, 1899), 339–40.

19. Opie, *Rebel Cavalryman*, 35–36.

along the hill, fighting continued: close, desperate, and costly to both sides. Jackson's brigade was engaged from the batteries across the slope to Henry House itself. Organization vanished as men fought individually and in small groups. Bronson Gwynn of the Fourth Regiment ran into a Federal soldier who rammed his bayonet through Gwynn's shirt, barely touching the skin. Before the Yankee could extricate the weapon, Gwynn shoved his musket into the man's face and blew his head to pieces.[20] A private in the Fifth Regiment exchanged shots at close range with a Federal. Both missed and quickly began reloading their guns for a second shot. When the Confederate saw that he was losing the race, he allegedly picked up a rock and hurled it with deadly accuracy at the blue-coat.[21]

But the Virginians also sustained their share of casualties. As the Thirty-third Regiment swept down the hillside in support, a Federal shell tore into its midst with a violent explosion. Found afterwards, lying side by side, were Holmes Conrad, Jr., his brother Tucker, and their cousin, Peyton Harrison.[22]

Hand-to-hand fighting continued bitterly for almost an hour. The Second Regiment succeeded in dragging off one of Ricketts' guns before Federal cannon and musketry again turned the area into a no-man's land. But the blue tide was beginning to ebb. With all Federal reserve units now engaged and barely able to hold their ground, Beauregard ordered a counterattack all along the line. Jackson's men were slowly pushing the bluecoats down the hill when in from their left rushed the fresh troops of General E. Kirby Smith's brigade. These men had double-timed to the battlefield from the train station at Manassas, and their arrival guaranteed Southern success. In a matter of minutes the battle was over. What shortly before had been an advancing Federal force confident of victory now became a defeated and somewhat demoralized mob, fleeing for the Stone Bridge and safety. Jackson's brigade joined in the pursuit and would have continued their harassment on into the night had not they, like the rest of the Confederate army, been stopped by Beauregard's orders. Just after sundown a rain began to

20. Lee (ed.), *Pendleton*, 151. 21. Opie, *Rebel Cavalryman*, 43.
22. McDonald, *Diary*, 29.

cool the hot air and settle the dust. As raindrops washed dirt from weary faces, the men of the First Brigade trudged back to Manassas and encampment. Some of the men not heavily engaged that afternoon were disappointed that the pursuit had been halted, but few were unappreciative of the order to fall back and rest.

Victory for Jackson's brigade had been dearly bought. Casualties totaled 111 dead, 373 wounded and missing out of 2,600 men engaged. The Fourth and Twenty-seventh Regiments, in the center of the line, appeared to bear the brunt of the losses, the former suffering 31 killed and 100 wounded, the latter 19 killed and 122 wounded.[23] Although officers reported some instances of cowardice by their raw troops, this was forgotten in the praise heaped upon the brigade. Jackson himself was overjoyed at its baptism into war. The day after the battle the newly dubbed "Stonewall" wrote to J. M. Bennett:

I am more than satisfied with the part performed by my brigade during the action . . . You will find, when my report shall be published, that the First Brigade was to our army what the Imperial Guard was to the First Napoleon—that, through the blessing of God, it met the thus far victorious enemy and turned the fortunes of the day.[24]

From all corners of the Confederacy, elation at the Southern victory singled out Jackson and his brigade more conspicuously than any other individuals or units engaged.[25] Virginia was justly proud of its accomplishments, as the Winchester *Republican* commented editorially: "If Virginia does nothing more than was done by this Brigade on the field of Manassas, she has repelled the imputation of degeneracy, and proved that she is equal to her best days." The paper then went on to poke fun at the Federals by stating:

---

23. *Official Records*, II, 482; William Fox, *Regimental Losses in the American Civil War, 1861–1865* (Albany, N.Y., 1889), 557, 560.

24. Roy Bird Cook, *The Family and Early Life of Stonewall Jackson* (Charlestown, W. Va., 1948), 161–62. In a letter written to his wife on the same day, Jackson said: "Whilst great credit is due in other parts of our gallant army, God made my brigade more instrumental than any other in repulsing the main attack." Mrs. Jackson, *Memoirs*, 178.

25. For example, see *Official Records*, II, 475, 500; William C. Rives to his wife, August 23, 1861, William Cabell Rives Papers, Library of Congress.

To take Manassas Junction
The Yankees thought was fun,
But greatly were mistaken,
For they only took the Run.[26]

Brigade members spent most of that Sunday night recounting personal feats of heroism. Tales of valor multiplied as the night passed, and humorous incidents made the rounds of the camp, greeted always with the hoots of laughter that come so easily when nervous tension gives way to relaxation. Probably the biggest laugh of all that rainy night was at the expense of Private T. C. Green of the Second Regiment. Before the battle Green had been outspoken in the number of Federals he intended killing, and at day's end he went through the camp recounting how many of the enemy he had shot before something went wrong with his gun. When a messmate examined the weapon, he found that the gun had not been fired at all, but was full of unexploded charges. In his excitement Green had gone through the motions of loading and firing, but had omitted some essentials, such as changing caps and pulling the trigger, and hence had done absolutely no harm to the enemy.[27]

For a week the brigade remained in camp near the junction, until sanitary conditions became so bad as to necessitate a move. The one stream that passed through the camp drained from the battlefield and brought with it all the odors associated with the bloated corpses still around Henry House Hill. Little wonder the brigade nicknamed the area "Camp Maggot." When typhoid fever began infiltrating the camp, Jackson received permission to move one mile east of Centreville. The change of base occurred on August 2, and was welcomed by all. Of the new site, named Camp Harman, Clem Fishburne of the Rockbridge Artillery wrote:

It was a pleasant camp and our life here was as pleasant as camp life could be. We got provisions in abundance, either from neighboring farms or from our homes, we had occasional visits from friends, and had many additions to our company—chiefly university students who

26. Winchester *Republican*, August 16, 1861.
27. Humphreys, *Heroes and Spies*, 200.

had no other more attractive commands with which to cast their fortunes.[28]

Fishburne's comment reflected the elated Southern spirit prevalent in that first autumn of the war. Morale was higher than it would ever be again. There were few rumors of battle. Men assigned to picket duty made friends with their foes across the way, for the Stonewall Brigade entered fully into the easy fraternization that characterized the Civil War. On occasion, incidents occurred to remind the men that they were a part of war. One night three pickets of the Second Regiment got into such a loud argument over secession that Federal sentries fired in the direction of their voices and killed one of them.[29] But the three things which most concerned the men were weather, Jackson's training, and furloughs.

Fall came early in 1861, and with it came cold, lazy rains that thoroughly soaked both skin and clothing. Because Jackson had strict orders against fires at night, the men were forced to endure the elements in their tents without benefit of any kind of heat. It was not at all uncommon for wind to blow the tents away in the middle of the night, or for rain to pour through the doors, which had to stay open, said Jackson, so that the men could hop out double-quick in case of alarm.

Not a man to watch time pass unused, Jackson trained and retrained his troops, determined to make them as perfect a brigade as existed in the Confederate armies. He marched and countermarched them, taught them every military movement in the tactics book, and so stressed the doctrine of obeying unhesitatingly every order issued them that the men became soldiers by reflex— the real secret of successful troops. Jackson knew First Manassas had proved their valor; he strove during the idle period to improve their discipline.

He was successful in almost every phase except where furloughs were concerned. Many feigned illness in an attempt to get home for a brief spell. Others, realizing the futility of sending a furlough request to Jackson, simply "went over the hill" on what were

---

28. Journal of Clement D. Fishburne, Alderman Library, University of Virginia.
29. Baylor, *Bull Run to Bull Run*, 26–27.

called "French furloughs" and came back to expected terms in the stockade. Just after Manassas an officer in the Stonewall Brigade received word that his wife was dying. He applied at once for an emergency furlough, and was stunned when told Jackson had refused it. The officer rushed to Jackson's tent and insisted in strong terms that he be allowed to go to his wife. In even stronger terms Jackson replied, "Man, man, do you love your wife more than your country?" The request again was denied, the wife died, and the officer never forgave Jackson.[30]

For the most part, however, these were happy and carefree days. Always at hand for concerts and serenades was the Fifth Regiment's "Stonewall Brigade Band." Organized in 1855 and given their new name soon after First Manassas, the musicians won additional laurels as medical assistants in battle. Jackson greatly enjoyed their music, though he confessed in private that he could not distinguish one song from another, regardless of who played it.[31] Religious services were held regularly, with at least two sermons on Sunday—a day the commander of the Stonewall Brigade was initially very strict in observing.

When on September 16 the brigade moved from Camp Harman to a less desirable site near Fairfax Court House, the "cheerfulness and spirit" which one officer thought so characteristic of Virginians in the unit seemed unimpaired.[32] Another officer, Captain Hugh White of the Fourth Regiment, wrote his sister: "If there be one in the army who does not find it more pleasant to endure the hardships of the camp, than to be at ease at home, he ought to be, if he is not, a Yankee." [33]

Apparently, few soldiers during those languid weeks shared the farsighted opinions of Major F. B. Jones of the Second Regiment, who stated in a letter home: "I have given up all hope of peace. A gloomy war, a long war, and a bloody one, you may depend upon it, is before us, and we may as well make up our minds to it." [34]

30. Douglas, *I Rode with Stonewall*, 236–37.
31. *Confederate Veteran*, VIII (1900), 304; Mrs. Jackson, *Memoirs*, 184, 192.
32. Caption of Events card, Company A, 27th Regiment, July–August, 1861, War Records Group, National Archives.
33. William S. White, *Hugh White*, 59.   34. Walker, *VMI Memorial*, 306.

On October 13 Jackson was promoted to major general. Eight days later the Confederacy established the Department of Northern Virginia, consisting of the Valley, Potomac, and Aquia districts. Jackson was soon ordered to take command of the Valley District, with headquarters at Winchester. Most of the men realized that the promotion foretold his transfer. The day of departure was November 4. Early that morning the regimental colonels went to his tent to say good-by. Later, on Jackson's invitation, a party from each company came in to pay its respects. As the contingent from the Second Regiment was leaving, young Kyd Douglas tried to tell Jackson how much his old brigade was going to miss him and how highly he was regarded in their eyes. Jackson expressed his pleasure at their sentiments and his disappointment at not being able to take them with him. "I shall never forget them," he told Douglas. "In battle I shall always want them. I will not be satisfied until I get them. Goodbye." [35]

The men in the ranks begged so earnestly for one last audience that Jackson agreed to speak to them before he left. At one o'clock that raw November afternoon he rode out into the field behind the Second Regiment's tents. There the regiments, with the exception of the Fifth, which was on picket duty, were drawn up in close order. The men did not applaud but the tears that streamed down rough and sunburnt faces told more than a thousand tongues of their devotion to their chief. Jackson sat astride his horse for a moment, looked over the men's heads into the distance, turned his eyes toward the troops, and began speaking:

Officers and men of the First Brigade, I am not here to make a speech, but simply to say farewell. I first met you at Harpers Ferry at the commencement of the war, and I cannot take leave of you without giving expression to my admiration of your conduct from that day to this, whether on the march, in the bivouac, the tented field, or on the bloody plains of Manassas, where you gained the well-deserved reputation of having decided the fate of the battle.

---

35. Douglas, *I Rode with Stonewall*, 15. According to Douglas, Jackson also stated to his chaplain, William White: "Had this communication not come as an order, I should instantly have declined it and continued in command of my brave old brigade." See also James H. Langhorne to his mother, November 4, 1861, Langhorne Letters.

Throughout the broad extent of the country through which you have marched, by your respect of the rights and property of citizens, you have shown that you were soldiers not only to defend, but able and willing both to defend and protect. You have already gained a brilliant and deservedly high reputation, throughout the army and the whole Confederacy, and I trust in the future by your own deeds on the field, and by the assistance of the same kind Providence who heretofore favored our cause, you will win more victories and add additional lustre to the reputation you now enjoy. You have already gained a proud position in the history of this, our second War of Independence. I shall look with great anxiety to your future movements, and I trust whenever I shall hear of the First Brigade on the field of battle, it will be of still nobler deeds achieved and higher reputation won.

Here Jackson paused for a moment. He dropped the reins across his horse's neck, rose in the stirrups, raised his hand to the troops who had made him famous, and continued in a high voice:

In the Army of the Shenandoah, you were the First Brigade! In the Army of the Potomac you were the First Brigade! In the Second Corps of this army you were the First Brigade! You are the First Brigade in the affections of your general, and I hope by your future deeds and bearing you will be handed down to posterity as the First Brigade in this, our second War of Independence. Farewell! [36]

For a few seconds no sound broke the stillness. Then the cheers began, individual and scattered at first, but soon swelling into a roar of voices that shook the countryside. Again and again the tribute rose in resounding hurrahs until Jackson, unable to stand the emotional display any longer, waved his cap at the men and rode rapidly off toward the Valley.

After Jackson's departure the camp was like a cemetery, save for brief but frequent periods of animation caused by rumors that the brigade was soon to rejoin its old leader. The rumors were inspired by hope; yet, unknown to the men, moves were already underway to fulfill their wishes. Jackson had no sooner arrived

36. The version given here is taken largely from Douglas, *I Rode with Stonewall*, 16–17, as Douglas and another member of the 2nd Regiment wrote out the text of Jackson's farewell less than half an hour after he delivered it. No two versions seem to agree. Henderson's account has thirty-one discrepancies when compared to the Douglas version, yet the latter account is largely substantiated by other transcriptions in Graybill, *Diary*, 9–10; Lexington *Gazette*, November 21, 1861; Couper, *One Hundred Years at V. M. I.*, IV, 166.

at Winchester than he was appalled by the lack of adequate and experienced defenders for the Valley. He immediately telegraphed Richmond for reinforcements, which by his special request were to include his old brigade.

On November 7 joy swept through the Fairfax camp. The First Brigade was ordered to Winchester "with the least practicable delay"—an order carried out to the letter.[37] Never again as long as Jackson lived would these men be separated from their beloved commander. But this they could not know.

---

37. *Official Records*, V, 389–90, 936, 958. General Johnston protested the transfer of the brigade from his command, but was reassured by Secretary of War Judah P. Benjamin that he would be sent twice the number of men as replacements. *Ibid.*, 940.

CHAPTER V

THE TEST OF PATRIOTISM

Not even a cold rain on Friday, November 8, could dampen the spirits of the Stonewall Brigade as it left camp at Fairfax Court House and marched to Manassas to board trains for the west. Several jubilant men fortified themselves along the way with whisky and, according to a member of the Thirty-third Regiment, "there was a jolly time quieting them." [1] The next morning only enough freight trains showed up to transport the Second, Fifth, and Twenty-seventh Regiments. The Fourth and Thirty-third had to remain behind for a day in a pouring rain, standing in what one member of the Fourth Regiment was certain was at least three feet of mud. [2] Finally, at 8:30 A.M. on an overcast Sabbath, the

---

1. Graybill, *Diary*, 10. See also Philip Slaughter, A *Sketch of the Life of Randolph Fairfax* (Baltimore, 1878), 20. Hereinafter cited as Slaughter, *Fairfax*.
2. James H. Langhorne to his mother, November 12, 1861, Langhorne Letters.

last of the brigade climbed aboard drafty boxcars and the trains lurched out of Manassas Junction.

Troops shivered in the damp air as the cars rumbled slowly through the Blue Ridge Mountains and down once more into the Valley of Virginia. Yet thoughts of returning to their native region warmed most of the men considerably. They whooped and sang, shouted at pretty girls along the way, and waved happily at friends and relatives. At sundown on November 10 the last train screeched to a halt at Strasburg. Lack of accommodations in town forced the soldiers to sleep in the uncomfortable and drafty boxcars. The march to Winchester began early the next morning. A bright sun soon dried damp uniforms. It even dried out the muddy road enough to make walking tolerable.

"Every little town we past through we were received with great pleasure," wrote a member of the Fourth Regiment's Montgomery Fencibles. "Every boddy seem glad to see us. The ladys said they had not forgotten the Stone Wall & had no fear of the Yankeys now." [3] Mrs. Judith McGuire affirmed this sentiment by stating: "We are greatly relieved to have that noble brigade in our midst." [4]

Early in the afternoon the last of the brigade marched into Kernstown, four miles south of Winchester. Word reached the troops that the citizens of Winchester had offered the tired soldiers the comfort of their homes, but that Jackson had declined the offer. Many grumbled at having to bivouac in a wet field, and for a few minutes the Fifth Regiment seemed on the verge of mutiny. [5]

The regiments spent one day at Kernstown, then marched through Winchester and four and one-half miles out the Stephenson road. Here they settled at a place officially called "Camp Stephenson," but known popularly among the men as "New Centreville." From the day they arrived, the elements seemed to turn against them. Freezing winds made the troops miserable; slashing rain and sleet turned the area into an icy quagmire. A large portion of the brigade was soon prostrated by influenza and measles. Hundreds of others went through the weakening throes

---

3. Jim P. Charlton to O. P. Charlton, November 18, 1861, Charlton Letters.
4. Judith W. McGuire, *Diary of a Refugee*, 72.
5. See Opie, *Rebel Cavalryman*, 48–50.

of diarrhea (which the Valley troops generally called "the Virginia quick-steps"). Men grew exceedingly anxious to know when they would go into winter quarters. And "the *colder the day*," wrote the Fourth Regiment's Jim Langhorne, "the more numerous the inquiries." [6] Others felt Old Jack was aware of their condition and would soon alleviate it. "All the troops have the greatest confidence in General Jackson," a member of the Liberty Hall Volunteers stated, "and know he will have everything done in its own proper time." [7]

The healthier men of the brigade tried to ameliorate their situation by slipping into Winchester "to enjoy the sights." Jackson issued orders forbidding troops from entering the town; to enforce the directive, he posted a protective ring of state militia around Winchester. To many of the adventuresome souls in the Stonewall Brigade (and there apparently *were* many), these hurdles were but challenges to their resourcefulness and ingenuity. On the very first night that Jackson's prohibitive order was in effect, some members of the Twenty-seventh Regiment tried to plead their way past the guards. When this failed, the veterans simply got their muskets, pretended to load them, and, emitting that high-pitched Rebel yell, charged the outposts. The totally inexperienced militia fled in panic.

Others acted with more finesse. Those who wanted the revelry of Winchester without any trouble with the sentries simply flanked the guard stations; a dozen or more men sauntered brazenly past the guards, brandishing forged passes from Old Jack himself. First prize for inventiveness, however, went to Jim Frazier of the Fifth Regiment. He armed a squad of men, marched them up to a sentry post, and informed the befuddled guards that General Jackson had ordered the squad into Winchester to round up the scoundrels who had disobeyed orders. The men marched with precision into Winchester, then broke ranks with loud guffaws as each man sought his pleasure. Through many and similar acts of subterfuge, Private George Baylor recalled, "I think it safe to say that fully half of the *First Brigade* visited Winchester that night."

6. James H. Langhorne to his father, November 25, 1861, Langhorne Letters.
7. Lexington *Gazette*, November 28, 1861.

Small wonder that by month's end a very harassed company commander in the Second Regiment was moved to report of his unit: "Its discipline is not such as its Commander would wish it to be, particularly in the matter of absence without leave which he has labored hard to arrest, but which cannot be stopped without the most rigorous measures." [8]

In the meantime, dispositions had been made for Jackson's successor as head of the brigade. Through the early part of November, Colonel James Preston of the Fourth Regiment was interim commander. Yet this elderly warrior, exposed to the coldness of that month, was soon so plagued with rheumatism as to be useless, and the command devolved on Colonel James Allen of the Second. On December 2 Jackson wrote the adjutant general in Richmond of the need for a good brigade commander; two days later Brigadier General Richard B. Garnett was assigned to the post. When Garnett reached Winchester, Colonel Preston escorted him to New Centreville to greet his troops, drawn up in silence to meet their commander. Many of them doubtless felt as Preston did— that command of the brigade should have gone to one of the regimental colonels. Yet their devotion to duty, and Garnett's personable nature, soon dissolved dissensions. [9]

Born in 1819 on his father's estate in Essex County, Virginia, Dick Garnett came from the best of Tidewater aristocracy. He and his cousin Robert (who was killed in western Virginia soon after the war began) attended West Point and were graduated together in the Class of 1841, Dick Garnett ranking twenty-ninth in his class. For the next twenty years he served at frontier garrisons from Florida to the Dakotas, and from Texas to the California gold mines. One of the most noted Indian fighters in the West, he won friends easily. Yet promotion was disappointingly slow; by 1861 he was no higher than a captain in the Sixth U.S. Infantry. When war loomed on the horizon, Garnett spoke pub-

---

8. Baylor, *Bull Run to Bull Run*, 28–31; Opie, *Rebel Cavalryman*, 48–51, 56–58; Casler, *Stonewall Brigade*, 68; Regimental Returns, Company I, 2nd Regiment, December, 1861, War Records Group, National Archives.

9. Elizabeth P. Allen, *The Life and Letters of Margaret Junkin Preston* (Boston, 1903), 125. Hereinafter cited as Allen, *Preston*. Obviously, Jackson did not consider any of his colonels experienced enough for brigade command.

licly of the crisis but once—and that was a strong plea to preserve the Union.[10] At Virginia's secession, however, he resigned from the army and hastened home to offer his services to the Confederacy.

During the first months of the war he served as a major of artillery. Conspicuous conduct brought him a brigadier's stars on November 14, 1861. On December 7 this handsome officer with brown wavy hair and finely cropped beard was ordered to the command of the Stonewall Brigade. The men's first impression of Jackson's successor was favorable. One brigade member wrote his father: "He is a man about 42–43 years old, light hair, blue eyes & light complexion & has rather a pleasant face. . . . He is said to be a competent officer." [11] In the weeks that followed, Garnett quickly gained the confidence of the officers and the admiration of the men. Even Old Jack came to grunt approval of his leadership.

Yet Garnett displayed a major fault, at least in Jackson's eyes. He pampered his brigade. He listened to the men's requests and tried to grant each one of them. To the Valley fighters he became as much a guardian as a commander—a benevolence that often ran contrary to Jackson's rigid schedule. For example, soon after taking command of the brigade Garnett saw how fatigued his men were becoming during a particularly strenuous march. Without waiting for Jackson's approval, he ordered them to stop marching, fall out, and cook their meals. That Jackson overlooked the incident might have been due to more pressing matters—or to the men whom Garnett commanded: Jackson's own Stonewall Brigade.[12]

Early in December, possibly to break the monotony at the Yankees' expense, Jackson decided to destroy Dam No. 5 on the Chesapeake & Ohio Railroad canal. Running alongside the Potomac from Cumberland, Maryland, to Washington, this waterway was the major channel for shipping coal into the North. By demolishing the dam, Jackson reasoned, the canal would be neutralized and Northern industry and transportation would suffer appreciably.

---

10. Walter Harrison, *Pickett's Men: A Fragment of War History* (New York, 1870), 19.
11. James H. Langhorne to his father, December 7, 1861, Langhorne Letters.
12. Henry A. White, *Stonewall Jackson* (New York, 1909), 105–106.

An attempt was made on December 8 to accomplish the task. Federals in unexpected strength blocked the move. On Monday night, December 16, the whole Stonewall Brigade left camp and marched fifteen miles to Martinsburg, rested a few hours, and then moved another thirteen miles to the bluffs overlooking the Potomac—and Dam No. 5. All baggage, tents, and wagons had been left at the Big Spring resting place near Martinsburg.

Throughout the following day (December 17) Jackson kept his men concealed, waiting for night to mask his operations. After chilly darkness had descended, thirty men (part of a company of New Market Irishmen) crept halfway across the dam and down into the icy waters of the Potomac, where they set to work hacking away at the dam's cribs. Their muffled blows went undetected by Federal guards on the opposite shore until nearly daybreak. Aroused bluecoats immediately opened fire on the workmen, but they soon saw through the mist that Jackson had piled up stones in the middle of the dam to form a crude but effective parapet.

As additional protection for the laborers, Old Jack posted the Rockbridge Artillery and R. P. Chew's battery on the overhanging bluffs to play on Federal buildings across the river. Their first few volleys created panic and scattered the bluecoats. Shortly afterward the Yankees returned—with a battery of their own. Concealed in a grove of woods, the Federal cannon played havoc with the Confederate artillerymen out on the top of the naked ridge. William T. Poague of the Rockbridge Artillery told of climbing the hill to his cannon and of finding part of Chew's gunners all crowded behind one small sapling, dodging first one way and then another as Federal shells exploded in the area.[13]

Jackson soon realized the futility of working in daylight, for laborers going to and from the stone parapet in the middle of the dam had to run a 250-yard gauntlet of Federal sharpshooter fire. On the second night Captains Frederick Holliday and Henry H. Robertson volunteered to take their companies of the Thirty-third and Twenty-seventh Regiments, respectively, and continue work on the demolition of the canal barrier. Comrades watched apprehensively from the bluffs as the two companies stole out onto

13. William T. Poague, *Gunner with Stonewall*, edited by Monroe F. Cockrell (Jackson, Tenn., 1957), 13–14.

the dam in the darkness and slipped waist-deep into water almost cold enough to paralyze.

The Federals were not napping that night. Union cannon soon after sundown opened fire on an abandoned mill on the Confederate side of the river. Not only was it housing sharpshooters, but once the Federals had managed to set it ablaze, they were able to use the light to fire at the men struggling along the base of the dam. At sundown the following day, however, Jackson countered. He allowed himself to be seen moving up the Potomac with pontoons, wagons, and men. Federals, concluding that he had given up trying to wreck Dam No. 5 and was now going after Dam No. 4, promptly dispatched their one battery and some infantry to guard against the new threat. With Jackson's successful ruse, Southerners worked unmolested on Dam No. 5 for several hours. Finally, after four and a half days of hard labor, a sizable breach was made in the barrier. Yet the arrival of enemy troops in strength again forced Jackson to halt operations. On December 21 the men retraced their steps, joined the remainder of the companies on the hilltop, and returned to Winchester. Total loss incurred on the expedition was one artilleryman killed.[14]

Throughout the next week the men fought extreme cold. The joy of Christmas Day celebrations was accentuated by the arrival of General William W. Loring and two brigades totaling 6,000 men who had been sent to Jackson as reinforcements. Many speculated through the last days of 1861 as to what their next move would be; they did so while struggling to withstand the freezing weather. All water had turned to ice and had to be melted over campfires for drinking purposes. At night soldiers wrapped themselves in as many as four or five blankets and bedded down on piles of hay and leaves placed in split timbers elevated off the ground. Those who slept on the ground wrote of waking up in the morning completely covered with frost. Cavalry scouts even found it necessary to dismount and walk, lest they freeze to death in the saddle.[15]

Such was the misery that closed the year. Jackson, however,

---

14. Joshua Parks of Lexington, a member of the Rockbridge Artillery, was the sole casualty. *Official Records,* V, 390
15. Paxton (ed.), *Memoir,* 31, 37–38; Graybill, *Diary,* 12–13.

still had no thoughts of going into winter quarters.[16] He was anxious to cement the western part of Virginia, his own native area, more closely to Virginia proper. Loring's 6,000 troops were not equal to the number needed for the task, but Jackson knew they were all he was likely to get. Moreover, he held firmly to the belief that "an active winter's campaign is less liable to produce disease than a sedentary life by camp-fires in winter-quarters." For two weeks after the Dam No. 5 expedition he formulated a plan to strike and occupy the strategic town of Romney. He then settled down to wait for a break in the weather.

It came on December 29, and Frank Paxton, just recently promoted from the ranks to Jackson's staff, wrote his wife: "If the bright sunshine of today is destined to last, you need not expect me [on a furlough], for Jackson is not disposed to lie idle when there is an opportunity to win laurels for himself and render service to our cause." [17] At 3 P.M. on New Year's Eve the brigade received orders to draw five days' rations, cook one day's food, and be ready to move out at three o'clock the following morning. Some of the men surmised that they were going to Romney; others reckoned they were heading back to Dam No. 5 to finish the pre-Christmas job.

At 5 A.M. on New Year's Day, 1862, the march began. The day was bright and pleasant as three brigades of infantry, five batteries of artillery, and Turner Ashby's cavalry started for Bath, northwest of Martinsburg. Behind the force slowly crawled brigade supply wagons. Jackson's strategy was comprehensive. The occupation of Bath would scatter the Federal forces at Hancock, an important rail junction just north of the springs. It would also destroy communications and thus split the Federal forces of General Nathaniel P. Banks to the east in Maryland and General Benjamin F. Kelley to the southwest at Romney. With Kelley cut off from the main army, the Federals would have to evacuate Romney, which would give the town—the eastern key to western Virginia—to the Confederacy.

The men started out in fine spirits and remained so even when

16. Mrs. Jackson, *Memoirs*, 218.   17. Paxton (ed.), *Memoir*, 39.

they realized that they were going farther northward than Dam No. 5. Because of the day's unusual warmth, most of the troops piled their coats, blankets, and tents in the baggage wagons that brought up the rear of the column. "This morning . . . was spring-like in its mildness," wrote a member of the Thirty-third Regiment. "The grass and limbs of the trees glistened and everything betokened one of those freaks in the weather which are not uncommon in the latitude of Virginia and Maryland." [18] Shortly after noon, however, the wind shifted to the northwest. By nightfall temperatures were approaching zero; snow and sleet laid the first of several icy coats on the countryside.

The wagon trains fell far behind. When Jackson called a halt to the march at dusk, the soldiers could only stand, hungry and cold, in the midst of the blizzard. It was soon obvious that the wagons would not catch up with the army before morning, so shivering troops hovered around fires for a while, then tried to sleep "hog-fashion." For greater comfort, four or more pooled what blankets they had and then wrapped up together. If curiosity got the best of one of the "bed brothers" and he poked his head out from underneath the blankets (thus allowing the elements to pour in on the rest), he was pommeled and upbraided until convinced to "haul in his horns." [19]

During the night, as one soldier rolled over in his blanket to allow the nearby fire to heat the other side, sparks set his covers afire. The blanket was a smoking tatters in a few chaotic moments. "I wish the Yankees was in hell!" he shouted.

"I don't," came a voice from underneath a blanket, "for if they were, Old Jack would be within half a mile of them, with the Stonewall Brigade in front." [20]

At dawn the Confederate soldiers arose from the icy ground, stretched stiff and aching muscles, and looked around in vain for the supply wagons with badly needed cartons of food and clothing. But the baggage train was bogged down miles to the rear, and the

18. Barton, *Recollections*, 18. 19. Casler, *Stonewall Brigade*, 73.
20. Douglas, *I Rode with Stonewall*, 20–21; Cooke, *Wearing of the Gray*, 48. Both authors noted that when Jackson was told of the conversation, he broke out with one of his rare, hearty laughs.

men resumed the march on empty stomachs. Throughout the day snow swirled and beat against them. The advance slowed to a crawl as they groped forward in the blinding storm and tried to maneuver through thick drifts. By nightfall the army of 8,500 men, straggling pitifully, had covered but ten miles. The second night seemed infinitely worse than the first; without food the troops found it increasingly difficult to ward off the cold. A reporter who accompanied the army for the first few days told of pickets standing in the open without benefit of fires, and of many collapsing in snow and being borne to the relative comfort of small campfires. "The soles of the shoes," he wrote of the other sentries, "actually froze to the ground, and the suffering of the men was awful to witness." [21]

The next morning—January 3—Jackson's soldiers again struggled to their feet. As they shook snow and ice from their blankets and pondered how much longer they could endure their present state, the Valley army heard the ring of wagon chains through the crisp air. The food wagons had arrived! But Jackson, anxious to compensate for the short distance covered on the preceding day, ordered the men to grab a mouthful and start moving out.

General Garnett, disturbed at the condition of his men, many of whom had not eaten for over thirty hours, dismissed the order and told the Stonewall Brigade to fall out and prepare decent meals. Great fires were soon roaring, and the odor of frying bacon and cornbread filled the air as other units trudged by on their way to Bath, ten miles distant. Jackson rode up and hotly demanded to know by whose orders those men were feasting.

"I have halted to let the men cook their rations," Garnett explained.

"There is no time for that," Jackson broke in impatiently.

"But it is impossible for the men to march further without them," Garnett insisted.

Jackson looked at the brigade, attentive to the conversation, spurred his horse, and said, as he wheeled back into the road: "I never found anything impossible with this brigade!"

---

21. Frank Moore (ed.), *Rebellion Record* (New York, 1862–68), IV, 16.

In a matter of minutes the Valley men were marching rapidly toward Bath.[22]

Snow and sleet set in again that afternoon, and the roads became so slick that the day's march was only six miles. Once again the wagon train fell behind; a third night was spent without food and with little shelter. The morning of January 4 broke overcast and freezing. With all haste Jackson pushed the army the last four miles to Bath and at noon arrived before the town. Loring's three brigades were ordered to move straight in, while the Stonewall Brigade and other militia were sent around both sides as flankers.

But the troops were exhausted, particularly Loring's three brigades, which were unaccustomed to Jackson's rapid pace. Even though he had the shortest approach to Bath, Loring had to halt his men several times in order to keep them together. Jackson grew impatient at the snail-like pace and sent Ashby's cavalry slashing into town, accompanied by the Fifth Regiment. This force routed what few defenders were left. Jackson sneeringly reported that he himself arrived in the town ahead of Loring's skirmishers.[23] With Bath now in Confederate hands, the army was ordered to pursue the Federals retreating toward Hancock, eight miles across the Potomac.

The troops bivouacked opposite the town. The next two days were spent in bombarding Hancock, but the Federals refused to give it up. Confederate cavalry combed the countryside, destroying railroad trestles, while Jackson began construction of a pontoon bridge two miles upstream from Hancock in order to flank the Federal force. By the afternoon of the sixth he realized that two days would be required to complete the bridge. Moreover, he received word that 1,500 Federal reinforcements were rushing to Hancock. The river crossing was abandoned, and on the morning of January 7 Jackson turned southward for Romney, the head of the column reaching Unger's crossroads at nightfall.

Men in the brigade and in the army never forgot that night. One of the heaviest snowfalls that many could remember blanketed the

22. Henry A. White, *Stonewall Jackson*, 105–106.
23. *Official Records*, V, 390–91.

countryside. The next morning men crawled out from coats and blankets covered with "a foot or more" of snow.[24] The army moved off slowly to Romney. Men and horses tramped the snow until it became packed and slick. The troops tried marching in the ditches and woods, but that proved no better. Men slipped, slid, and fell all along the way, breaking limbs and accidentally discharging rifles. "During this trip," a member of the Rockbridge Artillery wrote, "my patriotism was put to a test." [25] The long wagon train crept behind, drivers yelling and cursing as they beat horses that could advance only a few hundred yards before they too slipped down or fell exhausted to the ground. To keep the trains moving, four men were detailed to each wagon to hold it when the horses fell and to help it around icy curves. On at least one occasion Jackson himself was observed, his shoulder straining against a wheel, trying to prevent the loss of a wagon.[26]

The march reminded many of the men of Napoleon's retreat from Moscow. As the columns plodded on through the snow, the advance became slower. Soon the horse teams had to be unhitched and taken ahead to rest, while the men took ropes and chains and dragged wagons, cannon, and caissons along the lanes of ice. Jim Langhorne of the Fourth Regiment later wrote his mother: "I have endured and seen others endure that that if a man had told me 12 months ago that men could stand such hardships, I would have called him a fool." [27]

In a storm of driving sleet and freezing wind the army finally entered a deserted Romney at one o'clock on the afternoon of January 14. "When we marched into town," Langhorne wrote, "every soldier's clothing was a solid cake of ice, and icicles two inches long hanging from the hair and whiskers of every man." He added that at least one-third of the Fourth Regiment had fallen along the way from exhaustion and cold.[28] For three days the army rested, though a few men found the energy to gather up supplies abandoned by the Federals. Fatigue was plainly apparent in the

---

24. Baylor, *Bull Run to Bull Run*, 32.   25. Slaughter, *Fairfax*, 21.
26. Casler, *Stonewall Brigade*, 73–74; *Confederate Veteran*, XXXII (1924), 469.
27. James H. Langhorne to his mother, January 12, 1862, Langhorne Letters.
28. James H. Langhorne to his father, January 16, 1862, Langhorne Letters.

faces of soldiers who huddled in improvised shelters. No one knew what Jackson next planned to do, but the hope was paramount that he soon would put an end to this futile contest against the elements. "Two battles," Lieutenant Frank Paxton wrote his wife, "would not have done us as much injury as hard weather and exposure have effected." [29]

Of necessity the men devised a method of bedding down at night on the snow-packed ground. Tents were spread atop the snow, on which were placed first an oilcloth and then a blanket. The troops would lie on the blanket while comrades covered them with the remaining blankets and the sides of the tents. Men going on sentry duty customarily saw to it that the last men were so tucked away for the night.[30] The Rockbridge Artillery at this time was somewhat more fortunate; its members were quartered in a small church. In such closeness, however, the inevitable vermin began to infest the unit. Officers in the battery found a measure of relief by sleeping on the pews and in the pulpit.[31]

---

29. Paxton (ed.), *Memoir*, 46.
30. John O. Worsham, *One of Jackson's Foot Cavalry* (New York, 1912), 61–62.
31. Poague, *Gunner*, 17.

|||||||||||||||||||||||||||||||||||||||||||||||||||||||||||||||||||||||||||||||||||||||||||||||||||||||

CHAPTER VI

THE FIRST TASTE OF DEFEAT

The men in the ranks may have had their fill of winter fighting, but Jackson had not. Apparently oblivious to the misery within his army, he laid plans for a move on Cumberland, twenty-five miles to the northwest. Old Jack was particularly interested in destroying all Potomac River bridges in the area. On January 19, 1862, Garnett's Stonewall Brigade and William Taliaferro's brigade of Loring's division were ordered to ready themselves for the expedition. And then Jackson heard it: the murmurings of men so dispirited by suffering and fatigue that they openly declared their hostility to his brand of "fighting." The complaints were loudest in Taliaferro's command, where the troops were unaccustomed to Jackson's apparent inexhaustibility. Even some of the officers in the Stonewall Brigade, however, voiced their discontent, particularly when the weather warmed up enough for a driving rain to turn all roads into seas of mud and slush.

Jackson petulantly relented. He did not blame his old brigade for not wanting to continue the campaign; rather, his censure was aimed at Taliaferro's regiments, whom he classified in such an extent of demoralization "as to render the abandonment of that enterprise necessary." [1] Jackson's subsequent order to prepare for winter quarters occasioned loud cheering not heard since the army left Winchester three weeks before. Loring's heavy division was left at Romney to guard against another Federal infiltration; Garnett's brigade was ordered back to Winchester to block any Valley attack by General Banks's army, then encamped at Frederick, Maryland.

On January 26 the Stonewall Brigade stumbled to a stop just north of Winchester. "I think I am dirtier than I have ever been," Frank Paxton wrote home, "and may be lousy besides. I have not changed clothes for two weeks, and my pants have a hole in each leg nearly big enough for a dog to creep through." [2]

Yet Paxton's comments were mild in comparison to those of his compatriots. A private in the Stonewall Brigade affirmed that he suffered "right smart" on the expedition. The Winchester hospitals were full of men dying from pneumonia, "nine or ten every day. There is about three hundred in the hospital belonging to our brigade, the whole of them got sick by the exposure to the weather." [3] This was no exaggeration; reports of intense suffering even sifted into the Federal lines. Writing to his wife from Hancock, Union General Seth Williams confided of Jackson's campaign: "We have reliable information that he sent back over 1,200 frozen and sick men during the four days he lay [at Romney]. People who came over yesterday say that his sick and disabled fill every house from Bath to Winchester and that many amputations have taken place from frost-bite." [4]

---

1. *Official Records*, V, 393.   2. Paxton (ed.), *Memoir*, 48.
3. John Garibaldi, 27th Regiment, to his wife, January 28, 1862, John Garibaldi Letters, in possession of Stonewall Jackson Memorial Association, Lexington, Va.
4. Alpheus S. Williams, *From the Cannon's Mouth*, edited by Milo M. Quaife (Detroit, 1959), 58.

Rockbridge Artilleryman William Poague voiced the over-all sentiment of the Confederate troops by writing: "In all the war I never had a similar experience—never endured such physical and mental suffering as on this trip. The expedition seemed to everybody to be a dismal failure. Our confidence in our leader was sorely tried. Loring's part of the army was in a state of semi-mutiny, and Jackson was hissed and hooted as he passed them. This I had from a friend in the Georgia Regiment who teased me a great deal about the 'crazy general from Lexington.' " [5]

The only Confederate around Winchester or Romney to take a favorable view of the campaign was Jackson. To his thinking he had driven the Federals back across the Potomac, had restored Confederate sentiment in his home country, had established several bases, and confiscated large stores—all at a loss of four men dead and twenty-eight wounded. (Old Jack obviously did not count the hospitalized as casualties.) Failure to achieve greater success he attributed to Loring's "very much demoralized" division. On the other hand, he went out of his way to praise his old brigade. Throughout the campaign it had held up admirably, "still animated by the same spirit that characterized it at Manassas." Jackson felt confident that if an order had been issued right then for another march, the brigade "would have sustained its reputation, well earned during the recent expedition." [6] His enthusiasm was little shared by the subject of his praises.

But the Romney campaign did not end when the army went into winter quarters. A battle of commanders now exploded that surpassed any fighting the troops did while floundering in the snow. Jackson had left Loring's large division to cover the wide area around Romney. Yet to Loring in particular and to his men in general it seemed that they had been deserted in an "exposed and cheerless" village while their commanding general and "Jackson's pet lambs" (the Stonewall Brigade) returned to the warmth and hospitality of Winchester. Early in February, 1862, one of Loring's men wrote his father that all the troops confined at Romney "are abusing

---

5. Poague, *Gunner*, 18. See also *Official Records*, V, 1040–41; Casler, *Stonewall Brigade*, 78.
6. *Official Records*, V, 393–95, 1036.

Jackson mightilly and lay all their hardships at his door." [7]

Loring was enough of a military man (he had fought Indians for two decades prior to the war) to know that any entreaties for a change of address to a commander like Jackson would fall on deaf ears. Bypassing military channels, therefore, Loring and his officers sent a petition to Secretary of War Judah P. Benjamin asking to be transferred back to the Valley. The affable Benjamin, ever eager to please, ordered Jackson to recall the troops from Romney. To Jackson's point of view this withdrawal discarded all the fruits plucked during the expedition. Dutifully he recalled Loring's division—and then promptly tendered his resignation. Governor Letcher went into an uproar at the prospect of losing one of Virginia's leading commanders, while both Benjamin and President Jefferson Davis hastened to revoke the order and issue their apologies to Jackson. Old Jack received no interference from Richmond thereafter.[8]

Although the Stonewall Brigade had done its share of grumbling on the previous campaign, its members were, down deep in the heart, still devoted to Jackson. The news of his resignation had the effect of a thunderbolt when it reached the brigade's winter quarters, "Camp Zollicoffer," four and a half miles north of Winchester. Captain Hugh White of the Fourth Regiment summed up general opinion in a letter to his father: "There is but one feeling with us —that of perfect devotion to Gen. Jackson. With him we are ready to go anywhere, and to endure anything. But if he is to be run down, our spirit is utterly broken, and we can never re-enter the service with cheerful hearts."

Because men of other units did not share these sentiments— and went so far as to say so in the presence of Stonewall Brigade members—daily fist fights characterized one week's activities. Only when Jackson publicly announced his intentions of remaining at the head of the army did peace return to the winter quarters around Winchester.[9]

---

7. Charles E. Taylor, 10th Virginia, to George Taylor, February 6, 1862, letter in possession of Ted Blackburn, Xenia, Ohio.
8. *Battles and Leaders*, II, 282–83.
9. William S. White, *Hugh White*, 73; R. W. Waldrop, 21st Virginia, to his father,

The remainder of February passed quietly and, for the most part, pleasantly. True, Garnett kept the brigade in shape by constant drill and marches when possible, but long spells of stormy weather provided much relief from any strenuous exercises. Jackson even began a liberal granting of furloughs, and men in camp beat a path to Winchester for sleigh rides and companionship with the fairer sex.[10] Colonel Pendleton supervised the erection of a sixty-by-twenty-five-foot chapel, where church services were held regularly and well attended. All during this time the higher officers in the brigade were successfully re-enlisting men whose original terms with "Jackson's pet lambs" were expiring.[11]

The sunny days of early March signaled a natural end to the period of inactivity. Everyone knew something must soon happen, but no one was sure what it would be. "The army and the community here," wrote Captain White, "are kept in painful suspense, as to what is to be done. . . . But whatever comes, may we be ready to meet it. The only way to have any true peace of mind is just to be ready for anything."[12] Optimism was high, even though few members of the brigade knew the full scope of the military situation in Virginia that spring. The center of the Confederate army was anchored on "Uncle Joe" Johnston at Manassas. The right rested at Fredericksburg under aged and half-deaf General Theophilus Holmes, and Jackson in the Valley comprised the left. Under Abraham Lincoln's impatient probings, the Federal forces early in March began exerting pressure all along the Confederate line. General George B. McClellan moved out against Johnston and Holmes; General Banks left Frederick and advanced on Harpers Ferry to drive Jackson up the Valley.

At this time Jackson's force numbered 3,600 infantry, 600 cavalry under the indefatigable Ashby, and 6 batteries with a total of 27

February 14, 1862, R. W. Waldrop Letters, Southern Historical Collection, University of North Carolina Library.

10. James H. Langhorne to his father, February 7, 1862, Langhorne Letters; T. J. Jackson to J. E. Johnston, February 12, 1862, Hotchkiss Papers; Roger P. Chew, *Military Operations in Jefferson County, West Virginia* (Charlestown, W. Va., 1911), 17.

11. For example, see appeals in the Winchester *Republican*, February 14, 1862, and the Lexington *Gazette*, February 27, 1862.

12. William S. White, *Hugh White*, 75–76. See also James H. Langhorne to his father, March 8, 1862, Langhorne Letters.

guns. His army was divided into three brigades: Garnett's five regiments, three regiments and a battalion under Colonel Jesse S. Burks, and two regiments under Colonel Samuel V. Fulkerson. The units of the last-named officer were all that remained of Loring's division, for upon Johnston's recommendation Loring and most of his division had been transferred elsewhere. Banks's army totaled at least 25,000 effectives.

On March 9 the Federal columns started for Winchester. Two days later they were only four miles from the town. Jackson promptly moved out and offered to do battle on the short end of seven to one odds. Banks was reluctant to take the challenge, preferring instead to wait until crusty General James Shields and his division of 9,000 troops could join him.

Near nightfall on March 11 Jackson summoned the five regimental colonels of the Stonewall Brigade for a council of war. Heeding their advice, he ordered his army with all its supplies to move southward. Jackson's plan was to turn sharply at Newtown, race back down the pike, and deliver a night attack on Banks. But through misinterpreted orders the army moved through Newtown and continued so far southward as to make a night assault at Winchester completely out of the question. Jackson was furious. "That is the last council of war I will ever hold!" he shouted into the darkness. As history proves, he kept his word.[13]

The Confederate army continued up the Valley pike to Strasburg and thence to Mount Jackson, forty-two miles south of Winchester. Jackson's instructions from Richmond were to keep an eye on the Federal army in the Valley, to hold it there if at all possible, and to be ready to join Johnston's army at a moment's notice. The Valley troops knew that Shields's division of rough Midwesterners had followed them warily as far as Strasburg, where the blue regiments were then encamped. The men in Jackson's army were just as uncertain of Jackson's next movement as were their opponents. Frank Paxton, newly promoted to major, wrote at this time: "Jackson always shows fight, and hence we never know what he means." [14]

---

13. Henderson, *Stonewall Jackson*, I, 230. Dr. Hunter McGuire vouched for Jackson's statements.
14. Paxton (ed.), *Memoir*, 52.

On a raw and windy March 21 word reached Jackson from the scouting Ashby that Shields had abandoned Strasburg and was returning to Winchester. Old Jack interpreted the move as an indication that the Federals were leaving the Valley to concentrate against Johnston at Manassas. There was no time to waste. The Valley regiments moved down the Valley in immediate pursuit; wagon trains were left behind to catch up as best they could. Jackson's army left Camp Buchanan at dawn on Saturday the twenty-second; the Stonewall Brigade took the van to set a rapid pace. Stragglers by the score dropped along the wayside, but by nightfall the main body of the Confederate army was twenty-six miles down the pike and bivouacked at Cedar Creek (which two years later would be the scene of the Valley's dying gasp).

Brisk nighttime firing in front told that Ashby's men were having trouble in clearing the way. "It being evident that we would soon be engaged," Clem Fishburne of the Rockbridge Artillery later wrote, "we could see some of the tricks which the men's consciences were playing. Several well-worn packs of cards were thrown away, and men who had not been credited with a scrupulous knowledge of the difference between *meum* and *tuum*, where cooking utensils, &c., were involved, were seen to draw out their pocket 'Testament', and go to reading diligently." [15] Such eleventh-hour appeals for salvation were standard procedure for troops of both blue and gray.

The next morning was March 23—the Sabbath—but the accustomed observances were forgotten. Again the army set off at a rapid pace down the muddy pike. Early in the afternoon, after a ten-mile trek, the lead columns of the Stonewall Brigade filed into Kernstown, a hamlet four miles south of Winchester. The sound of spasmodic firing in the distance was indication that Ashby was still skirmishing with Federals. At this point, few of the infantrymen displayed any great concern, for in a sense three-fourths of the army was out on its feet. The Stonewall Brigade had marched thirty-six miles since the preceding morning. Straggling had depleted Jackson's army to no more than 3,000 men. When orders passed down the line to go into bivouac, the men did so willingly —and blessed Jackson's piety for finally observing the Sabbath.

---

15. *Southern Historical Society Papers*, XXIII (1895), 130.

But the men had hardly stacked arms when they heard the officers shouting commands to prepare for battle. Unbelievingly, troops fell into ranks. The Fifth Regiment smartly moved into position behind a stone fence that ran in front of a broad field bordered by woods to the left and the Valley pike on the right. The rest of the brigade marched off to the left in the direction of a high ridge roughly paralleling the main road. Carpenter's battery (formerly Company A, Twenty-seventh Regiment) led the way, protected by Fulkerson's two regiments (Twenty-third and Thirty-seventh Virginia), and supported by the Twenty-first Virginia of Burks's brigade. Gaining the ridge, Carpenter broke the silence on the field by lobbing a few shells toward the opposite rise of ground. Immediately Pritchard's Hill exploded with a roar as masked Federal batteries answered Carpenter's call. Men in the brigade looked at each other, their weary eyes expressing disbelief. After all that marching, Jackson was taking them into battle—and on Sunday to boot!

Old Jack had not planned it that way. Upon reaching Kernstown with his fatigued regiments, he had decided to encamp for the night and assault the Federals the following morning. But a combination of factors quickly changed his mind. Ashby sent him word that only Shields's rear guard—four regiments—stood in front of him. Then Jackson learned that the Federals had a clear view of his position and could easily rush up reinforcements before morning to put him on the defensive. To make a check of the condition of his army, Old Jack rode through the camp of the Stonewall Brigade. He mistook their jubilation at the order to bivouac for "good spirits at the prospect of meeting the enemy." He promptly formed a battle plan that was basically sound: Ashby and a part of Burks's small brigade were left on the right to create a diversion; the bulk of the artillery unlimbered in the center to guard the Valley pike; the main body of the army was to strike Shields's right through the woods and cover of the high ground.[16]

Though the afternoon was half gone, it was apparent within the ranks of the Stonewall Brigade that Jackson wanted to turn the Federal right by a sledge-hammer assault. Two batteries dashed past double-timing infantry, joined Carpenter's battery on the other

16. *Official Records*, XII, Pt. 1, p. 381.

side of the ridge, and began to direct their fire at the Federal position. Colonel J. M. Patton's Twenty-first and Colonel John Echols'
Twenty-seventh Regiments were thrown out as skirmishers across
the ridge and in advance of the artillery. In a matter of minutes they
were slugging it out with Federals in great strength. The Thirty-
seventh and Thirty-third Regiments, moving together, emerged
from the woods to the left and spied a stone wall toward which
Federals were already moving. Control of that fence was all-important to both sides. The Confederates got there first and delivered
a point-blank volley that left Federals scattered like new-mown hay
on the grassy field.

The battle on Jackson's left increased in fury, the smoke of exploding gunpowder covering the ridge like a dense fog. In some
places hand-to-hand fighting broke out; in others, men on both
sides were lying on the ridge, exchanging volleys at short range, and
reloading muskets adroitly from prone positions. Federal reinforcements poured into the area in a steady stream. Jackson, certain
that he was fighting more than a four-regiment rear guard, ordered
Garnett's Second and Fourth Regiments and Burks's Irish Battalion to assist the Twenty-seventh and Twenty-first Regiments,
now sorely pressed. Having made two futile efforts to drive Fulkerson from the cover of the stone fence, the bluecoats had veered
to the left and were concentrating their fire against Garnett and
his brigade in the center of the sector.

For two hours the fury of battle swelled and ebbed across the
rolling hills. General Shields, an Irish emigrant who owed his stars
largely to his service in the U.S. Senate, became increasingly
alarmed at the tenacity of the Confederates. Frantically he rushed
the equivalent of six regiments from his left to the critical area
on the right.[17] To the men of the Stonewall Brigade, it was like
trying to stem a tidal wave. At times regiments had to hug the
ground as artillery fire and volleys of musketry blanketed the entire
area. Then, in the lull of Federals reloading, the Valley fighters

---

17. These Federal reinforcements, largely responsible for turning the battle in
Shields's favor, were the 5th and 62nd Ohio, 13th and 14th Indiana, 84th Pennsylvania, seven companies from the 67th Ohio, and three companies of the 8th Ohio.

would jump up and charge the opposing lines with a yell. Each time one rank of bluecoats was driven back, confused and bleeding, fresh Federals rushed in to breach the gap and drive tiring Confederates back to the cover of their woods, stone fences, and artillery.

On the left the strain began to tell, first on the Fourth and Thirty-third Regiments that had seen the most severe fighting. To their right the Twenty-seventh Regiment, still in the forefront of action, was gamely holding on, despite the fact that its commander, tall and pugnacious John Echols, had been borne from the field with a shattered arm. Colonel James W. Allen's Second Regiment rushed onto the field and charged into the thick of action—only to be shot to pieces in less than an hour. The Second's battle flag was riddled by fire; seven of its color-bearers went down in rapid succession.[18] Colonel Raleigh Colston saw his own brother fall mortally wounded, and was powerless to reach him.[19] Federals had now advanced to another stone wall, from which they raked the taut Confederate lines across the ridge. Allen's men made a gallant charge on the stone barrier, but Federal fire was so rapid that only the right of the regiment reached the objective. It held on desperately until lack of support forced its recall.[20]

Time was now definitely on the Federal side. The sun was dipping toward the western range of mountains. Company after company in Garnett's Stonewall Brigade began to give out of ammunition. The gray line was thinning. Across the smoking ridge could be seen a solid mass of blue; hundreds of bayonets glistened in the waning sunlight. The terrible noise of battle, clearly audible to anxious citizens standing in the streets of Winchester, was described by one artillery officer as "the most incessant I ever heard." [21]

Suddenly the Confederate line began to bend dangerously. Jack-

---

18. Charlestown *Spirit of Jefferson*, February 16, 1904.
19. Lieutenant Colonel Lawson Botts of the 2nd Regiment saw an advancing party of Federals bearing down rapidly on the stretcher-bearers in the process of carrying William Colston to the rear. He rode over quickly and gave his horse to the wounded man. Walker, *VMI Memorial*, 124.
20. *Official Records*, XII, Pt. 1, p. 388.
21. R. P. Chew, *Stonewall Jackson* (Lexington, Va., 1912), 20.

son, far on the right with the artillery, summoned the Forty-second and Colonel Bill Harman's Fifth Regiment—all he had left—to rush up and save the day.

But Garnett had already reached a crisis. Many of his companies were lying helpless on the ground, their ammunition expended. Regiments had broken into smaller units and were struggling to check a flood of Federals who swept across the field from three directions. The Stonewall Brigade was shattered and utterly fatigued; bluecoats were in a position to assault its front and both flanks. It was senseless to continue, thought Garnett, and suicidal to remain.

Spying the Fifth Regiment as it approached the field at double time, Garnett sent a courier to Harman to stop and form a secondary position on which his men could retire. At the same time he passed the word down the line for his brigade to fall back. Some of the men mistook the withdrawal order as a signal that the line had collapsed. Just at this time Jackson rode forward and was startled to see men rushing headlong to the rear. "Where are you going?" he shouted angrily to a running soldier.

The man replied that he was out of ammunition and did not know where to find more.

Jackson, face flushed and trembling with rage, leaned forward and snapped, "Then go back and give them the bayonet!" [22]

Galloping forward, Old Jack suddenly jerked his horse to a stop. Instead of seeing the Fifth Regiment in line of advance, as he had ordered, he found the Staunton companies fanning out atop the wooded ridge and behind a sturdy stone wall. Below them their sister regiments were breaking apart. The Rockbridge Artillery had pounded the Federal line furiously until bluecoats infiltrated both flanks. The death of a wheel horse forced the battery to leave one gun on the field. Ordered "to cut the traces and make the best time in getting away," the young gunners from Lexington carried out the order "in Bull Run style." [23]

---

22. Worsham, *One of Jackson's Foot Cavalry*, 68. For a survey of how unreliable the bayonet was considered in the struggle of the 1860's, see *Civil War History*, VII (1961), 128–32.
23. Slaughter, *Fairfax*, 23.

In the tumult Old Jack hailed a nearby drummer boy, led him to a slight rise, and shouted, "Beat the rally! Beat the rally!" The small lad began a steady rhythm on his drum, but his efforts were drowned out by the chaos now attendant to the battle. From his position a frustrated Jackson could see the entire Confederate line melting away as Federals swarmed all over the scarred and littered ridge. The Union troops now had the advantage, wrote Colonel E. H. C. Cavins of the Fourteenth Indiana. "Yet many of the brave Virginians who had so often followed their standards to victory, lingered in the rear of their retreating comrades, loading as they slowly retired, and rallying in squads in every ravine and behind every hill—or hiding singly among the trees. They continued to make it hot for our men in the advance." [24]

The Fifth Regiment, so far not engaged, made it even hotter for the Federals. It and Colonel Burks's Forty-second Regiment met the Union advance up the hill with six hundred defiant men. From behind the stone wall and nearby trees the two units raked the advancing lines again and again as Federals by weight of numbers tried to break the Confederate position. The Fifth Ohio fell apart, its flag pierced eighty-four times. The Sixty-second Ohio lost twenty-five per cent of its complement. The Eighty-fourth Pennsylvania was hurled back twice and did not break until its colonel plunged bleeding from his horse.

At the height of the struggle the color-bearer of the Fifth Virginia leaped over the stone wall and advanced toward the Federals, waving the banner and daring them to advance farther. From one end of the Federal line to the other ran the shouts: "Don't shoot that man! He is too brave to die!" A hush settled over the area. The color-bearer was ordered to take cover, which he did with a parting salute, and the roar of battle swelled up again.[25]

Soon Federals were pouring in on Burks's left flank. Harman gave quick orders and his men backed off slowly, following Jackson's whole army into the woods. As night descended the Fifth took up a third position in a narrow lane with a fence toward the Federal side. It was a position of desperation, both flanks lying wide open.

24. *Battles and Leaders*, II, 307 n.
25. *Confederate Veteran*, XVII (1909), 125.

"A single ramrod," one of the Confederates wrote, "would have spitted the whole battalion." [26]

The rest of the army—baffled, overwhelmed, and worn out—slowly retraced its steps for five miles up the Valley pike to the wagon trains waiting at Newtown. Many of the brigade did not make it. Some, "so exhausted after the battle [they] could not run," sank to rest in fence corners, under trees and along the way.[27] Those who staggered into Newtown collapsed wherever they halted. No one bothered to eat. With their appetites and thoughts numbed by defeat and fatigue, the men stared silently at the ground or into the darkness.

The army wallowed in despondency. In his official report Colonel Arthur Cummings of the Thirty-third Regiment wrote of his men: "Owing to the severe march, they were not in a physical condition to meet equal numbers, much less immense odds." [28] J. C. Wade of the Fourth Regiment seconded Cummings' sentiments. "It was a terrible fight . . . The boys that are here are tolerably well but very much broken in spirit." [29] William T. Poague of the Rockbridge Artillery made the observation: "Had 'Old Jack' commanded on the other side he would have pressed forward and doubtless gobbled up a big lot of us." [30] Frank Paxton wrote forthrightly to his wife: "We had a severe fight to-day and are pretty badly whipped." [31]

Indeed, the brigade was badly whipped, almost one-fourth of its membership listed on the casualty sheets as follows: [32]

	Strength	Killed	Wounded	Missing	Total
2nd Regiment	320	6	33	51	90
4th Regiment	203	5	23	48	76
5th Regiment	450	9	48	4	61
27th Regiment	170	2	20	35	57
33rd Regiment	275	18	27	14	59
	1,418	40	151	152	343

26. Henderson, Stonewall Jackson, I, 246.
27. J. C. Wade, 4th Regiment, to his wife, March 26, 1862, letter in possession of Virginia Historical Society.
28. Official Records, XII, Pt. 1, p. 396.
29. J. C. Wade to his wife, March 26, 1862.
30. Poague, Gunner, 19.   31. Paxton (ed.), Memoir, 54.
32. Official Records, XII, Pt. 1, p. 384. Jackson's total loss at Kernstown was 700

Most of the Valley fighters felt that Jackson had erred in attacking Shields, that he had rushed headlong into action without ascertaining fully the strength of his foe.[33] Few of the men realized, on the other hand, that even in defeat Jackson had gained valuable military advantages for Virginia. Two heavy divisions scheduled to leave the Valley and join General Irvin McDowell's assault on Richmond (in collaboration with McClellan's move up the Peninsula) were ordered to remain where they were, while a third division was dispatched to the Valley by Lincoln to assist Banks. A total of 35,000 Union troops congregated at the northern end of the Valley to take care of 3,600 defiant Rebels.

And, according to Valley newspapers, Jackson's men were still defiant—the Stonewall Brigade in particular. Displaying faith, even in the face of contrary facts, the Lexington *Gazette* stated: "The 'Stone-wall' may be removed, but can never be broken. A little crevice may be made in it now and then, but the balls of the enemy can never make a fatal breach in its unyielding mass. Wherever and whenever the Yankees try their strength upon it, they will find it the same well-built, and closely cemented line of defence—movable, it is true, but breakable—never." [34]

The next day Jackson ordered the army back to Mount Jackson. Just as the regiments were forming to march out, a Federal battery appeared on a nearby hill and began lobbing shells into the area. The Rockbridge Artillery returned the fire. During the exchange one Federal shell went screaming into the ranks of the Twenty-seventh Regiment, standing in the road, killing and wounding twelve men.[35]

men. *Southern Historical Society Papers*, XLIII (1920), 163. Despite John Casler's assertion that "the enemy's loss was much greater than ours in killed and wounded, as they stood so thick that a bullet could hardly miss them if aimed low," Shields's casualties numbered only 590 men. Casler, *Stonewall Brigade*, 84; *Official Records*, XI, Pt. 1, pp. 346–47.

33. See Casler, *Stonewall Brigade*, 83.

34. Lexington *Gazette*, April 3, 1862. Similar praises are given in *ibid.*, April 10, 1862; Richmond *Whig*, April 8, 1862.

35. Casler, in *Stonewall Brigade*, 87, stated that Colonel A. J. Grigsby, temporarily commanding the 27th Regiment and "always rather headstrong," charged straight down the road toward the battery. Other accounts noted that the regiment was standing idly in line when the bombardment started. See Graybill, *Diary*, 18; Poague, *Gunner*, 19; George M. Neese, *Three Years in the Confederate Horse Artillery* (New York, 1911), 38–39.

After reaching Mount Jackson, the army settled down and replenished its ranks with men gathered from throughout the Valley.[36] While the troops regained their composure, however, Jackson had one more task to perform. On April 1 General Garnett was relieved from command of the Stonewall Brigade and ordered south to Harrisonburg under arrest. Indignation swept through the ranks of the five Virginia regiments at what was considered a gross injustice, and promises were many that Garnett's successor was in for a rough tenure, and a short one, if he lacked patience or fortitude.

In Jackson's army, however, Garnett became an example not to be followed. After Kernstown, when Jackson gave orders for a general to have his troops in a certain place at a particular time or to hold a position until otherwise ordered, the memory of Dick Garnett spurred him to unquestioning punctuality and obedience.

---

36. See Staunton *Spectator and General Advertiser*, March 25, 1862; Robert L. Dabney, *Life and Campaigns of Lieut.-Gen. Thomas J. Jackson* (New York, 1866), 326–27. Hereinafter cited as Dabney, *Jackson*.

!!!

CHAPTER VII

HIDE-AND-SEEK IN THE VALLEY

Brigadier General Charles Sidney Winder did not appreciate the cold reception he received from the Stonewall Brigade, but he was too much of an army man to allow it to influence his ideas of strict military training and discipline. Born in Talbot County, Maryland, on October 7, 1829, he was a product of one of that state's most privileged families. His uncle (and later his father-in-law), Colonel Edward Lloyd, owned thousands of choice acres in Maryland, Louisiana, and Mississippi. Twenty-second in the West Point graduating class of 1850, Winder was assigned to the artillery, the branch of service he most preferred. In 1854 his unit, the Third United States Artillery, was ordered to duty in California. En route around South America a severe Atlantic hurricane struck his ship, the *San Francisco*, blowing it so far off course that for several weeks it was thought to be lost with all hands. The troops were eventually rescued and delivered to their destination. For heroic conduct during this critical period, Winder was promoted to captain. At the age of twenty-six he was one of the youngest captains in service.[1]

Reassigned to the Sixth United States Infantry, Winder quickly added laurels to his reputation by his valor in the campaigns of the 1850's against the Spokane Indians in Washington. But, like Garnett, he gave up his army position when civil war approached. He hastened to Richmond and on April 5, 1861, was appointed major of artillery. He was soon raised to colonel and given command of the Sixth South Carolina Infantry, which he molded into one of the most highly regarded units in Confederate service.[2] His achievements did not go unnoticed. In February, 1862, General Joseph E. Johnston, commander of the Virginia theater, listed Winder as one of six colonels most deserving of brigade command.[3] President Davis concurred. On March 1 Winder was promoted to brigadier and given command of the Manassas garrisons; a month later he was transferred to the Valley to take Garnett's place at the head of the Stonewall Brigade.

In appearance and personality Winder was the type of officer not easily forgotten. Tall, thin, and graceful, he had a face that reflected both assurance and sensitiveness. A precisely trimmed mustache and beard, an extraordinarily high forehead, dark, curly hair combed straight back, large brown eyes that flitted restlessly in quest of minute weaknesses or errors, all stamped this officer as an unusual man of exceptional talents. He was an immaculate dresser—not a dandy, just a perfectionist in his apparel—and he insisted upon having the finest steed available.

No one called Winder "Charlie." To even his closest associates he was "General" or "Sir." He was a "Regular," imbued with the high standards and severe discipline of the old army. Whatever unit he commanded was noted for precision, order, and efficiency.

1. Clement A. Evans (ed.), *Confederate Military History* (Atlanta, 1899), II, 166.
2. Two sources state that Winder served as an aide to General P. G. T. Beauregard during the Fort Sumter bombardment. *Ibid.*; McHenry Howard, *Recollections of a Maryland Confederate Soldier and Staff Officer under Johnston, Jackson and Lee* (Baltimore, 1913), 110.
3. *Official Records*, V, 1058.

He was determined that the Stonewall Brigade should be no exception.

Winder wasted no time putting his ideas into practice. Although warned that he would last only a few weeks under Jackson's demanding scrutiny, he did not waver in his determination to refine the brigade to the spit and polish perfection he himself practiced. The first days proved particularly rough for him. The men in the brigade were so incensed at the removal of Garnett that, for the first and only time during the war, they refused to cheer Jackson whenever he rode through camp. As for Winder, only scorn and ridicule initially greeted him from the ranks. Had he succeeded Jackson, he undoubtedly would have met the high trust and affection which his experience and expertness merited. Yet he was Dick Garnett's opposite in bearing and personality; moreover, he was not a Virginian—a point that bore much weight among the fighting clans of the Valley.

Trouble first came with an order from Jackson curtailing the amount of baggage that was to accompany the army. This meant that all items not of absolute military necessity had to be carried in knapsacks or sent home. The men in the Stonewall Brigade placed the blame for the reduction on Winder, and when he rode through camp he was greeted with the cry of "More baggage! More baggage!" [4]

Winder decided to overlook the incident as a rash display by men whose sense of decorum had been momentarily blotted by anger. But on his next ride through the camps he was again greeted by hissing and mumblings. He rode on, seemingly oblivious to the hostility aroused by his appointment. In a few minutes the colonel whose regiment was responsible for the action was summoned to Winder's tent and told curtly that any further displays of disrespect would result in the punishment of both the regiment and the commander.[5]

If Winder received open hostility from the men in the ranks, he likewise was treated with apathy by the regimental officers. So great was their resentment of Garnett's dismissal that most of them refused to extend to Winder the courtesy of a visit. Then, after

---

4. Casler, *Stonewall Brigade*, 73.   5. Howard, *Recollections*, 82–83, 99–100.

Colonel John Neff of the Thirty-third Regiment was placed under arrest following an unexplained argument with Winder, no officer went to the headquarters tent unless ordered to report there.[6] Colonel William Harman of the Fifth Regiment finally broke the ice and paid Winder a social call. Soon thereafter came the Twenty-seventh Regiment's Andrew Grigsby, who was to become a frequent nighttime visitor around Winder's campfire. Most of the other officers abandoned their aloofness when Turner Ashby displayed a warm cordiality toward the new commander.[7]

Until the middle of April, 1862, the army lay at Rude's Hill, south of Mount Jackson. No action took place other than minor brushes between skirmishers. Morale began to climb upward. Failure of the Yankees to push forward vigorously after Kernstown was interpreted as bespeaking wholesome respect for the Confederates. Moreover, the Confederate Congress and newspapers had heaped praise on Jackson's force. Wounded comrades were returning to the ranks; new recruits were trickling in daily. On April 16 Congress passed a conscription act providing for the drafting of men between the ages of eighteen and thirty-five. When he learned of this new measure, Old Jack turned to his quartermaster, John Harman, and barked, "Now, Major, we'll have war in earnest. Old Virginia has waked up!" [8] His observation was in part true. Many Valley residents who had remained at home rushed to volunteer for service in the Virginia forces, since the conscription bill allowed those who entered the service voluntarily to join extant and—in the case of the Stonewall Brigade—already famous units. By the end of the month the ranks of the brigade had swelled to 3,681 men—the largest complement it would ever have.[9]

---

6. Walker, VMI Memorial, 403.
7. This association between Winder and Ashby soon proved valuable to the stability of the Valley army. Toward the end of April, Jackson was urged by Richmond to bring some semblance of order to Ashby's overloaded and somewhat disorganized cavalry companies. Jackson divided the twenty-two companies, assigning part of them to William Taliaferro's command and the remainder, Ashby included, to Winder's brigade. When Ashby promptly submitted his resignation, Winder took it upon himself to go to Jackson and mediate the case—whereupon Old Jack rescinded the order. Howard, Recollections, 90.
8. A. M. Garber, "Recollections of A. M. Garber," unpublished manuscript, Hotchkiss Papers.
9. Official Records, XII, Pt. 3, p. 879.

Yet Jackson still needed reinforcements to combat the large number of Federals massing against him. Accordingly, General Richard S. Ewell's division of 8,000 men was dispatched to the Valley. To facilitate a junction with Ewell, Jackson on April 18 began moving his army to Swift Run Gap. The men marched a day and a night in driving rain and hail and through mud which one soldier described as "up to our knees nearly all the time." By the time the Stonewall Brigade reached Conrad's Store, at the foot of Swift Run Gap, this same soldier swore that neither Congress nor the draft could keep him in the army once his term of enlistment had expired.[10]

The reorganization of the army (as provided by the Conscription Act) took place right after the encampment at the base of the mountain. Those youths not of draft age were eligible to return home at the end of their one-year term of enlistment. But most of these lads agreed to stay on for another term. Kyd Douglas expressed pleasure at "the wonderful unanimity" with which the members of the Old Brigade re-enlisted.[11] Such devotion, however, was not uniform among the new elements joining the Valley forces. When a Rockingham County militia company refused to adhere to the law calling them into active service, four companies of the Thirty-third Regiment, assisted by cavalry and a battery of artillery, went after them and brought them forcibly into camp.[12]

Some changes occurred in the spring elections of Stonewall Brigade officers. Popular James W. Allen continued as colonel of the Second Regiment. Charles A. Ronald was elected to command the Fourth Virginia. With the retirement of Colonel Harman, Will Baylor succeeded him as commander of the Fifth Regiment. New colonel of the Twenty-seventh was Andrew Jackson Grigsby, whose caustic nature quickly singled him out among his fellow officers. In the Thirty-third Regiment Colonel Arthur Cummings resigned after a strong disagreement with Jackson. That Cummings could have retained his position otherwise is doubtful. Few of the men had much affection for the hard disciplinarian—especially after an

---

10. E. D. Cottrell, 4th Regiment, "Confederate Letters," *Tyler's Quarterly Historical and Genealogical Magazine*, X (1928–29), 185–86.
11. Douglas, *I Rode with Stonewall*, 29.
12. *Southern Historical Society Papers*, XLIII (1920), 171.

incident over a fence. When some of the members of the Thirty-third violated Jackson's orders and used the rails of a fence for firewood, Cummings asked the guilty men to report themselves. No one stepped forward for punishment, whereupon Cummings ordered the entire regiment into the woods and made the men cut trees and replace the fence.[13]

The men in the ranks were aware that Federals in great strength were pouring through the Valley, but knew little else of the military situation. They did not know that Banks, at Harrisonburg with 19,000 men, stood in their front, waiting to move on Jackson as soon as two brigades (6,000 men) of John C. Frémont's western army could gobble up General Edward Johnson's force of half that number stationed to the west of the Allegheny Mountains. Jackson's force consisted of 6,000 men, with Ewell's division expected before the end of the month. The plan Jackson devised was both sound and simple: using Ewell as a buffer against Banks, he would move secretly with his own division to Johnson's aid, crush the majority of Frémont's army, then hasten back to Ewell and assist him in defeating Banks. In this manner, Jackson could destroy two armies before they united in overwhelming strength against him. Speed and deception were all-important for success.

Jackson had left half of his wagon train at Staunton—a town that became a central depot for Jackson's army throughout the Valley Campaign. Food, ammunition, and other supplies were crammed in all available spaces. One resident wrote about this time of railroad boxcars loaded with supplies being drawn through the streets to warehouses by horses.[14]

On the night of April 30 Ewell's division filed through Swift Run Gap. Many of the men could see Jackson's campfires and looked forward to meeting their compatriots in Old Jack's army. They threaded through the sleeping camp and then bivouacked for the night. When reveille sounded the next morning, Ewell's men jumped up in their eagerness to see the Valley troops. "To our utter amazement," wrote one soldier, "when we turned our faces to where we had passed his army the evening previous, nothing met

13. Casler, *Stonewall Brigade*, 61.
14. Diary of J. Addison Waddell, typescript, Hotchkiss Papers.

our gaze but the smouldering embers of his deserted camp-fires." [15]

To lull Banks into a sense of false security, Jackson led his men over the mountains, ostensibly heading toward Charlottesville or Richmond. Old Jack by this time had adopted the habit of telling no one of his plans. Consequently, there was dejection and bitterness in the ranks at leaving the Valley. Bad weather heightened dissatisfaction. "We are making our way toward Charlottesville," a member of the Fourth Regiment wrote. "It has been raining for five days and it is nothing but mud everywhere and we are without tents, too." [16] Except for the absence of snow and sleet, the march was almost as painful as the Romney expedition. Men and horses floundered in the mud as the army crept through the Blue Ridge and then veered southward toward Mechum's River Station and the Virginia Central Railroad. Averaging little more than five miles a day, the army half crawled and half waded through the quagmire for three days.

As if to signal the end of the march, the clouds parted on May 3. The sun was shining when the men trudged into Mechum's River Station and boarded waiting cars. To their amazement, however, the cars headed westward. Cheers echoed across the rolling hills as the men realized, for the first time, that they were returning to the Valley.

The infantry arrived at Staunton on Sunday, May 4. Artillery and wagon trains, moving through the mountains by road, reached the supply depot the following day. Jackson's army encamped all around the city. The Stonewall Brigade pitched its tents two miles east of town near the local cemetery where, a scant four months later, the remains of the Fifth Regiment's Colonel William Baylor would be borne. On May 7 the army started northward down the pike; after a short distance Jackson cut diagonally to the left and headed westward toward McDowell, twenty miles away. The Stonewall Brigade formed the rear guard of the army, following the wagon train that creaked and groaned over roads softened by fresh

---

15. W. W. Goldsborough, *The Maryland Line in the Confederate States Army* (Baltimore, 1869), 43–44.
16. Jim P. Charlton to Oliver P. Charlton, April 30, 1862, Charlton Letters. See also George R. Bedinger, 33rd Regiment, to his sister, April 29, 1862, Caroline D. Dandridge Papers, Duke University Library.

rains. The wagons soon churned the mud into slush which some-times extended to the knees of the men plodding along in the rear.[17]

In the early afternoon of Thursday, May 8, Jackson, now united with General Johnson's brigade, struck the divisions of General Robert H. Milroy and General Robert C. Schenck at McDowell. This was one of the few battles of the war fought solely with small arms, as the terrain proved too mountainous for either side to get its artillery into position. The Stonewall Brigade was not engaged in the battle but remained on alert near the wagon train, guarding supplies and protecting the rear. Late that night the Federals fled toward Franklin with Ashby hot on their heels. Although Jackson had been victorious, his casualties exceeded those of the Federals.[18]

Naturally, Old Jack was not satisfied. The defeated Federal units were still a threat so long as they could conceivably unite with Banks. On the morning of May 10, therefore, Jackson pushed off in pursuit of the Federal forces. The Stonewall Brigade, almost by cus-tom, took the van and set the pace. The going was rough: the Yankees laid a smoke screen by setting fire to everything in their path; broken terrain slowed the Confederates as they strove to overcome the comfortable lead of the bluecoats; lack of cavalry cover rendered the gray infantry columns very susceptible to Federal snipers, who methodically pecked away at the men throughout the morning.

After seven miles of moving warily up and down hills, the lead elements of the brigade came to a fork in the road. Winder had received no instructions as to which direction he should move. Sending a courier back to Jackson for orders, he then ordered his men to stack arms and rest. The bearded Marylander was pacing up and down the dusty road when Major Douglas Mercer, the brigade quartermaster, rode up. It was reported at Staunton, he informed Winder, that Jackson had placed him under arrest for not having his brigade in battle position at McDowell.

Winder was in the process of expressing his incredulity at the news when a battery of artillery galloped down the narrow road.

---

17. William S. White, *Hugh White*, 82.
18. Jackson's losses at McDowell totaled 461 men; Federal casualties numbered 256. Henderson, *Stonewall Jackson*, I, 298–99.

The men had to break their musket stacks in order to let guns and horses pass. Then up through the dust of the battery rode Jackson. Winder, flushed cheeks plainly visible, mounted his horse and, after saluting briskly, immediately demanded to know if Jackson had placed him under arrest.

"I did not," Jackson curtly replied.

Winder began, "I have always obeyed your orders—"

"But General Winder," Old Jack interrupted, "you are not obeying my orders now. My order is that whenever there is a halt, the men shall stack arms."

The Stonewall Brigade commander, trying to curb his anger, spoke rapidly. "I did obey your order, but had to break the stacks to let a battery pass." Then, returning to the original subject, he added: "I intend to have my rank as second in command of the army respected by everybody."

Jackson drew himself up in the saddle and was about to snap something back when a messenger dashed up and handed him a message. Old Jack read it hastily; then, in a gesture that told much, he passed the paper to Winder. Quickly the Stonewall Brigade shouldered muskets and took the right (north) fork. For the moment, at least, Winder's rank became secondary to the more pressing demands of the campaign.[19]

The Fourth Regiment led the way through woods and across open fields. It soon came to a spot where the road swerved gently down to the right of a high ridge. Winder ordered Colonel Ronald to disperse his men and sweep up the wooded height to clear away any skirmishers. A few minutes later Winder himself rode up the eminence to reconnoiter. Instead of finding Ronald's men advancing, he discovered the entire regiment backing down the hill in an orderly retreat.

Winder's nerves were still taut from the exchange with Jackson. Spying Ronald, he pointed to the retiring troops and hotly demanded: "What is the meaning of this?"

"Why," Ronald answered matter-of-factly, "we came upon the enemy."

Measuring his words carefully, Winder replied: "Why did I put

19. Howard, *Recollections*, 98–100.

you here for but to come on the enemy? Face your men about and move forward!"

Ronald reversed his regiment. At the top of the ridge the men came upon a camp where food was still cooking. There were other indications of a hasty retreat.[20]

The following day, May 12, Jackson gave up the pursuit. As became his custom when unable to observe the Sabbath, he decreed the weekday (Monday) as the Lord's Day. Religious services were held in the morning at all the regimental camps. Two days later the army filed across the battlefield and into McDowell, then turned eastward toward Staunton. On the sixteenth the march was halted for a day of prayer and feasting. This observance was ordered by President Davis to give thanks for the victory at McDowell.

On this day occurred the only mutiny in the history of the Stonewall Brigade. Several companies in the Twenty-seventh Regiment whose original terms of enlistment were ending asked to be discharged. Because of the seriousness of the military situation, and because most of the members were between eighteen and thirty-five (and hence obligated by the Conscription Act to remain in the service), their request was denied. Many of the men promptly threw down their muskets and refused to march or fight. Colonel Grigsby informed Jackson of this situation and asked for instructions.

Old Jack's reply was terse. "Why does Colonel Grigsby refer to me to learn how to deal with mutineers? He should shoot them where they stand."

Grigsby immediately ordered the remaining companies of the regiment to fall in with their muskets and surround the insurgents. Once the move had been executed, Grigsby ordered the mutinous companies to surrender or die. The men promptly "re-enlisted" and thereafter could not be distinguished "from the rest of the regiment in their soldierly behavior." [21] The episode pointed out clearly to the brigade that while it held a special place in the affections of its first commander, his sympathies had definite limitations.

One other incident of note occurred on the McDowell expedition. Following the battle General Winder rode through a portion of the camp and was greeted with a loud cheer by the men. This

---

20. *Ibid.*, 101–102.   21. Dabney, *Jackson*, 354.

first display of admiration for the conscientious commander was received, wrote a staff officer, with "evident gratification." [22]

On May 18 the army was in camp at Mount Solon, ten miles southwest of Harrisonburg. Pleasant weather signaled the coming of spring, and morale was high. While the men speculated as to their next movements, Jackson and "Old Baldy" Ewell were mapping out strategy. Jackson's plan was one of deception. He would march eastward, as if going to Richmond, but as soon as he had crossed over the Massanutten Mountains, and was shielded from observation by Banks, he would rush down the narrow Luray Valley between the Massanuttens and the Blue Ridge. Then, he would swoop down on the flank of the unsuspecting Federal army and destroy it.

Preparations were hastily made. From Staunton loaded wagon trains moved to Harrisonburg, where an advance supply depot was established. The march began on Monday, May 19. Walking four abreast, the gray regiments entered Harrisonburg and were told to deposit their knapsacks at the courthouse. The men perked up at this order. "We knew there was some game on hand then," John Casler wrote, "for when Gen. Jackson ordered knapsacks to be left behind he meant business." [23]

The next day the army, reinforced along the way by General Richard Taylor's Louisiana brigade of Ewell's division, reached New Market. With Ashby's cavalry masking Jackson's moves, the army turned off to the right at New Market, filed through the Massanuttens, and virtually disappeared. So effectively did Old Jack conceal his whereabouts that the Lexington *Gazette* stated: "We know little of Gen. Jackson's movements, but we are expecting to hear of him creating a *stir*, somewhere between Harrisonburg and the Potomac before many days." [24] On the day this story appeared Jackson united at Luray with the rest of Ewell's division.

The long gray line now swung down the Luray Valley, the Stonewall Brigade in the rear. Fearful that the Federals might escape before he could pounce upon them, Jackson set a tremendous pace. For fifty minutes of every hour the men marched rapidly. When

22. Howard, *Recollections*, 103–104.   23. Casler, *Stonewall Brigade*, 96.
24. Lexington *Gazette*, May 22, 1862.

halted, the soldiers stacked arms and enjoyed ten minutes' rest before renewing the march. Thirty minutes were allowed for lunch.[25] Once the march was resumed, Jackson rode up and down the lines, urging the troops on with "Close up, men, close up. Push on; push on." The rapidity of their march quickly earned the men the title of "foot cavalry." The Stonewall Brigade proved the appropriateness of this nickname on May 23, when it marched twenty-six miles to Front Royal in sixteen hours. "Verily," Major Paxton of the brigade wrote his wife, "it is a moving life we lead." [26]

25. Jackson's Order Book, May 13, 1862, Confederate Museum.
26. *Official Records*, XII, Pt. 1, p. 734; Paxton (ed.), *Memoir*, 57.

||||||||||||||||||||||||||||||||||||||||||||||||||||||||||||||||||||||||||||

C H A P T E R   V I I I

JACKSON'S FOOT CAVALRY

In the meantime, at Strasburg, General Nathaniel P. Banks tugged nervously at the ends of his bushy mustache. The one-time Massachusetts politician was finding with each passing day in Jackson country that army life was far more complex than he had ever imagined. Fancied dangers and false reports of Jackson's whereabouts had rubbed his nerves raw. Moreover, the aristocratic New Englander wrote, Strasburg was "the dirtiest, meanest town of all the dirty, shiftless villages of the valley." [1] His only consolation was the belief that his army was larger than Jackson's and that Federal forces stood between the Confederates and the escape route to Winchester and the Potomac.

Suddenly, on May 23, 1862, Jackson "popped out of his hole"

---

1. A. H. Quint, *The Record of the Second Massachusetts Infantry, 1861–65* (Boston, 1867), 77–78.

at Front Royal and after a three-hour engagement drove the Union defenders down the Valley pike in confusion. Banks, ten miles west at Strasburg, received the news of Jackson's strike with complete consternation. Not only was the Confederate general not in his front, he was making for Banks's only route out of the Valley. Now Banks began a dash for Winchester to extricate himself from the closing jaws of Jackson's army.

The Stonewall Brigade, still relegated to rear guard, did not participate in the Front Royal fight. On May 24 it moved out behind the army shortly before 8 A.M. Soon the sound of firing at Middletown drifted back to the end of the column. Sensing battle, Winder ordered the Second, Fourth, and Fifth Regiments to move forward at double-quick time. A few minutes later a courier rode up with instructions from Jackson to turn the brigade northward and strike for Newtown. From the messenger Winder also learned that Jackson had fallen upon Banks's retreating army at Middletown and was even then routing the rear elements. Quickly the three regiments were recalled, while the Twenty-seventh and Thirty-third started northward. The order of march was reversed. The Twenty-seventh and Thirty-third, accompanied by the Rockbridge Artillery, were in front; the Second, Fourth, and Fifth, originally in the van, now brought up the rear.

Winder's lead columns arrived at Newtown simultaneously with Jackson's army, which had threaded its way down the pike clogged with abandoned wagons and burning supplies. Townspeople rushed out joyfully to greet their "liberators." Captain William Poague wheeled the Rockbridge Artillery through town to answer the rearguard fire of a Federal battery. His men saw a portly matron standing on her porch with outstretched arms and shouting lustily, "All of you run here and kiss me!" [2]

Jackson, having tasted success, now pushed for total victory. Poague had cleared the Federal artillerists from the road. At 3 P.M. the chase was resumed, the Stonewall Brigade in the front of the army. Having marched eighteen miles since morning, the Valley troops began to grumble in their weariness. Yet spirits soared appreciably when the Twenty-seventh and Thirty-third Regiments

2. Edward A. Moore, *Cannoneer*, 54.

rushed into Newtown, for there they found abandoned wagons loaded with such luxuries as canned peaches, pickled lobsters, and new underwear. The Confederate pursuit stalled momentarily as men broke from the ranks to grab clothing and to fill stomachs that had not received food since dawn. An exasperated Jackson soon got the men moving down the Valley pike—now so choked with re-treating Federals, Negroes, sutlers, prostitutes, and Union civilians that one Federal officer likened it to "a miniature Bull Run stampede." [3]

By sundown Jackson's regiments were nine miles from Win-chester. The gray sky glowed from burning wagons and supplies discarded in Banks's hasty effort to escape. "Push on, push on," Jackson repeatedly urged. His troops struggled forward in the gathering darkness. Progress was rough—and dangerous. With no light to show the way, the tiring soldiers stumbled over rocks and honeysuckle vines, moved laboriously over swampy terrain, and splashed across several small streams that meandered through woods and fields. Private Edward Moore of the Rockbridge Artillery seemed to catch the full drama of the succeeding hours:

> Night soon set in, and a long, weary night it was; the most trying I ever passed, in war or out of it. From dark till daylight we did not advance more than four miles. Step by step we moved along, halting for five minutes; then on a few steps and halt again. About ten o'clock we passed by a house rather below the roadside, on the porch of which lay several dead Yankees, a light shining on their ghastly faces. Occasion-ally we were startled by the sharp report of a rifle, followed in quick succession by others; then all as quiet as the grave. Sometimes, when a longer halt was made, we would endeavor to steal a few moments sleep for want of which it was hard to stand up. By the time a blanket was unrolled, the column was astir again, and so it continued throughout the long, dreary hours of the night. [4]

A new and deadly obstacle—ambush—confronted the men as the hours passed. The Twenty-seventh Regiment was fired on as it was attempting to ford a creek. The Thirty-third ran into a second

---

3. *Official Records*, XII, Pt. 1, p. 743; William S. White, *Hugh White*, 85–86; David Strother, "Recollections," *Harper's New Monthly Magazine*, XXXIV (1871), 442–43.
4. Edward A. Moore, *Cannoneer*, 54–55.

ambuscade of such intensity that it was driven back in confusion. Colonel Grigsby bellowed orders to his Twenty-seventh Regiment to move up in support. In contrast, the quiet Jim Allen cautiously edged forward with his Second Regiment as red flashes of musketry continually broke the darkness.[5]

At 2 A.M., four miles from Winchester, Jackson halted the advance. The troops were given one hour to rest on their arms. But Colonel Baylor's Fifth Regiment, in the advance, was not allowed that small respite. The companies stood in column while Baylor rode to the front and listened apprehensively for any sound of movement. Soon he had company. Jackson joined him and remained in the advanced position until 4 A.M., when word was passed down the line for the men to prepare for action.

Shortly thereafter the 1,529 men of the Stonewall Brigade began moving through the mist as skirmishers. Just beyond Hollingsworth's Mill the men spotted Federals posted atop a long, commanding ridge southwest of town. Winder rode forward with his staff to reconnoiter. As the officers swung their horses around to start back, a Federal cannon shell whistled through the air and clipped off the tail of Captain John O'Brien's horse. Whether or not the assistant adjutant general intended it, he led the return to the rear by a comfortable margin.[6]

Winder reported to Jackson that the Federals were in strength all along the hill. "You must occupy that hill," Jackson snapped. Winder saluted and rode quickly to make dispositions. Baylor's Fifth Regiment was thrown forward as skirmishers; Grigsby took his Twenty-seventh and moved to the left to occupy a wooded rise opposite the Federal position; the Second, under Colonel Allen, was posted on Grigsby's right; to Allen's right was Ronald's Fourth Regiment, placed in a wheat field adjacent to the Valley pike; John Neff's Thirty-third dropped back in reserve.[7]

The Sabbath stillness was suddenly broken by the loud, deep booms of Jackson's artillery. With a shout Winder's men bounded forward through the smoke and fog and rushed for the hill. Dick Taylor's brigade supported them on the left, and the remainder of

5. *Official Records*, XII, Pt. 1, p. 734.   6. Howard, *Recollections*, 109.
7. *Official Records*, XII, Pt. 1, pp. 736, 746.

Ewell's division made a simultaneous assault down the pike. The brigade reached the crest of the hill as Federals dashed down the other side toward Winchester. Before the graycoats could take up pursuit, Federal artillery on the hill opened fire. The Confederates quickly backed behind the brow and sought cover in ravines and washouts. For two hours they were pinned there "under a most galling fire," Grigsby wrote.[8]

The Rockbridge Artillery rode up and began unlimbering. Before it could fire a volley, a Federal battery dashed to the crest of a ridge obliquely to the left, wheeled beautifully into action, and delivered a salvo at Poague's battery that cleared one piece of all its gunners. Jackson, galloping from one point to another, saw a Federal regiment filing behind a stone wall to protect the cannon now blazing away with deadly accuracy.[9] Carpenter's battery was dispatched to Poague's assistance.

Before Carpenter's four guns could get there, the Yankees behind the wall had not only picked off another of Poague's crews but were thinning Andrew Grigsby's Twenty-seventh Regiment, which was trying to protect the Confederate guns. Grigsby himself narrowly escaped injury when a musket ball passed through the sleeve of his coat, causing the colonel to fling a string of oaths at Federals in general.[10] Soon Poague's Parrotts were in action. When canister showed no effect on the bluecoats, Poague ordered his guns loaded with solid shot and literally hammered to pieces the wall and the men who were back of it.[11]

Jackson, riding to the rear to accelerate the movements of Taylor's brigade, came upon Colonel John Neff and his Thirty-third

8. *Ibid.*, 752.
9. These Federals were Colonel George L. Andrews' 2nd Massachusetts of Colonel George H. Gordon's 3rd Brigade.
10. Elihu Riley, *Stonewall Jackson* (Annapolis, 1920), 167.
11. *Official Records*, XII, Pt. 1, pp. 761–62; Howard, *Recollections*, 110. Although numerous infantry officers on both sides during the Civil War stated that their men encountered grapeshot in charges, artillery officers do not mention the use of grape in field pieces and grape does not appear in the ammunition lists for light artillery. Authorities on Civil War artillery are of the opinion that grape was rarely if ever used by field artillery, despite the fact that in this engagement both Grigsby and Andrews reported grape being fired into their troops. *Official Records*, XII, Pt. 1, pp. 622, 752.

Regiment. The two officers exchanged salutes. Jackson asked quickly, "Colonel, where is your regiment posted?"

"Here," Neff answered, "the right masked in this depression of ground, and the left behind that fence."

"What are your orders?" came the next question.

"To support that battery," replied Neff, pointing to W. E. Cutshaw's battery of four pieces wheeling into position.

Jackson pointed to a nearby hill, clenched his fist, and then said to Neff in a voice of stern determination, "I expect the enemy to bring artillery to this hill, and they must not do it! Do you understand me, sir? They must not do it! Keep a good lookout, and your men well in hand; and if they attempt to come, charge them with the bayonet, and seize their guns! Clamp them, sir, on the spot!"

Neff calmly answered, "Very well, General, but my regiment is rather small." (This was an understatement; the Thirty-third numbered only 150 men.)

"Take it!" Jackson ordered, then rode off swiftly.[12]

The Thirty-third moved over behind the guns. From one end of the gray line to the other, as Confederate artillery hotly contested the guns across the ridge, the infantrymen poised for action. Jackson rode hurriedly to prod Dick Taylor's brigade into position. Until the Federal right could be turned, the battle was in doubt. As Jackson passed the Stonewall Brigade at full gallop, the men looked at him affectionately. They had been ordered not to cheer, but somehow they had to show him how they felt. Silently the men removed their hats. Jackson acknowledged their tribute with a similar gesture and rode on.[13]

At 7:30 A.M. Taylor's brigade charged so furiously that the Federal right seemed to melt from the heat of the assault. This was the moment Jackson had sought. The entire Confederate army surged forward under the warmth of the early morning sun. "All were eager for the charge," Winder stated of his Stonewall Brigade, "and moved forward rapidly and in good order, sweeping the entire field,

---

12. This interchange between Jackson and Neff is from accounts in *Official Records*, XII, Pt. 1, pp. 755–56; Dabney, *Jackson*, 378; *Southern Historical Society Papers*, IX (1881), 235.
13. Douglas, *I Rode with Stonewall*, 57–58.

the enemy leaving his position some time before we reached it." Across the rolling hills toward Winchester, Confederates pursued Banks's army, Federal wagon trains already rumbling toward the Potomac. Because of the "exhausted and disabled condition" of the Valley troops, Winder wrote, the effectiveness of the chase was greatly impaired; but it continued with all the enthusiasm of a weary army a few steps from total success.[14] Randolph Fairfax of the Rockbridge Artillery wrote of the scene outside Winchester: "Such a [Federal] rout has not been seen since Manassas; arms, knapsacks, blankets and all sorts of accoutrements, were strewn along the route of their flight." [15]

Banks's retreat had indeed degenerated into a rout. From her front parlor Mrs. Cornelia McDonald watched the blue army filing down Winchester's streets. "Nothing could be distinguished, nothing but a huge moving mass of blue, rolling along like a cloud in the distance." At that moment, from passageways and upstairs windows, scores of townspeople began banging away at the Federals with shotguns and flintlocks. Panic now seized the Union troops; "like a muddy torrent with the sunlight glittering on its turbid waves," regiments scurried northward without organization or intent. General Banks himself rode among the confusion, trying to restore a semblance of order.

"My God!" he shouted at a mob of fleeing soldiers. "Don't you love your country?"

"Yes," came a reply from some unknown soldier, "and I am trying to get back to it as fast as I can!" [16]

By this time the Stonewall Brigade, the Second and Fifth Regiments in front, had double-timed into Winchester. "Old men and women, ladies and children, high and low, rich and poor," rushed into the streets, "shouting for joy at the entrance of the victorious Stonewall Brigade." One woman was heard screaming above the rest, "Oh, you brave, noble, ragged darlings, you! I am so glad to see you!" Jubilant citizens passed out food to soldiers who snatched

---

14. *Official Records,* XII, Pt. 1, p. 737.   15. Slaughter, *Fairfax,* 28.
16. McDonald, *Diary,* 68; *Southern Historical Society Papers,* IX (1881), 235; Strother, "Recollections," *loc. cit.,* 445; E. E. Bryant, *History of the Third Regiment of Wisconsin Veteran Volunteers* (Madison, 1891), 69–71.

a mouthful and then continued up the streets in pursuit of Banks's army. But now the task became difficult. Townspeople overwhelmed with happiness kept impeding the advance to greet loved ones and to inquire of the well-being of relatives. Meanwhile, pockets of Federals had barricaded themselves at street intersections and strategic locations. Some fought stubbornly until overrun or flanked. Colonel Will Baylor was conspicuous in the mopping-up operations. He personally captured two Federals, turned them over to a lady to whom he gave his pistol, and then raced down Loudoun Street to rejoin his Fifth Regiment. A bystander who noticed Baylor's leg drenched in blood offered to escort him to a doctor, but the fiery officer replied that he was not wounded; it was his horse.[17]

By this time the whole brigade was rushing through town. David Barton of the Thirty-third Regiment ran down Cameron Street and momentarily broke from the ranks to embrace his mother on the front porch of their home. Resuming his chase, young Barton spied his old Negro "mammy" standing along the curb farther down the street. He stopped and tearfully informed the woman that his younger brother Marshall had been killed earlier that day. And he instructed the Negro not to tell his mother until she had had the opportunity of enjoying the day's victory.[18]

For five miles Jackson's army chased the remnants of Banks's forces. Near Stephenson's Depot, Jackson himself galloped past the loping Stonewall Brigade and was greeted with loud cheers and a scattering of hats thrown into the air. Soon the chase was stopped. The Federals had lost control of the Valley and its stores; in addition, Banks's army had suffered casualties totaling 3,000 men, 800 of whom had been expended at Winchester. All this Jackson had achieved at a cost of 400 men, 37 of whom came from the Valley brigade.[19]

---

17. McDonald, *Diary*, 68; *Official Records*, XII, Pt. 1, p. 737; C. A. Porter Hopkins (ed.), "An Extract from the Journal of Mrs. Hugh L. Lee of Winchester, Va., May 23–31, 1862," *Maryland Historical Magazine*, LIII (1958), 386.
18. Louisa M. Green (ed.), *True Stories of Old Winchester and the Valley* (Winchester, 1931), 9–11. See also Barton, *Recollections*, 16.
19. *Official Records*, XII, Pt. 1, p. 737; *Battles and Leaders*, II, 301.

Monday, May 26, the day after the victory, was dedicated to rest, celebration, and prayer. While the Stonewall Brigade encamped just north of Winchester, newspapers in the South began reprinting a short poem:

> Whilst Butler plays his silly pranks,
> And closes up New Orleans banks,
> Our Stonewall Jackson, with more cunning,
> Keeps Yankee Banks forever running. [20]

It was probably during this two-day rest period at Winchester that a woman rebuked Jackson for "marching the dear boys so hard." Old Jack stared at her for a moment, then replied sharply, "Legs are cheaper than heads, Madame." [21]

On May 28 Winder's brigade, with the batteries of Carpenter and Poague, was ordered northward to Harpers Ferry. Jackson then directed that all available wagons in the Valley gather at Martinsburg without delay to help haul off captured stores. These included 9,300 small arms and large quantities of badly needed medical supplies. The Stonewall Brigade was thrown forward to provide protection against a sneak attack.

Leaving Winchester at 5 A.M., high-spirited men began a leisurely march for Charlestown. Presently a Rebel cavalryman dashed back from a visit in Charlestown and informed Winder that Federals were entrenching south and west of the town. Winder relayed the news to Jackson in Winchester. But to the admiration of both Jackson and the men in the Stonewall Brigade, the dark-haired Marylander, instead of expending precious time waiting for reinforcements, gave orders for his men to fall in and quick-march to Charlestown.

A mile south of town the Confederates ran into skirmishers, who were quickly brushed aside by two companies of the Fifth Regiment. After moving through a clump of woods to the edge of an open field, Winder saw Federals drawn up in line of battle. Their

---

20. Charleston *Mercury*, quoted in Frank Moore (ed.), *Rebellion Record*, VI, Pt. 3, p. 10.
21. Garber, "Recollections."

strength was estimated at 1,500 men, roughly equal to Winder's force.[22] Two Federal cannon began to play on the graycoats. Quickly Carpenter's battery unlimbered its guns and answered with a ten-minute bombardment of such intensity that the bluecoats fled in disorder, leaving arms, blankets, food, and other matériel in their wake.

The streets of Charlestown were lined with cheering citizens as the Confederates passed through en route to Harpers Ferry. Four miles outside the city Winder halted his men. Federals in larger numbers were clearly visible atop Bolivar Heights, the south-westerly range overlooking the Ferry. Winder deemed them too numerous for his force to handle, and withdrew his brigade to within one mile of Charlestown. Early the following morning Jackson arrived with the Second Regiment, quickly sized up the situation, and sent the Second to Loudoun's Heights to dislodge the Federals from Harpers Ferry. The rest of the army bivouacked at Halltown.

In the meantime, on May 28, an elderly gentleman informed Jackson that Federals were moving in strength on Front Royal. Sometime during the night of May 29–30 Ashby's couriers confirmed this report and added that John C. Frémont's army was moving east toward Strasburg and a rendezvous with James Shields's division. Jackson realized that if these pincers were closed, he would be trapped, for Banks was also preparing to march southward from Williamsport. Yet Jackson remained a picture of imperturbability. He watched the Fifth Regiment skirmish with Federals; then, when a light rain began to fall, he leaned back against a tree and instantly fell asleep.[23]

By noon, however, orders had been issued. Jackson would take the bulk of the army to Winchester. Winder and the Stonewall Brigade would remain at Halltown until the Second Regiment could return from Loudoun's Heights. Then it would rejoin the

---

22. The men of the 2nd Virginia were left at Winchester as provost guards. Winder placed the strength of his four regiments at 1,337 men. This figure did not include the two batteries accompanying him on the expedition. *Official Records*, XII, Pt. 1, p. 739.
23. Freeman, *Lee's Lieutenants*, I, 413.

army. Soon Jackson was gone. Winder spent the rest of the day waiting for Colonel Allen's regiment.

Late that night Lieutenant McHenry Howard, one of Winder's aides, was awakened by someone stumbling over his tent ropes. Walking out into the cool air, Howard recognized Jed Hotchkiss of Jackson's staff. Hotchkiss had become lost trying to find the Stonewall Brigade, and the hours wasted only intensified the seriousness of the news he bore. Jackson had been forced to evacuate Winchester in order to keep Shields and Frémont from uniting at Strasburg. Winder's brigade was to start southward with all possible haste. If Winchester were occupied, Hotchkiss told Winder, he was to take him "through the mountains" in an effort to rejoin Jackson.[24]

The Second Regiment wearily marched into camp at dawn, whereupon, wrote the Rockbridge Artillery's Launcelot Blackford, "we decamped with undignified haste." [25] The Second Regiment did not have time either to grab a bite to eat or to rest before the whole brigade was moving down the road toward Winchester. Winder and his officers were well aware of their perilous position. The regimental colonels tried to keep the four-abreast columns moving at rapid speed. It was impossible. A pouring rain hampered vision and turned the roads into loblollies that impeded wagons and exhausted the men. All through the gloomy day the columns moved toward Winchester. They reached the abandoned town at dusk, passed through silently, and continued up the Valley pike.

On into the darkness the march continued. Rain now beat down in torrents; stragglers in scores scurried out of ranks and sought cover in nearby woods. At 10 P.M. the brigade filed into Newtown. Winder, unwilling to push his men any farther, issued orders to bivouac for the night. The men fell out along the streets and utilized every possible shelter from the rain; without bothering to cook rations, most of them dropped immediately into a sleep of

---

24. Although many in the Stonewall Brigade came to feel that Jackson had deserted them, Hotchkiss wrote later that Old Jack "fully appreciated the situation and manifested more anxiety about getting the Stonewall Brigade back to his command in safety than I ever saw him do at any other time." Jed Hotchkiss to A. C. Hopkins, September 2, 1896, Hotchkiss Papers.

25. L. Minor Blackford (ed.), *Mine Eyes Have Seen the Glory*, 192.

exhaustion. Four of the regiments had marched twenty-eight miles
that day. The Second had covered thirty-five—and had not eaten
for two days.[26]

For the first time since assuming brigade command, Winder de-
parted from his usual military silence. Tired and wet, bitter at having been ordered to do the impossible, he resolved then and there
that "he might as well lose his men in battle as on such a march." [27]
And although Jackson's instructions were for the Stonewall Brigade
to rendezvous with his command at Strasburg by seven o'clock the
following morning, Winder lingered at Newtown until that hour
to allow stragglers to rejoin their units.

The men in the ranks were still almost out on their feet, and the
prospect of continuing the march in mud and rain was extremely
depressing. As the Stonewall Brigade shuffled off toward Strasburg,
ten long miles away, one Confederate soldier noted: "Officers and
men were silent as the grave—occupied all with the same gloomy
apprehensions. I fancied that even the gallant and intrepid General
Winder . . . looked chagrined and gloomy." [28] On two occasions
horsemen of Ashby's cavalry dashed up with rumors that the pike
had fallen into Federal hands. The sound of artillery booming in
the distance was audible proof that the Yankees were closing the
trap.

As the lead columns reached a road junction north of Middletown, Winder and his staff suddenly saw a group of horsemen standing in the mud. McHenry Howard rode forward to ascertain their
identity and was overjoyed when he recognized General Turner
Ashby. The colorful cavalry leader returned the young aide's salute
and asked: "Is that General Winder coming up?"

When Howard replied in the affirmative, Ashby smiled and said,
"Thank God for that!"

Winder rode up and Ashby took his hand warmly. "General," he
said, "I was never so relieved in my life. I thought that you would
be cut off and had made up my mind to join you and advise you to
make your escape over the mountain to Gordonsville." [29]

---

26. Douglas, I Rode with Stonewall, 69; Casler, Stonewall Brigade, 105.
27. A. C. Hopkins to Jed Hotchkiss, August 26, 1896, Hotchkiss Papers.
28. Randolph H. McKim, A Soldier's Recollections (New York, 1910), 107.
29. Howard, Recollections, 116–17.

With Ashby's cavalry covering both flanks, the Stonewall Brigade moved painfully up the Valley pike and at noon filed slowly into Strasburg. Jackson's army was facing east to meet Shields, while General Ewell had his men and guns to the west, holding Frémont at bay with taunts of battle. The Stonewall Brigade continued south from Strasburg for a few miles and then fell out to bivouac. Most of the men simply dropped down into the muddy road where they had been standing. In the condition of indifference that comes from fatigue, hunger, and dampness, troops fell asleep with little concern for the dangers about them. The ordeal of the past two days had sorely tried even Jackson's foot cavalry. Chaplain A. C. Hopkins of the Second Regiment wrote later: "I venture to say that there is no military march on record, for distance and unfavorable conditions, equal to that march of Saturday of the Second Regiment of Va. infantry! And very few equal to that march of the Brigade!" [30]

---

30. A. C. Hopkins to Jed Hotchkiss, August 26, 1896, Hotchkiss Papers.

CHAPTER IX

"FIGHTING IS BECOMING
QUITE FASHIONABLE"

The next morning, June 2, Jackson resumed his retreat up the Valley. At the same time, from Staunton some 275 fully loaded wagons started down the pike toward his army. Loaned by farmers and manned largely by Mennonites whose faith opposed the bearing of arms, these wagon trains always seemed to come from nowhere when Jackson stood in need of supplies.[1]

Winder's Stonewall Brigade brought up the rear of the army. The men had covered only a short distance when the sound of firing was heard from the pickets in the rear. Winder quickly wheeled the brigade into battle position astride the pike. The advance of the Federals was checked, but they appeared strong enough

---

1. Waddell Diary, entries of May 28–June 2, 1862.

to pin the brigade down where it was. General Dick Taylor offered to bring his Louisianians back to help Winder extricate himself, but the Marylander declined any assistance. To the admiration of both Jackson and Taylor, he was able to remove the brigade by a novel procedure. The regiments on the two flanks turned and moved toward the center, giving cover to the other units who were falling back. The Stonewall Brigade units rejoined Jackson's army and resumed the withdrawal.[2]

Jackson reached Harrisonburg on June 5. For two days the Confederates rested in battle position while the sick and wounded were transported by wagon to Staunton. On June 7 Jackson turned eastward for Port Republic. His reasoning was this: if forced to leave the Valley, he would be near the Virginia Central Railroad; if forced to fight, he had the shelter of the mountains to protect his flank. Moreover, Port Republic was of far more importance than its size indicated. It lay in the angle formed by the South and North rivers as they merged into the South Fork of the Shenandoah. Two important roads met there and Brown's Gap lay a short distance to the east. In essence, control of the village meant control of the upper Valley.[3]

Destroying all bridges behind him, Jackson reached Port Republic on June 6. Ewell remained four miles northwest at Cross Keys to keep an eye on Frémont. Jackson's army encamped around Port Republic, with the Stonewall Brigade posted on knolls just north of the village. Old Jack would watch the east for signs of Shields's division. His sole strategy was to keep the two opposing armies divided. Frémont's force numbered 15,000 and that of Shields, 10,000. With but 16,000 troops, the Confederates' best hope of success was to fight the two armies one at a time.

Sunday, June 8, dawned warm and still. After a march of over three hundred miles, the Valley troops lay on the grass, basking in the sunshine; many sauntered down to the river banks to fish, using their muskets for poles. At his headquarters south of town Jackson mounted his horse and prepared to ride leisurely to the front. A

---

2. Howard, *Recollections*, 117–18; Richard Taylor, *Destruction and Reconstruction* (New York, 1879), 68–69.
3. Vandiver, *Mighty Stonewall*, 268–69.

courier suddenly rode up at a gallop and informed him that Federal troops were filing into Port Republic from the east. Just then the roar of cannon broke the stillness. At the first shot McHenry Howard of the brigade staff, who was unpacking his bag, rapidly began repacking. "What are you doing?" a fellow aide asked. Howard, who like other members of the brigade had grown accustomed to Old Jack's strange strategy, replied, "Well, it's Sunday and you heard that shot." [4]

Jackson, convinced that Shields was launching an attack, rode furiously to the bridge and the north bank of the river. Although two of his aides were captured during the ride, he made the crossing safely under a shower of bullets. He proceeded straight to Winder's tent and ordered him to get a regiment across the river on the double. Five minutes later Colonel Allen was advancing toward the bridge with his Second Regiment. Jackson then rode up to the crest of a hill overlooking the bridge and the village. He found Poague's Rockbridge Artillery already there, banging away at Federal columns approaching the bridge from the east. The remainder of the Stonewall Brigade and Taliaferro's regiments were ordered to move quickly and secure the bridge. If the Federals took it, Jackson's wagons—strung out all along the Mount Meridian road south of town—would be lost. Little wonder that to Captain Poague, Jackson's anxiety seemed to border on irrationality.[5]

As Old Jack was watching the action below, he saw some blue-clad gunners heading for the bridge with a six-pounder. Jackson turned quickly to Poague. "Fire on that gun!" he shouted.

Several members of the Rockbridge Artillery yelled out, "General, General, those are our men!"

"Fire on that gun!" Jackson bellowed again.

"General," Poague interjected, "I know those are our men." He went on to say that he had seen a new battery (Carrington's) ride into camp the preceding day, and for lack of uniforms the men were wearing blue clothing "borrowed" from the Federals.

Jackson listened impatiently, then rode up to the top of the ridge opposite the bridge and cried out to the gun crew that he had just left, "Bring that gun up here!"

4. Howard, *Recollections*, 122.   5. Poague, *Gunner*, 26.

The men, torn between Jackson's order and their conviction that the gunners at whom he wished them to fire were friendly, stood immobile.

This time Jackson rose in his stirrups, turned a deathlike gaze on the men, and roared, *"Bring that gun up here,* I say!"

At that moment the blueclads in the street turned their gun so as to rake the ridge where Jackson stood. The move was unmistakably hostile and removed any doubt of their true identity. "Let 'em have it," snarled Jackson. The Parrott gun beside him barked once and sent a ball bouncing by the Federals. The Yankees fired a wild shot over the heads of the Confederates and then abandoned their piece in order to escape from grayclad infantry racing down the hill toward them.[6]

This threat removed, Poague, now reinforced by Carpenter's battery, began bombarding the blue columns moving toward the bridge. In quick fashion the Federals fell back, "stunned, riddled and scattered," to the cover of a ridge a mile northeast of town.[7] In the meantime, Winder had moved his Stonewall Brigade into position at the bridge. The Second and Fourth Regiments were sent to the left so as to cover the span obliquely. The Fifth was posted behind Poague's battery, and the Twenty-seventh took up a similar position with Carpenter's battery. John Neff's Thirty-third Virginia was held in reserve. Total strength of the brigade at this point was 1,134 men.[8]

The action around the bridge—principally probing skirmishes by both sides—lasted an hour. The Stonewall Brigade remained quietly in position for the remainder of the day. To their left, "Old Baldy" Ewell taught John C. Frémont's fighters painful lessons in the art of war at Cross Keys. By nightfall Frémont's army was half-paralyzed from shock, injury, and death.

Around the flickering light of a campfire Jackson planned the next day's strategy. A combination of Shields's inactivity and Frémont's defeat made him think in bold terms. He decided to attack both armies in succession. While holding Frémont at bay, he would

6. Edward A. Moore, *Cannoneer,* 68–69; *Southern Historical Society Papers,* XLIII (1920), 271; Freeman, *Lee's Lieutenants,* I, 441–42.
7. Douglas, *I Rode with Stonewall,* 86.
8. *Official Records,* XII, Pt. 1, p. 740.

assail and destroy Shields, then turn and finish the damage Ewell had inflicted on Frémont.

At 3:45 A.M. on June 9, Winder's Valley regiments began filing silently across a makeshift bridge to get in battle position. They followed the Federal line of retreat for a few hundred yards, then halted to wait for dawn and the scheduled assault. The Second Regiment was in front, two of its companies thrown out as skirmishers. By 6:30 A.M. the men were still waiting for the battle order. The sun should have been up, but a haze partially cloaked the area —not enough, however, to conceal the battle arena.

The site left much to be desired by the attackers. Open ground ran from the bridge for almost a mile and a half, then rose gradually to a wooded slope.[9] Behind and to the left (east) of the ridge was a small opening formed by a charcoal clearing—known as a "coaling." Jackson was sure Shields would have guns posted over there. What he did not know was that Shields's division, now under General Erastus B. Tyler, had been strengthened with troops from Ohio and western Virginia, hardy men as resolute in their fighting as the veterans of the Valley. Except for an apple orchard on the right and a clump of woods farther to the east, the entire area between the two lines was a vast wheat field, its greenness now beginning to glisten in a coat of dew.

Jackson was in a hurry to raise the curtain on his strategy. Without waiting for General Dick Taylor's men, en route from Cross Keys for the assault,· he ordered the Stonewall Brigade to move out unsupported. Winder sent the Second Virginia toward a clump of trees to the right, with the Fourth to its left and in support. Across the open plain moved the Fifth and Twenty-seventh Regiments in battle line. The Thirty-third Virginia was on picket duty and, owing to a mixup in orders, did not reach the field in time to assist its sister regiments.[10]

---

9. Jackson estimated the distance at a mile and a half; Winder thought it to be a mile across the river bottom. *Ibid.*, 714, 740.

10. Neither Neff nor the messenger who brought him word to join the Stonewall Brigade knew exactly where it was. Moreover, as the 33rd Virginia moved toward the river, the Valley troops found the way clogged with wagons, ambulances, artillery, and other units. As a result, Neff's regiment was three hours late in arriving on the field. *Ibid.*, 757; Walker, *VMI Memorial*, 401–402.

The Valley fighters easily drove back Federal pickets and advanced unmolested a third of the way across the wheat field. Suddenly whiffs of smoke curled up from the coaling, followed by deep booms. Seconds later, shells screamed and whistled overhead, plowing up the field all around the advancing Confederates. Volley after volley came quickly and accurately. The foot cavalry were helpless, for the cannon were well beyond the range of their muskets. The advance stalled; gaps began to appear in the gray lines.

Jackson, who was directing the assault, ordered troops to be sent through the woods to flank the six-gun battery playing havoc with his infantry. Colonel Allen moved out with the Second and Ronald's Fourth Virginia; Carpenter's battery followed them as a support.[11] The rest of the Stonewall Brigade, aided by the Rockbridge Artillery, remained in position on the left.

While the flank attack was materializing, Poague waged a valiant but futile effort to protect the troops in his front. Only his two Parrott guns could reach the coaling. He managed to get in two shots before the Federal cannon pinpointed his position. "More accurate shooting I was never subjected to," gunner Ned Moore wrote later.[12] The brigade was further hampered by the absence of the Thirty-third Regiment, still trying to get across the homemade bridge at Port Republic.

Meanwhile, on the right the Second and Fourth Regiments had encountered unforeseen obstacles. In moving through the woods to the ridge, the men ran into honeysuckle and mountain laurel of such density as to make passage almost impossible. Foot by foot they hacked their way forward. Captain Joe Carpenter, finding the route impenetrable, returned with his battery to assist Poague, who certainly needed help.[13]

Allen and Ronald finally got their regiments through the woods to within one hundred yards of the Federal battery, which had two regiments in immediate support and two others within calling dis-

---

11. The two regiments totaled 541 men. *Southern Historical Society Papers*, XLIII (1920), 281.
12. As Federal shells tore up the ground around Poague's two guns, Bob Lee, the son of Robert E. Lee, crawled up to E. A. Moore and said good-naturedly, "Ned, that isn't making batter-cakes, is it?" Edward A. Moore, *Cannoneer*, 73–74.
13. *Official Records*, XII, Pt. 1, p. 741.

tance. Despite the overwhelming odds, Allen was determined to try to silence the guns. The two companies of the Fourth Virginia nearest the battery loosed a volley that knocked down a handful of gunners and sent the remainder scurrying for cover. When General Tyler saw that his battery had been abandoned, he ordered an immediate counterassault. The Fifth and Seventh Ohio sprang forward across a ninety-yard field toward the guns. The Virginians poured a concentrated fire into their ranks. Five color-bearers of the Seventh Ohio went down before Lieutenant Leicester King (awarded the Congressional Medal of Honor for his feat) picked up the flag and led the regiment into the works. This successful assault, and the subsequent heavy fire from the Federals, was such, Colonel Allen stated, "as to throw my men into confusion." Both Virginia regiments fell back down the hill in disorganized fashion. Jackson's daring flank attack had failed.[14]

Back in the wheat field Winder was faring no better. The Federal battery had now pinpointed the Stonewall Brigade with shells; supporting Federal infantry behind the cover of a fence to the left were pouring a deadly cross fire into the gray ranks. A brigade of Federals began advancing down the ridge. Winder sent an urgent plea to Jackson for reinforcements: the Stonewall Brigade was being hacked to pieces. At this moment the lead elements of Dick Taylor's brigades appeared on the field—but Jackson, seemingly oblivious to the plight of his old brigade, sent Taylor's men doubletiming to the right to overrun the Federal battery.

Disaster seemed to be staring Winder in the face. If the Federals charged, his thinned line would collapse. He would not give the enemy such an opportunity, he concluded; the best defense was an offense. He ordered the Fifth and Twenty-seventh Regiments, along with Colonel Harry Hays's Seventh Louisiana, temporarily under his command, to prepare for assault. Orders were rushed to Poague and Carpenter to follow the infantry and to unlimber as close to the Federals as possible. These dispositions made, Winder raised his arm and signaled the advance.

A chorus of shouts rose from the field as cheering Confederates

---

14. *Ibid.*, 745, 747; George L. Wood, *The Seventh Regiment: A Record* (New York, 1865), 118.

swept forward in two lines. Shoes and trouser bottoms became wet as the men raced through the shin-deep, dew-covered wheat; ranks quickly took on irregular shapes. On and on the troops advanced, firing as they ran, rubbing arms across foreheads in an effort to stem perspiration that blinded eyes and gave lips the thirst-rising taste of salt. Colonel Grigsby was directing his Twenty-seventh Virginia and cursing Yankees when his horse went down from a succession of wounds. Undaunted, Grigsby squirmed from under the dying animal and led his men forward on foot—still uttering a stream of oaths. The assaulting regiments reached a fence halfway across the field and were promptly pinned down by canister and Minié balls raining from the ridge. The supporting batteries of Poague and Carpenter proved feeble help at the most. For two hours the Stonewall Brigade endured a deafening and deadly bombardment. Winder again called for help; again his pleas were of no avail.

Ammunition soon began to run low, and the wavering of the Valley ranks gave ominous signs of impending disaster. Winder must have asked himself a hundred times what was detaining Taylor. Why did he not silence that battery? Perhaps in that moment the memory of Dick Garnett drifted across the anxious general's mind. This was Kernstown all over again: pinned down by a crushing fire, out of ammunition. What Winder most feared now began to occur. Here and there a soldier broke from cover and ran back across the wheat field. Soon men by the scores were following their example. Seeing his line slowly melt, Winder quickly ordered the two batteries back to safety. He and his regimental colonels rode back and forth across the field—beseeching, ordering, cursing, and shouting at the men to go back before the day was lost. Their entreaties fell on deaf ears; the stampede was on. The Fifth Virginia tried to regroup in the orchard; but before it could reform, the Seventh Louisiana bolted through and scattered the Virginians.[15]

Federals were now pouring down the hill in a counterattack. Winder saw at once that they must be held back until his troops could be rallied. He sent a courier to Poague, instructing the artillery officer to halt his withdrawal and to hold the Federals at bay as long as possible. The Rockbridge Artillery wheeled about hand-

15. *Official Records*, XII, Pt. 1, p. 750.

somely and raked the advancing blue ranks. But the tide could not be checked. Faced with complete envelopment, Poague hastily hitched his guns and started off. Not hearing his order, the crew of one six-pounder was left in a forward position. Federal shells pounded the area, killing an officer and two horses, and forcing the gun to be abandoned.[16]

At this critical moment the Second Brigade of Ewell's division arrived on the field from Cross Keys. Three regiments double-timed to Winder's right; but before they could form battle ranks, the Federals veered to the left and drove them in confusion back into the woods. Ewell's troops were disorganized, and Winder was in the midst of trying to reorganize his command. Into the chaos galloped Jackson. Dashing back and forth among his old brigade, he shouted, "The Stonewall Brigade never retreats! Follow me!" [17] Just then Neff led his Thirty-third Virginia onto the field. He had been stalled for hours without instructions; but, as he later wrote, "orders now came in abundance." [18]

Suddenly the Federal battery in the coaling that had boomed away all day abruptly ceased firing. A cheer swept through the Confederate ranks. Dick Taylor had finally silenced the guns! Three bloody assaults were the price, but the guns had been captured!

Federals had swerved to counter Taylor's flank attack. Just as they turned, the Stonewall Brigade rushed back across the field and poured a deadly fire into their flank while the Louisianians delivered a volley in front. Tyler's army fell apart. For four hours it had waged a masterful struggle, but this Confederate cross fire was too much. The bluecoats broke and fled down the road to the north, with the brigades of Winder and Taliaferro hot on their heels. For five miles the chase continued until men "worn-out and exhausted from the hard labors of the day" began to fall along the roadside.[19]

That afternoon a weary Stonewall Brigade encamped atop the Blue Ridge at Brown's Gap. Considering the severity of the action, their losses had been relatively slight: 15 killed, 145 wounded, and 31 missing.[20] Jackson's total losses, more than 800, were the highest

16. *Ibid.*, 715, 741, 763.
18. *Official Records*, XII, Pt. 1, p. 758.
20. *Ibid.*, 717.

17. *Battles and Leaders*, II, 295–96.
19. *Ibid.*, 750–51.

yet suffered on the campaign.[21] But the Valley was now his. In one of the most brilliant campaigns of all times, Old Jack with little more than 16,000 men had defeated three Union armies aggregating 60,000 troops.

On June 12, 1862, the army went into camp at Weyer's Cave near Mount Meridian. For five days it licked its wounds and pondered Jackson's next move. Artillery Captain Carpenter used this lull to write his father in Covington:

'Tis useless for me to tell you of the fights that we have had as no doubt you already know. But it appears to me now that fighting is becoming quite fashionable, especially in Jackson's army. We have had three days rest in the last two months—the balance of the time either on a forced march or fighting—one or the other. A few more marches and fights will ruin his Old Brigade unless he allows them to recruit now but the enemy appears to be determined to press us hard in our unorganized condition. But thank God we have been able to overcome them on every occasion as yet.[22]

On Tuesday, June 17, the army broke camp and headed eastward for the mountains. The ranks were silent as the long gray lines swung through Brown's Gap. Then the men heard the magic word that was their destination: Richmond! They were going to reinforce Robert E. Lee's army, besieged before the capital by General George B. McClellan's Army of the Potomac.

On the night after the march began, Lieutenant Colonel Raleigh Colston of the Second Virginia wrote his mother. "The soldier's life," he said, "is one of so much excitement and toil that he has no time to give way to unhappiness . . . But you must cheer up and not allow yourself to be so anxious about me. We are in fine health and spirits, and trust we shall get down in time to turn the tide of battle." [23]

---

21. Shields's losses were placed at 1,018 men. *Ibid.*, 712, 717, Pt. 3, p. 690.
22. Joseph Carpenter to his father, June 16, 1862, letter in possession of Joe Carpenter, Covington, Va.
23. Walker, *VMI Memorial*, 124–25.

CHAPTER X

SERVICE ON THE PENINSULA

Spirits in the Stonewall Brigade were high as the march to
Richmond began. Some of Jackson's army boarded trains
for the long trip, but the men of the brigade were ordered to walk
toward Gordonsville. Yet, boasted John Casler, "we could break
down any cavalry brigade on a long march," and the regiments
swaggered down the road to the east.[1] Even the men of the Rockbridge Artillery strapped knapsacks on their backs and followed the
infantrymen. They held up well, despite the fact that Dick Taylor's
men chided them with taunts of "There go Jackson's mules!"[2]

On a particularly sunny day, as the ranks were winding down
a dusty wagon trail, the men saw Jackson and his staff standing by

---

1. Casler, *Stonewall Brigade*, 116.
2. *Confederate Veteran*, XXXII (1924), 469.

the road. A loud cheer went up for Old Jack; then catcalls and hoots filled the air. On the other side of Jackson was Major Robert L. Dabney, his chief of staff and minister. The Reverend Mr. Dabney was attired in his usual Prince Albert coat and beaver hat, and sat holding a large umbrella as a shield from the glaring sun. The men whooped it up as they passed: "Come out from under that umbrella! Come out! I know you're under there; I see your feet a-shaking!" "Fraid you're gonna get your geegum spoiled?" "Fraid you'll get wet?" When Jackson angrily turned and rode off, the spectacle became even funnier. Dabney was not an expert horseman. In his frantic effort to catch up with the rest of the staff, his horse bolted through some bushes. The major lost his umbrella and most of his Prince Albert coat as he sought to stay in the saddle and to hold in place his beaver hat, which teetered dangerously to one side of his head.[3]

As the army moved into the Piedmont, the march became more strenuous. Recent rains had left the roads spongy with mud. Creeks were over their banks, necessitating time out to build temporary bridges. The whole march became a series of stops and starts. On June 25 the Confederates marched twenty-one miles, a good distance in view of the obstacles. But this was too slow for Jackson. He had ridden ahead for a conference with Lee two days earlier. The two officers had devised a large-scale plan to cave in the right flank of McClellan's army. Jackson's presence at Mechanicsville on the twenty-sixth was necessary for success. Yet the Valley men were behind schedule. Reports of Federal cavalry in the front caused additional concern, for if they discovered the Confederate army moving in from the Valley, the advantage of secrecy would be lost. The wagon trains lagging far to the rear only heightened Jackson's anxiety.

On the night of the twenty-fifth the brigade commanders reported to Jackson for instructions. Old Jack looked at Winder and said, "You must have your men cook their rations and be ready to move at dawn."

Winder answered quickly, "That is impossible, because of the position of my baggage-train."

---

3. Thomas C. Johnson, *Robert Lewis Dabney*, 270.

Jackson glared at him a moment, then replied curtly, "General Winder, it must be done." [4]

But it was not done. The troops did not finish eating their rations until almost eight o'clock. The day—Thursday, June 26—was intensely hot. Steam rose from the swampy flatlands through which the army moved, and heavy perspiration caused clothing to stick to damp skins. By 9 A.M. Jackson was fuming with impatience. He was already six hours late. The march slowed to a crawl; occasionally the army was halted to remove fallen trees that Federals had dragged into the road to delay an advance.

By 5 P.M. the army had reached a point just north of Mechanicsville. To the south the roar of musketry told of the terrific struggle going on as Powell and Harvey Hill tried to dislodge FitzJohn Porter's men from the hills overlooking Beaver Dam Creek. It "exceeded anything I ever heard during the War," William Poague wrote.[5] Too late to lend assistance, Jackson encamped his army at Hundley's Corner, four miles northeast of Mechanicsville. While he rode off to find Lee, men in the brigade fell out of ranks and sought relief from the heat. Some lounged beneath trees; others began gathering wood for cook fires. After meager rations and idle chatter the weary troops slumped on blankets and snatched some much-needed sleep.

The regiments were roused before dawn. Despite the early morning heat, the Valley men were in good spirits as they cooked bacon and bread. They were anxious to get on with the task for which they had been summoned. At 5 A.M. the Stonewall Brigade moved out with the rest of the army. Throughout the morning and early afternoon the troops marched up and down narrow country lanes, while constant firing to the south gave indication that the Federals were stubbornly contesting Lee's assault. Around 4:30 P.M. a courier rode up with orders from Ewell to hurry the brigade forward.

The Twenty-seventh Regiment, leading the column, wheeled southward across an open field, followed by the Second, Fourth, and Fifth Regiments, with the Thirty-third bringing up the rear.

---

4. Major Dabney, who recorded the scene, wrote that Jackson was "scarcely courteous" to the devoted Winder. Freeman, *Lee's Lieutenants*, I, 504.
5. Poague, *Gunner*, 28.

In columns of four the men double-quicked through woods and swamps toward the sound of battle. They soon came to an open field on the north side of Telegraph Road. Winder halted the regiments and closed them up tightly while he awaited further instructions. The loud roar of artillery and musketry told him that the battle was in or beyond the woods ahead; ignorance of the terrain, however, made him reluctant to advance.

Winder rode a short distance forward and soon encountered General A. P. Hill. Asking for orders, Winder was told by Powell Hill to remain in his present position until it could be ascertained where he was most needed. In a few minutes Hill called for two regiments to serve as artillery supports. Winder immediately dis- patched the Second and Fifth Regiments. The two Valley units, unfamiliar with the lay of land and further confused by the smoke and gunfire that blanketed a wide area, missed Powell Hill's posi- tion. They soon came up on James Longstreet's right flank, which virtually formed the extreme Confederate right wing of Lee's cres- cent front. Yet their presence had a tremendous psychological effect. As Longstreet's hard-pressed troops gazed with bloodshot eyes at the veterans expertly filing into position, they set up a shout that roared down the gray line: "Jackson's men! The Valley men are here!" [6]

Back on the road, the other three regiments of the Stonewall Brigade fidgeted. Although in battle position—the Thirty-third on the right, the Twenty-seventh manning the center, and Fourth anchoring the left—they were still a full half mile from the front. Thirty minutes passed; grumblings increased in volume. The Valley troops were not accustomed to stand by idly while a battle raged— especially one with the intensity of this struggle near Gaines' Mill.

Then came an urgent order to Winder from caustic Harvey Hill on the extreme Confederate left: bring up all men for a grand as- sault on the Federal right. The troops quickly discarded blankets and baggage and double-timed obliquely to the left and over swampy ground. Neff's Thirty-third Regiment, on the right, found it difficult to keep up with the brigade. The regiment had to bypass a Georgia unit standing in the woods; several companies then be-

6. Dabney, *Jackson*, 484.

came entangled in the swamp. As a result, the Thirty-third was the last regiment to enter into the action.[7]

By this time most of Winder's men had emerged into an open field, where they were soon joined by the Second and Fifth Regiments, returned to Winder by Powell Hill. Other units were helping Winder close the gap between the divisions of Powell and Harvey Hill. To the front (south) the Federal position was now visible. The Union commander, skillful and fearless FitzJohn Porter, had chosen an almost perfect position from which to hold off the combined armies of Lee and Jackson. The Federals were posted on a high bluff that dipped from twenty to forty feet down into a mushy bottom. On the opposite bank was swampy woodland so dense, wrote one of Jackson's men, "that a man ten yards in front could not be seen." Farther beyond the trees were broad, bare fields that clearly revealed to Porter any Confederate movement. From the hilltop Porter's massed batteries were hurtling shells into the cleared areas with such rapidity that a member of the Stonewall Brigade likened it to "the roar of falling water or rising and falling like the groaning of heavy machinery in motion in an old building." And he added, "It was the only field I had seen on which the smoke of battle rested, through which the setting sun shone red and dim." [8]

At a little past six o'clock Winder ordered his men forward. The Valley veterans signaled their entry into battle with a high-pitched yell. Their shout caused Jackson to jerk a half-sucked lemon from his mouth in startled fashion. An aide soon rode up to say the old brigade was moving into action. Pleased, Jackson replied, "We shall soon have good news from that charge. Yes, they are driving the enemy!" Then he raised his lemon aloft, as if it were a battle standard.[9]

The men charged across the field and plunged into the darkness of the pines. A portion of the brigade passed through the First Maryland, standing immobile in battle line. Lieutenant Howard

---

7. *Official Records*, XI, Pt. 2, p. 584.
8. Worsham, *One of Jackson's Foot Cavalry*, 99; Howard, *Recollections*, 140. Porter's batteries became so hot from rapid firing that many of the gunners could load the pieces only "by jamming the rammers against the trees." Jennings C. Wise, *The Long Army of Lee* (Lynchburg, Va., 1915), I, 212.
9. Douglas, *I Rode with Stonewall*, 104.

reined up his horse and shouted at the men, "Are you going to remain here like cowards while the Stonewall Brigade is charging past?" One soldier angrily leveled his musket at Winder's aide, but quickly lowered it and followed his comrades toward the Federal line.[10]

The cheering Confederates burst from the woods and started up the ridge. The ground trembled as Union artillery belched fire and iron into the ranks; Federal muskets rattled back and forth across the ridge. Men in the Stonewall Brigade began dropping and in a short while the whole hillside was covered with bodies. But the assault continued. The Second and Fifth Regiments, caught in the heat of battle, rushed forward with such determination that they got in front of the line, ran headlong into a concentrated volley, and were ripped to shreds. Colonel Jim Allen of the Second was killed while leading the assault.[11] His second-in-command, Raleigh Colston, had to retire with blood pouring from a leg wound. Major Frank B. Jones, next ranking officer in the regiment, sank to the ground after a shell shattered his leg.[12] The rest of the men held on desperately, firing from a prone position. Winder's main line soon swept past; the Second and Fifth rejoined it and the ridge was carried. It was 7 P.M. and almost dark.[13]

Because of the lateness of the hour and his ignorance of the terrain, Winder halted his brigade. Soon orders came from Harvey Hill to retire to a crest one hundred yards in the rear and bivouac.[14] In the darkness it was difficult to distinguish friend from foe. A

10. Howard, *Recollections*, 40. Cf. Goldsborough, *Maryland Line*, 89.

11. Allen, struck in the head, died instantly. He was buried in Richmond's Hollywood Cemetery on June 29, 1862. Richmond *Enquirer*, June 29, 1862.

12. Jones lay on the battlefield all night, attended by one lone soldier. On the following day he was borne to a hospital and the shattered limb was amputated. He died of complications on July 9. Walker, *VMI Memorial*, 308.

13. In his official report Will Baylor of the 5th Virginia wrote that, because of the darkness, he could barely see the men of the 2nd Regiment on his immediate left. "But I urged my men forward, being guided more by the cheering than by the sight of that regiment." *Official Records*, XI, Pt. 2, p. 580.

14. Winder wanted to continue the pursuit on into the night, General Harvey Hill wrote, but uncertainty over Federal strength and position caused him to refuse the request. Yet Hill went on to state that Winder was right, and that all of them had underestimated the routed condition of the Federal army. *Battles and Leaders*, II, 357.

group from the Thirty-third Regiment wandered off in quest of water, stumbled upon Federal pickets, and received a volley that killed one and wounded two. After the firing quieted down, several of the men crept out on the field and began a systematic robbing of the dead.[15] Others lay on their arms through the night, listening to the cries of the wounded. The casualties in the Valley regiments numbered 30 killed and 149 wounded.[16]

Soon after daylight on June 28 pickets of the Stonewall Brigade advanced through the woods and captured a large number of prisoners, including Brigadier General John F. Reynolds.[17] The brigade remained in this position throughout the hot day. Corpses lying on the battlefield became offensive to the living. Accordingly, the brigade spent the following day as a burial detail for both blue and gray; in the process, large quantities of arms were gathered up. At 2:30 A.M. on the thirtieth the brigade left camp, crossed the Chickahominy, and continued southward. Throughout the day heavy firing was audible in front. Yet in the middle of the afternoon the men halted at White Oak Swamp and, by Jackson's order, proceeded no farther. Jackson's reasons for remaining in the swamp while Longstreet and Powell Hill were fighting desperately at Frayser's Farm are unknown. That night Jackson overheard several of his staff discussing their inactivity and blurted out, "If General Lee had wanted me at Frayser's Farm, he would have sent for me!" [18]

Before sunrise the next morning the brigade moved out toward Malvern Hill. Winder ordered the batteries of Poague and Carpenter to proceed to the front, where action had already begun. The two captains soon unlimbered their guns in a wheat field behind a slight ridge. For six hours Confederate guns tried to dislodge the Federal batteries on Malvern Hill. Their efforts were futile. Indeed, Carpenter's battery barely escaped annihilation when Federal guns found the range and began what Carpenter termed "the most severe

15. Casler, *Stonewall Brigade*, 120–22.
16. *Battles and Leaders*, II, 316. Winder prematurely listed his losses at 15 killed and 64 wounded. *Official Records*, XI, Pt. 2, p. 573.
17. *Ibid.*, 578. After his exchange Reynolds returned to active service and was killed on the first day's fighting at Gettysburg.
18. Hunter McGuire to Jed Hotchkiss, June 15, 1896, Hotchkiss Papers.

fire I think I ever experienced." [19] Randolph Fairfax of the Rockbridge Artillery stated that "shot and shell seemed to pour over in one successive stream and burst into our midst." [20] Four hundred yards to the rear, one of the gunners was resting under an oak tree when a shell passed through the thirty-inch trunk and cut off his head.[21]

Throughout the day the Stonewall Brigade moved slowly toward Malvern Hill. It left the road at Willis Church and moved into the protection of a large clump of woods. Dense underbrush and foliage soon separated the Second and Fifth from the other three regiments. Before the units could reform, Winder ordered them forward to support Harvey Hill's assault on Malvern Hill.

After a brief and unsuccessful effort to get down a road filled with wagons, ambulances, and men hastening to the rear, the brigade abandoned the thoroughfare and double-timed across a field under a shower of Federal shells, then plunged into a dense pine grove and through swamps and briar bushes. It was now 7 P.M. and all was confusion in the Stonewall Brigade. The growing darkness, the rough terrain, the rapid move to get on the Federal right had scattered regiments over a large area. Yet Winder had no time to stop and reform his brigade. The assault must be made quickly if the ridge were to be carried that day.

Couriers rushed through swamps and woods trying to establish a battle line. Winder himself fell in with the Thirty-third and part of the Fourth Regiments. Night was descending fast and the men could barely see. Winder rode up and down a wooded bottom, trying to animate his men and organize a battle line. A few were too demoralized to know what was happening. Many in the rear were loading and firing, paying no attention to the direction in which their muskets were pointed. Winder rode angrily up to one man, grabbed him roughly by the shoulder, and shouted, "Scoundrel! You have shot one of your own friends! I saw you do it!" Moving forward a little farther, he found a group of his men behind a tree, standing in a file six men deep and swinging right or left whenever

19. *Official Records*, XI, Pt. 2, p. 574.   20. Slaughter, *Fairfax*, 35.
21. Edward A. Moore, *Cannoneer*, 89–90; Poague, *Gunner*, 29–30.

a shell exploded nearby. He ordered them forward in unpolite terms.[22]

To the right the Twenty-seventh and the remainder of the Fourth Regiments had staged a "hare-race" to get across an open field.[23] Colonel R. D. Gardner's horse was eviscerated by an exploding shell. The dead animal fell atop Gardner and pinned him to the ground until several of his men pulled him free. Farther across the field Colonel Andrew Grigsby was leading his Twenty-seventh forward in the darkness when a Minié ball struck him under the left arm and spun him around. The wound, more painful than serious, evoked a string of oaths from the commander.

To Winder's left, the Second and Fifth had taken cover in a ravine behind a fence. Colonel Will Baylor's Fifth was trapped in the gully and came under a severe fire that killed six and wounded thirty-two in his regiment. By now Federals were delivering what Winder termed "the most terrific fire I have ever seen." [24] The brigade consisted of pockets of men lying bewildered behind trees and fences. A few men fired aimlessly at the Federal position. At 10 P.M. Winder called off the attack, ordered the men back into the woods, and determined to resume the assault the following morning.

Because of the darkness, which hampered the aim on both sides, casualties in the brigade were few. Total losses were eighteen killed and ninety wounded. The Fourth, Fifth, and Thirty-third Regiments had borne the brunt of the Federal fire.[25]

Later that night Colonel Grigsby walked up to a group of soldiers sitting around a spring and asked them to pour some cool water on his wound. As they leaped forward to lend assistance, one private looked at the picturesque officer and inquired politely, "Colonel, does it hurt?"

"Yes, Damn it!" came the reply. "It was put there to hurt." [26]

Promptly at dawn on Wednesday, July 2, the Stonewall Brigade pushed up the ridge, only to find that the Yankees had retired

---

22. Howard, *Recollections*, 153–54.   23. *Official Records*, XI, Pt. 2, p. 578.
24. *Ibid.*, 571.
25. *Ibid.*, 576, 579, 582–83, 586. Losses in the batteries of Poague and Carpenter were four killed and fifteen wounded. *Ibid.*, 573–75.
26. Casler, *Stonewall Brigade*, 130.

during the night. In a drizzly rain the men moved with the rest of Jackson's division toward Harrison's Landing, McClellan's base of supplies on the James River. Early the following morning the Stonewall Brigade drove in the pickets and moved on the landing. Suddenly the Valley men came under a bombardment such as they had never experienced before. High-caliber deck guns on ships anchored in the river began blazing away at the infantrymen. Shells richocheted through the ranks, uprooted trees, and tore gaping holes in the ground.

Being the Confederate unit closest to the river, Jackson's foot cavalry received the most severe fire. Winder halted his regiments and sent word to Jackson that his men were very much afraid of the shells. Jackson sent the courier back with the curt reply: "Tell General Winder that I am as much afraid of the shells as his men, but to continue his advance." [27] Old Jack wanted to assault McClellan on the riverbank, yet his men were utterly fatigued. No officer could be found who exhibited any desire to do battle. Even Winder informed his superior that his men were not "boiling over" to make any attack. The order was soon given for the units to go into encampment.[28]

On July 4 a portion of the Thirty-third was on picket duty when the men spied a large field of blackberries. On learning that Federals were in the woods at the opposite end of the field, the Confederates proposed a truce. For the remainder of the day, Yankees and Rebels picked berries, swapped tobacco, coffee, newspapers, and war tales "as peaceably and kindly as if they had not been engaged for the last seven days in butchering one another." [29]

Elation filled the brigade camp on July 8. The men were ordered to pack up and start for Richmond. Only a few days before, the regimental doctors had agreed that the men were physically unable to endure much more activity. Yet, at the mention of Richmond, they forgot sore feet, loose bowels, and general fatigue. Gleefully

27. William C. Oates, *The War between the Union and the Confederacy* (New York, 1905), 122–23. Hereinafter cited as Oates, *Union and the Confederacy*.
28. George W. Booth, *Personal Reminiscences of a Maryland Soldier in the War between the States, 1861–1865* (Baltimore, 1898), 55.
29. Casler, *Stonewall Brigade*, 134.

they moved westward up the Peninsula and into camp on the Mechanicsville Turnpike. They were three miles from Richmond at Glenwood, the farm of Hugh A. White, whose nephew and namesake was an officer in the Fourth Regiment. William Poague wrote:

These were the halcyon days of Jackson's troops. Well earned rest, good rations, abundant supplies from their Valley homes, proximity to the capital with its varied attractions, the praises and admiration of its people for Stonewall and his followers all combined to make it most pleasantly remembered ever afterwards. [30]

30. Poague, Gunner, 32. See also Henderson, Stonewall Jackson, II, 76.

||||||||||||||||||||||||||||||||||||||||||||||||||||||||||||||||||||||||||||||||||||||||||||||||||||||||

CHAPTER XI

"INTO THE JAWS OF DEATH"

The rest ended on July 17, 1862. The men left Richmond and marched northward. They encamped at Hanover Junction for two days, then headed for Gordonsville through Louisa County and pitched their tents at what McHenry Howard called "the edge of the rich 'Green Spring' oasis." [1] Drill was held to a minimum. Major Frank Paxton, only three months away from command of the brigade, wrote of the welcome rest the men were enjoying: "Everything here seems so quiet . . . considering the severe hardships through which the men have passed since the war began, it is very much needed. Everything has a happy quiet appearance, such as I have not seen in the army since we were in camp this time last year after the battle of Manassas." [2]

1. Howard, *Recollections*, 161.
2. Paxton (ed.), *Memoir*, 59. Cf. William S. White, *Hugh White*, 110.

After a week's encampment the brigade doubled back through Gordonsville, marched three miles out the Madison Court House road, and went into camp on the farm of Oliver H. P. Terrell. By now most of the men knew that they had been sent to confront a new foe. Major General John Pope had come out of the West to lead "The Army of Virginia" southward toward Richmond.

This meant hard battle, Winder knew, and he was determined that his regiments should be prepared for it. As soon as the Stonewall Brigade had made camp north of Gordonsville, Winder issued orders that any man not present for the evening roll call would be "bucked" from sunrise to sunset the following day. That night thirty men were absent from the camp. Winder proved as good as his word. The following morning the thirty men were taken into the woods, their hands bound at the wrist, their arms slipped over their knees, and a stick run beneath the knees and above the arms. Until sundown the men remained in this cramped and humiliating condition. When released, half promptly deserted. Then, following a brief training march, several loafers who straggled badly were stripped to the waist and strung up by their thumbs. On learning of such disciplinary measures inflicted on his old brigade, Jackson angrily rode to Winder's tent and told the brigadier in no polite terms never again to impose such punishment.[3]

But the damage had been done. The men quickly forgot Winder's real character—his extraordinary traits of leadership, his valor, the warmth and courtesy that lay beneath the icy surface of harsh inflexibility. Not even his desire to have his brigade well disciplined for the action that lay ahead made any difference now to the men. In their eyes he had become a "tyrant," and mutterings ran through the camp that the next battle would be Winder's last—one way or the other.[4] Strange talk indeed from one of the most devoted of Confederate brigades!

The army was in motion before sunrise on August 7. Jackson's

---

3. Unidentified newspaper clipping, Hotchkiss Papers. An original member of the Stonewall Brigade wrote of Winder and Jackson: "At first their relations were not very cordial and each certainly underrated the other; in many things, they were too much alike to fit exactly." Douglas, *I Rode with Stonewall*, 125.

4. Casler, *Stonewall Brigade*, 141–43. Cf. Freeman, *Lee's Lieutenants*, II, 3–4.

objective was to strike his old Valley foe, General Nathaniel P. Banks, at Culpeper before General Pope could reinforce that part of his army. Unknown to Jackson, however, Pope had ordered Banks to the south of Culpeper. The Union army was moving into position at Slaughter Mountain, eight miles from town. On the eighth the Stonewall Brigade forded the Rapidan while Ewell's division, in the lead, drove back a cavalry picket with little difficulty. But the march was woefully slow, Jackson's prodding notwithstanding. The sun beat down with such intense fury that several men dropped dead in the road from sunstroke.[5]

Colonel Charles Ronald of the Fourth Regiment was temporarily commanding the brigade. Winder was so ill with fever that he had remained behind—but only after Jackson's unusual assurance that no battle was anticipated within the next twenty-four hours.[6] Late in the afternoon of August 8 the brigade went into bivouac a mile north of the Rapidan. A few hours later Winder was borne into camp unannounced and taken straight to his tent. Although some of the men in the ranks may not have been glad to see him, the regimental officers were intensely relieved at his presence. When McHenry Howard informed one of the colonels that Winder had rejoined the brigade, the man replied, "Thank God for that!" [7]

At 4 A.M. on a Saturday that proved to be blistering, Winder was placed in command of Jackson's division.[8] The gallant officer's health was little improved; he was pale and obviously weak. But he promptly left his bed and rode to the head of his column, ignoring the pleas of the brigade medical director. The army moved out at 7 A.M. The Stonewall Brigade, in columns of four, was third in the line of march. Slowly the Valley men trudged through the dust kicked up by those ahead.

By noon the men had covered seven miles, but they were weary

5. Casler, *Stonewall Brigade*, 146; Henderson, *Stonewall Jackson*, II, 88.
6. Howard, *Recollections*, 162–63.
7. *Ibid.*, 164. Commanding the regiments at this time were: 2nd—Lieutenant Colonel Lawson A. Botts; 4th—Lieutenant Colonel R. D. Gardner; 5th—Major H. J. Williams; 27th—Captain Charles L. Haynes; 33rd—Lieutenant Colonel Edwin G. Lee.
8. *Official Records*, XII, Pt. 2, 183.

and badly scattered. The heat was unbearable and the dust seemed to be growing thicker. At least 10 of the 160 men in the Thirty-third Regiment collapsed from heat exhaustion before Slaughter Mountain became visible on the right.[9] Word passed down the ranks that Federals were in battle position a short distance ahead.

Ewell's division in front filed off the road and went into battle position at the base of the mountain. The Stonewall Brigade and the rest of Jackson's division continued down the road for a few hundred yards and then halted. Officers rode forward to survey the terrain preparatory to making troop dispositions.

The country between the road and Slaughter Mountain was open. Thick woods ran southward from the hill. To the left of the pike were dense pine woods, broken only by a cornfield near the Madison Court House road junction and a harvested wheat field a few hundred yards farther to the east. A line of Federal cavalry was visible in the wheat field and the rolling land across the road. The Union army, the men thought, was undoubtedly masked in the woods behind the cavalry picket.

Jackson's plan was a double flank attack. Ewell would move around the face (east) of the mountain and turn the Federal left. Jubal Early's brigade would move straight down the road, while Winder's division, constituting Early's left, would sweep through the woods and assail the Union right. The Stonewall Brigade was to take a position on Winder's right and Early's left, in order to lend assistance to either commander. Accordingly, it filed off the road to the left and formed a battle line in the cornfield.[10] While Early rode forward to reconnoiter, Winder began bringing up his artillery to support the center.

It was near four o'clock. With his division now moving to the left, Winder rode forward to place his guns. Ewell's artillery was already booming on the right. To assist in softening up the Federal

9. *Ibid.*, 199.
10. *Ibid.*, 229. Although the Stonewall Brigade and its sister units did not know it, Jackson erred twice in opening the battle. He assumed first that the Federal strength was concentrated in the open and broken ground to the right, when the exact opposite was true. Secondly, he began the battle while a majority of his 20,000 men were still strung out as far as seven miles down the road. See Vandiver, *Mighty Stonewall*, 339–40.

position, Winder ordered up Poague's two Parrotts, Carpenter's Parrott, and the long-range guns of Captain William Caskie. Poague fired one shot to test the range. Federal batteries concealed in the woods on the left-center answered with a deafening roar. Intense artillery fire commenced on both sides.

Winder, his coat off and his sleeves rolled up, appeared oblivious to the shells exploding around the guns. He gazed intently through his binoculars and calmly called out range adjustments to the gunners. The artillerymen were struggling to maintain a steady fire, for Union batteries had pinpointed their position and were pounding them with shells. Suddenly Captain Carpenter slumped beside his Parrott, mortally wounded by a shell fragment in the head. His brother John jumped forward to take command of the gun. Other gunners were dropping into the dust. But the Confederate fire was beginning to have a telling effect. Federal batteries in the distance began backing off to new positions.

Winder was elated. This was the fighting he most enjoyed: artillery driving the opposition to cover. He turned quickly and shouted an order to Poague's Parrott on his immediate right. In the roar of the cannon the men could not hear him. Ned Moore of the Rockbridge Artillery started over to Winder to ask him what he had said. Winder cupped his hand to his mouth to repeat the order. He shouted one or two words; at that instant, a Federal shell struck him, knocking his binoculars into the air and tearing his left arm and side to shreds. Quivering frightfully, Winder wavered for a moment, then slumped to the ground.[11]

A surgeon rushed up, examined wounds that extended all the way back to the spine, and pronounced them fatal. Winder had just been placed on a stretcher when his aide, McHenry Howard, rode up. "General, do you know me?" Howard asked in a voice shaking with emotion.

"Oh yes," Winder replied, then painfully mumbled a few words

---

11. Lexington *Gazette*, August 28, 1862; Poague, *Gunner*, 33. Winder was struck by one of the first shots fired by the 2nd Maine Battery, Captain James A. Hall, commanding. Hall had just arrived on the field in the woods to the north side of the road; his was one of four batteries rushed up to answer Winder's telling fire. *Official Records*, XII, Pt. 2, pp. 171–72.

concerning his wife and children. The battle was still raging around him, but his mind had returned to the peaceful countryside of his native Maryland.

A chaplain bent over him and said, "General, lift up your heart to God."

"I do," said Winder feebly, "I do lift it up to Him."

As the stretcher-bearers carried the dying officer to the rear, they passed the Stonewall Brigade moving forward to attack. Officers crowded around the stretcher with sorrow in their eyes. The ranks filed by silently, men gazing sympathetically at the man a few of them had sworn to kill in this battle. Winder saw their compassionate stares and inquired how the battle was progressing. After Lieutenant Howard reassured him that all was well, the stretcher was carried to the rear. Two hours later Charles Winder was dead.[12]

The forward move of the Stonewall Brigade came from Early's urgent plea. Banks's whole army of 9,000 appeared to be pouring in on the Confederate center and left. Early sent word of the move to Jackson, who now realized that the Yankees wanted to take advantage of the dense woods on the left of the road. Old Jack hastened to move up the reserves. He rode into the cornfield where the brigade was waiting, ordered the Valley units forward at double-quick, and shouted after them, "Remember that you are the Stonewall Brigade!"[13] The men leaped through the woods and down the road, many of them setting up a chant of "Stonewall Jackson! Stonewall Jackson!"[14] After passing the dying Winder, however, the ranks grew quiet and grimly resolute.

At 5:45 P.M. the woods seemed to explode with the crash of cannon and the staccato of musketry. Shells began falling into the area through which the brigade was passing. Will Baylor was assisting the Rockbridge Artillery when a shell exploded in the ranks of his Fifth Regiment, killing or wounding six men. Baylor rushed over to his disorganized troops and in a calm but firm voice said, "Steady, men, steady! Close up!" In like manner, the other regi-

---

12. Howard, *Recollections*, 170–71.
13. Jed Hotchkiss to his brother, August 14, 1862, Hotchkiss Papers.
14. James D. McCabe, Jr., *Life and Campaigns of General Robert E. Lee* (New York, 1866), 197.

mental colonels sought to preserve tight ranks.[15] Soon the Valley troops encountered demoralized units, many men without arms and shouting warnings of impending disaster. In columns of regiments the Stonewall Brigade quickened its steps. Near the end of the woods Colonel Ronald, temporarily in command, ordered the men into brigade battle line. The Twenty-seventh Virginia, in the lead, swerved to the right, its right flank one hundred yards from the road. The Thirty-third Regiment moved to the left, while the Fifth continued straight ahead as the center unit. The Second Virginia moved thirty degrees to the left, and the Fourth Regiment veered sharply to form the extreme left of the line. Shrapnel was spraying the woods, and canister rattled ominously against trees and rocks.

Ronald halted the brigade at the fence enclosing the field. He asked Jackson for instructions, and was ordered to continue the advance.[16] The Valley regiments tore down the fence and moved out into the clearing, men glancing left and right in search of Federals. Soon they found them: massed ranks standing defiantly four hundred yards in their front.

The Stonewall Brigade halted. Silently, methodically, the men bit open the paper cartridges, poured powder into their muskets, rammed home the lead balls, and placed the metal caps into position. While the Southerners gazed intently at the Federal ranks now advancing, hammers clicked up and down the ranks. Officers cautioned the men not to fire until the Yankees were within easy range. Suddenly the first line of bluecoats broke into a run; when they did, the Valley regiments loosed a sheet of flame and lead that tore the Federal wave into segments.

Loading and firing as they went, the Confederates then moved across the field. The second blue line was caught in the rout of the first, and both fell back on the third. In the ensuing confusion the Stonewall Brigade delivered volley after volley into the woods where Yankees were crouching. Disregarding their dead and dying, the Federals moved backward. Colonel Ronald, new in the role of a brigade commander, momentarily forgot the units sup-

15. Susan L. Blackford (ed.), *Letters from Lee's Army* (New York, 1947), 104.
16. *Official Records*, XII, Pt. 2, p. 192.

porting his flanks. Here was victory to be had; pressing forward at moments like this had won the Stonewall Brigade its reputation. "Forward!" Ronald shouted again, and the men continued their pursuit across the field.[17]

Severe and sudden fire on his right made Ronald rein his horse abruptly. For the first time he realized that the right of the Stonewall Brigade was not resting on the left of the Second Brigade. A gap existed between the two units—a gap the Federals had also seen and were now moving forward to penetrate! [18]

Ronald moved desperately to meet the new threat. At his command his men scampered back across the field and plunged into the woods. Cheering Yankees continued to race toward the gap on Ronald's right. To meet them, the Stonewall Brigade veered into a north-south position that ran obliquely to the general northeast-southwest battle line. Its position ran from the southern edge of the woods to the northern end of the wheat field. The Twenty-seventh Virginia on the right was posted in the woods, with its flank still open. Next to it, the Thirty-third covered an area from the woods to the edge of the field. The Fifth and Second Regiments, in the open, piled the fence boards into a crude but effective parapet. Far to the left and facing the field was the Fourth Virginia, its left flank bent and resting on the edge of a clearing covered with undergrowth.

The Confederates had scarcely taken their new positions when the Federals slammed into the front and flank of the Twenty-seventh Virginia. Hand-to-hand fighting with bayonets and clubbed muskets broke out in the woods. Shouts of combatants and screams from the wounded rent the air as men on both sides were captured and recaptured. Grigsby's Twenty-seventh Regiment bent back before the Federal onslaught; some of the men broke and bounded to the rear while others fell back in disorder on the right of the Thirty-third Virginia.

When Colonel Edwin G. Lee, commanding the Thirty-third,

---

17. *Ibid.*, 194–95.
18. Sandie Pendleton of Jackson's staff was of the opinion that "owing to bad management of some of the officers, incident upon the loss of Winder, some confusion resulted" in the assault. He obviously was referring to Ronald and William B. Taliaferro, who had assumed command of Jackson's division. Lee (ed.), *Pendleton*, 203.

saw the Twenty-seventh Regiment giving way, the dapper Virginia aristocrat quickly ordered Companies A, D, and F of his own regiment to form a line perpendicular to the rest of the regiment so as to cover the right flank. The move was executed hastily but expertly, the men of the Thirty-third parting to allow the disorganized elements of the Twenty-seventh to pass through to the rear. As the Federals moved northward toward the Thirty-third, the three companies, formed in two ranks, poured a withering fire into them and abruptly checked their advance. This brief respite gave the Twenty-seventh Virginia the opportunity to reform hurriedly and take position behind the right companies.

Just as the Federals regrouped and started forward again, a cheer rose from the woods to the left. Moving up at double time and plainly discernible were the lead columns of Powell Hill's crack light division. The approach of fresh reinforcements gave the Stonewall Brigade renewed confidence, even in the face of overwhelming odds. In columns of regiments the men leaped up from their firing positions and charged the Federals, who recoiled from this new thrust and raced back across the trampled field where scant hours before buds of wheat had strained toward the sun. The Stonewall Brigade was now after victory and would not be halted. The men swerved to the left in pursuit of the Federals. Staccato bursts of gunfire and the shouts of determined troops filled the air as the five regimental colonels, all on foot, led their men toward the distant woods.[19]

The Twenty-seventh Virginia was so anxious to redeem itself that it pushed too far to the front, causing the line to shift from an easterly to a northeasterly direction. The brigade reached the far edge of the clearing, started into the woods—and ran headlong into a point-blank, concentrated fire. The Twenty-seventh Regiment, as well as the Fourth on the other flank, veered to bring the line into correct position as the center regiments took cover behind the fence enclosing the field.

In trying to pivot, however, the Twenty-seventh caught a close

---

19. *Official Records,* XII, Pt. 2, p. 198. Jackson had rushed Hill's Virginians from their position far down the road into the action on the left. Because of the long jaunt, many of the men were near exhaustion when they entered the fray.

volley on both front and flank. The regiment wavered for a moment, then fell apart a second time. Some of the men made for the fence; others turned and ran back toward their own woods across the field. General Lawrence Branch was rushing forward with the lead brigade of the light division when he saw some of the Valley men scurrying to the rear. Branch's ranks parted, permitting the fragments of the Twenty-seventh to pass through. The fresh troops of Hill then moved quickly to the assistance of the main body of the Stonewall Brigade.[20]

The routed elements of the Twenty-seventh Virginia continued their panicky flight until they saw Jackson riding toward them rapidly. Old Jack, blue eyes blazing in the afternoon sun, snatched a battle standard from a surprised color-bearer. Waving it high over his head, the General shouted, "Rally, men! Remember Winder! Where's my Stonewall Brigade? Forward, men, forward!" The rout instantly ceased, and men half-embarassed and half-rejuvenated turned back and fell in with Powell Hill's division, which was now moving across the wheat field. The Valley men would have followed Jackson, wrote one Confederate, "into the jaws of death itself; nothing could have stopped them and nothing did." [21]

On the opposite side of the clearing, the bulk of the Stonewall Brigade held on doggedly. To the right could be heard the roar of Jubal Early's counterattack in the center of the line. The Federal fire was still severe on the left, but regimental commanders realized that this was the time to grasp victory. Ronald ordered his men over the fence and into the Federal-held woods. Colonel Raleigh Colston jumped in front of the Second Virginia, grabbed its flag, and told the troops to follow him. The whole brigade, with the exception of a few individuals in the Thirty-third Regiment,

20. In his private journal Branch erroneously stated that his men had advanced only one hundred yards "before we met the celebrated Stonewall Brigade utterly routed and fleeing as fast as they could run." *Confederate Veteran*, XXV (1917), 415. Powell Hill's report, in *Official Records*, XII, Pt. 2, pp. 214–16, contained a similar criticism. Yet William T. Poague, in *Gunner*, 34, stated that Hill's censure may have been a product of his jealousy of Jackson and the Stonewall Brigade.
21. Susan L. Blackford (ed.), *Letters*, 105. A more dramatic account is in Alexander Hunter, *Johnny Reb and Billy Yank* (New York, 1905), 371.

clambered over the fence. Seeing the shirkers, Major Frederick Holliday rode up to the color-bearer of the Thirty-third and said confidently, "Get over the fence with the colors and I know the men will follow!" The sight of the flag moving off into the woods rallied even the most demoralized, and the whole regiment charged *en masse* with the brigade.[22]

The Fourth, Second, and Fifth Regiments wheeled to the right behind the Thirty-third and Twenty-seventh. Now the solid gray ranks moved through the thick timber, shooting, clubbing, and capturing Federals in the reddish glow of sunset. In quick order the Valley men routed the Fifth Connecticut, Twenty-eighth New York, and Forty-sixth Pennsylvania, captured three battle flags, and killed or disabled every field officer and adjutant in the three regiments.[23]

By sundown Banks's army again was in retreat. With other Confederate units the brigade continued the chase until darkness rendered further pursuit impossible. The men then walked slowly back to the battlefield, where stripped trees, ruined crops, and wounded men lying everywhere showed the intensity of the ninety-minute struggle. The Valley men, soon joined by the Rockbridge Artillery, bivouacked in the wheat field over which they had fought. Few of the men bothered to eat; most of them fell out of ranks and dropped off instantly into a sleep of fatigue and nervous exhaustion. And, wrote Launcelot Blackford of the Rockbridge Artillery, "I do not believe anything short of the enemy could have revived them to action." [24]

In his official report Colonel Ronald stated: "I attribute so few casualties to the fact that the brigade charged at the proper time." [25] What Ronald meant is not certain, but the brigade's losses, considering the severity of the action, were amazingly small: 10 killed, 52 wounded, and 1 missing. That the Twenty-seventh Regiment

22. Casler, *Stonewall Brigade*, 146–47. See also Walker, *VMI Memorial*, 125.
23. Caught in the wake of the brigade's assault, the three units suffered a combined loss of 687 out of 1,244 men engaged. *Official Records*, XII, Pt. 2, pp. 147, 152–53.
24. Susan L. Blackford (ed.), *Letters*, 106.
25. *Official Records*, XII, Pt. 2, p. 193.

suffered the least number of losses (3 killed, 1 wounded) of the units in the brigade caused some to wonder why it had become so easily disorganized.[26]

Praise of the brigade's over-all conduct poured from superior officers. General Taliaferro wrote: "The First Brigade sustained its ancient reputation. It captured a number of prisoners and four stands of colors." [27] Jackson stated that although the brigade always fought well, on that day it fought gloriously.[28] But the men were too weary to bask in such praise or to celebrate their hard-earned victory. More than that, the fight at Slaughter Mountain had cost them Charles Winder. True, some of the troops had rebelled at his disciplinary measures; yet no one could deny his capacities of leadership and courage.

Sympathy at his death was widespread—and genuine. One company commander in the Stonewall Brigade wrote that he was "a most gallant soldier, and by his admirable discipline, was not only keeping the brigade efficient, but was making it better, I think, than it ever was before." [29] Kyd Douglas classed him as "the most brilliant of the many officers Maryland gave to the Confederacy." Douglas was certain that "had he lived he would have been the commander of a corps before the war ended." [30] Of the many tributes to Winder, however, one of the greatest came from the man least prone to bestow praise. "I can hardly think of the fall of Brigadier General C. S. Winder without tearful eyes," Jackson wrote. And in his report of the battle he added: "It is difficult within the proper reserve of an official report to do justice to the merits of this accomplished officer . . . Richly endowed with those qualities of mind and person which fit an officer for command and which attract the admiration and excite the enthusiasm of troops,

26. *Ibid.*, 177–99.
27. *Ibid.*, 190. Brigadier General Alpheus S. Williams wrote in his official report of the battle that three of his Federal regiments were able to escape with their colors. *Ibid.*, 147.
28. Lexington *Gazette*, August 28, 1862. Jackson's remarks were contained in an account of the battle submitted to the paper by an unnamed member of the Rockbridge Artillery. As the same wording is given in Slaughter, *Fairfax*, 36, the newspaper writer was probably youthful Randolph Fairfax.
29. William S. White, *Hugh White*, 113.
30. Douglas, *I Rode with Stonewall*, 126.

he was rapidly rising to the front rank of his profession. His loss has been severely felt." [31]

31. *Official Records*, XII, Pt. 2, p. 183. Colonel Charles Ronald of the 4th Virginia wrote that in Winder's death "the brigade was deprived of his great services, the army of an able and accomplished soldier, the country of a good citizen, and society of an ornament." *Ibid.*, 193. For other praise of Winder, see Howard, *Recollections*, 134, 174; Taylor, *Destruction and Reconstruction*, 68; Dabney, *Jackson*, 498–99.

CHAPTER XII

GROVETON AND ANOTHER MANASSAS

Masking his movements with burning campfires, Jackson retired from Slaughter Mountain early on the morning of August 10 and moved to the vicinity of Gordonsville, where the army rested for five days. During this period Winder's successor was named. On August 15 the officers of the Stonewall Brigade sent a petition to Adjutant General Samuel Cooper in which they asked that Colonel Will Baylor of the Fifth Regiment be named their new commander. The petitioners, after calling attention to Baylor's consistent gallantry and devotion to duty, went on to state: "The Brigade has never asked anything, but we think that it has done enough to entitle it to this consideration." [1] Officers not even connected with the brigade wrote letters to Richmond, reinforcing the

---

1. The petition is in Baylor's personal file, War Records Group, National Archives.

plea that Baylor be appointed.[2] Jackson concurred with the request, and the appointment was made.

William Smith Hanger Baylor was born in Augusta County, deep in the Valley of Virginia, on April 7, 1831. His father was an ex-judge who owned a prospering farm near Staunton. Even in his early youth Baylor displayed an unusually pleasing personality. He entered Washington College at the age of sixteen and was graduated with honors in 1850. He showed outstanding skill in debate. Three additional years of study at the University of Virginia brought a law degree. Baylor then returned to Staunton and became a practicing attorney. In 1857 he was elected commonwealth attorney for the city and held the post until his death.

When a local militia company was organized in the late 1850's, Baylor's personality compensated for his lack of formal military training, and he was elected captain of the West Augusta Guards. This unit was one of the first called out to repel John Brown's raid in October, 1859. But Baylor was not there to lead it. He had gone to New York on his honeymoon, where he was stricken with typhoid fever. When told that his unit had been ordered to Harpers Ferry, in his delirium he imagined himself there and had to be restrained by his doctor and wife from leaving immediately for Virginia.[3]

When several volunteer companies from Augusta County were organized in the spring of 1861, Baylor was chosen their colonel. In April the units were ordered to Harpers Ferry and mustered into Confederate service. In the reorganization Baylor was appointed major. Command of the companies—now officially the Fifth Infantry Regiment, Virginia Volunteers—went to Kenton Harper, a native Pennsylvanian who had fought in the Virginia Regiment in the Mexican War and was then promoted to major general of militia. Baylor took the demotion in stride, feeling that it would only be a short time before he was restored to a colonelcy. After First Manassas, however, there was no indication that he was to

2. See Lieutenant Colonel U. H. Skinner, 52nd Virginia, to General Samuel Cooper, August 19, 1862, *ibid*.
3. Undated biographical sketch from Lottie Baylor Landrum to Jed Hotchkiss, Hotchkiss Papers.

receive promotion. Jackson wrote at least one letter to Richmond in which he upheld Baylor as his most dependable and deserving subordinate during the critical weeks of organization at Harpers Ferry.[4]

When Colonel Harper resigned, all the officers of the Fifth Regiment signed a petition asking that Baylor be appointed to succeed him.[5] But the colonelcy was given to another and Baylor made up his mind to resign. "You may say to the President," he wrote a Richmond official, "that whilst I would rather remain in Virginia, I am so anxious to serve my country in an honorable position, that I will cheerfully go any where the good of the service demands." [6] Someone, possibly Jackson, persuaded him to remain with the brigade. This he did, the more gladly when Jackson appointed him to his staff as inspector general. With the reorganization of the Stonewall Brigade in mid-April, 1862, Baylor was named to the command of his old Fifth Regiment.

From that moment on, in a unit distinguished for its valor, he set an example. In every fight his heavy-set figure was to be found where the battle raged most perilously, his blue eyes flashing fire, his long hair disheveled, his face flushed with excitement. At Winchester, when a horse dropped dead from under him, he led the final assault on foot. During the Seven Days he was cited several times for conspicuous bravery. If valor had been the sole criterion for brigade command, Baylor's appointment would never have been in doubt.

But because his undaunted courage and complete disregard of personal safety made him an easy target in battle, Baylor's first campaign at the head of the Stonewall Brigade was his last. Barely ten days after assuming command—even before his promotion to brigadier could be confirmed—he was killed.

Late on the afternoon of August 15 Jackson's army broke camp at Gordonsville, passed through Orange Court House, and spent the night near Pisgah Church. Here the men gained an additional five

---

4. T. J. Jackson to unidentified addressee, August 5, 1861, Confederate Accessions 21500, Virginia Archives.
5. The petition, dated September 6, 1861, and signed by twenty-seven officers, is in Baylor's file, National Archives.
6. W. S. H. Baylor to A. T. Bledsoe, October 15, 1861, *ibid.*

days of rest while Baylor tried to acclimate himself to the new responsibilities of brigade command. Jackson, as usual, said nothing of his intentions, leaving the troops to speculate on their next movement. Although some of the foot cavalry expected a pursuit of Pope's army, a few had hopes of returning again to the Valley. They did not know that after Slaughter Mountain their Army of the Valley had ceased to exist. The Valley regiments were now an official part of the Army of Northern Virginia.[7]

Yet something was in the wind; of that the men were positive. Jackson became very strict about organization and straggling. And on August 18 the men witnessed an illustration of Old Jack's feelings about desertion. Prior to leaving Gordonsville, four deserters from Jackson's division had been brought into camp from the Valley. Three were from the Tenth Virginia; the other was a member of the Fifth. Early in the afternoon of the eighteenth the division was assembled in a three-sided formation, the Stonewall Brigade facing the open end. Into the center of the hollow square came the condemned men under heavy guard. Each man was blindfolded and then placed in a kneeling position beside an open grave. Twenty paces away twelve riflemen stood at attention, half the rifles loaded with balls, the other half with blanks. After the death sentences were read to the condemned, a lieutenant barked out commands, the crack of musketry split the still air, and the deserters toppled backward into the pits. Officers then marched their regiments past the graves, to impress indelibly upon them the awful consequences of desertion.[8]

The army broke camp on the nineteenth, waded across the thigh-deep Rapidan, and continued in a northeasterly direction. After two days of marching in the rain, the brigade encamped at Jeffersonton, where it remained for two more days, with no shelter and little food. What few wagons Jackson had permitted to accompany the army were mired miles to the rear. On the night of August 24

7. Freeman, *Lee's Lieutenants*, II, 63.
8. Casler, *Stonewall Brigade*, 164. A discrepancy exists as to the actual number executed. Edward A. Moore, in *Cannoneer*, 99–100, stated that only three were shot. Mercer Otey, like Moore a member of the Rockbridge Artillery, put the number at five. *Confederate Veteran*, VII (1899), 262–63.

the men were told to prepare three days' rations. They cooked their bacon—then promptly ate it. A long march lay ahead, most of them thought, and the less to carry, the better. Before dawn they received sixty rounds of ammunition.

When the troops received orders to leave all knapsacks in a vacant building nearby, "we then knew what was up the same as if 'Stonewall' had told us," John Casler wrote. "It simply meant a 'forced march and a flank movement.' " [9]

Casler's guess was correct. What the men in the ranks did not know was that they were embarking on one of the most famous flanking movements of the war. After slipping behind the cover of the Bull Run Mountains, the brigade and its sister units were supposed to file through Thoroughfare Gap, dash behind the right flank of Pope's army, and slash his communications with Washington. If the plan worked, the Federal army would be caught between the two wings of Lee's army. Secrecy and speed were essential and, on the basis of their past achievements, the Valley men had been chosen for the difficult flank movement.

On August 25 the army left Jeffersonton in high spirits, laughing and joking over the prospects of meeting Yankees. According to James Hendricks of the Second Regiment, "Each felt that something extraordinary was contemplated." [10]

Ewell's division took the lead; behind it came Jackson's division, with the Stonewall Brigade in the van. The march proceeded pleasantly; occasionally, to shorten the distance, the army veered from the dusty roads and cut across fields and streams, sometimes passing through farmyards before the wondering gaze of residents. No halts were permitted except the customary ten minutes' rest per hour.

Late in the afternoon of August 26, as the tired men of the Stonewall Brigade came around a curve in the road, they saw Old Jack standing on a large boulder. He was gazing westward at the sinking sun. The troops forgot their weariness and broke out in loud cheering. Over and over they hurrahed their old commander. Jackson finally sent an officer to stop the shouting, lest the sounds reveal their position to Federal scouts.

---

9. Casler, *Stonewall Brigade,* 150.
10. *Confederate Veteran,* XVII (1909), 549.

"No cheering, boys," the officer said, riding up and down the lines. "The General requests it."

Some of the men quieted down; but others behind them continued their loud yelling, and again the cheers rolled up and down the line.

Jackson, obviously pleased, turned to a member of his staff and said, "Who could not conquer with such troops as these?" [11]

The brigade and the army bivouacked at Salem after a march of twenty-five miles. Men stacked their muskets and dropped to the ground too tired even to unroll their blankets. All too soon the company commanders were rousing them for the next day's march. The soldiers went without breakfast, for all rations had been consumed the preceding day.

Throughout August 27 the men moved slowly through heat and dust. Sometimes a man would break from the columns, scamper into a nearby cornfield to gather an armful of green ears, and quickly return to his place in the ranks. Officers rode up and down the long columns, repeatedly urging, "Close up, men, close up; push on, push on." By mid-afternoon the men were too fatigued to talk, but their spirits soon rose when the army filed through Thoroughfare Gap. Below them, green in the summer sun, lay the broken and rolling country around Manassas.

Marching eastward the long gray lines passed through Hay Market and Gainesville. At sunset the brigade was near Bristoe on the Orange & Alexandria Railroad. Firing broke out in front. The men knew instantly that elements of Dick Ewell's division had encountered something hostile. When they entered Bristoe, they learned that a Federal train had just passed through town, headed for Washington, and that although two other trains had been captured, a fourth had stopped short of the village and then headed back in reverse toward Pope's army with the news of the Confederate advance.

The men had marched more than fifty miles in the past forty-eight hours.[12] Most of them wanted desperately to bivouac at

11. Dabney, *Jackson*, 516–17. Because Dabney witnessed the scene, his version is accepted over John Esten Cooke's more dramatic account in *The Life of Stonewall Jackson* (New York, 1866), 275.
12. *Official Records*, XII, Pt. 2, p. 670.

Bristoe, but Jackson wished to push on to Manassas Junction, Pope's supply depot. General Isaac Trimble's brigade left at midnight; three hours later the Stonewall Brigade followed it. Near dawn of August 27 Baylor's skirmishers shoved aside a cavalry picket and entered town. The lead columns of the brigade filed through the railroad yards just as the sun arose. The Valley veterans, their stomachs empty, their clothes tattered, and their feet half-shod, could not believe their eyes. All around them were warehouses, sheds, railroad cars, and literally piles of every conceivable item an army could use. It was like a dream come true: 50,000 pounds of bacon, 1,000 barrels of corned beef, 2,000 barrels of salt pork, and 2,000 barrels of flour—and this was just the beginning.[13]

But the men were forbidden to touch it. They had been ordered to proceed north of the junction and take up a defensive post to guard against a surprise attack. Standing vigil while the rest of the army plundered was the price of being the trusted Stonewall Brigade. The men grudgingly fell into a loose battle line as instructed. But temptation got the best of many of them, and they soon joined other Rebels in a wild looting of the storehouses.[14]

The major part of Jackson's army arrived in mid-morning. At 11 A.M. word came back from the Stonewall Brigade that a Federal column was approaching town from the northwest. Jackson hastened to the area with the light division and the batteries of Poague and Carpenter. When a New Jersey brigade under General George W. Taylor advanced across an opening, it was raked up and down by the Confederate batteries until it broke in confusion and retired hastily from the field. Yet it was plain that Pope was on his way to Manassas.[15]

When Ewell's division arrived from Bristoe, Jackson ordered the abandonment of Manassas Junction. The men in the Stonewall Brigade stuffed pockets, belts, and shirts with all they could carry. Canteens were filled with brandy, molasses, and sugar. The Rockbridge Artillery did not return from chasing Taylor's men until the choicest items had been taken. "What we got," Ned Moore wrote

---

13. *Ibid.*, 644.   14. Casler, *Stonewall Brigade*, 151–54.
15. See *Official Records*, XII, Pt. 2, pp. 260, 543; Edward A. Moore, *Cannoneer*, 104–105.

disgustedly, was "disappointing, and not of a kind to invigorate, consisting, as it did, of hard-tack, pickled oysters, and canned stuff generally." [16]

In mid-afternoon the columns moved off toward the northwest with two sutlers' trains filled to overflowing. Behind them large flames licked skyward from the depot. Soon the ammunition dumps caught fire. Spasmodic explosions shook the ground and filled the air with a roar that sounded as if a terrible battle were in progress.[17] Darkness came but the men continued on by the light of the burning depot. The Stonewall Brigade had been marching for three days and three nights, with a total of four hours' sleep. "Nothing but exhiliration at our unwonted success kept us up," one member wrote.[18]

At midnight the brigade reached its destination, a high ridge near Groveton. A mile to the east across broken country loomed Henry House Hill. Baylor's brigade was posted on the far right of the ridge, facing southward. A thick clump of pine and oak ran halfway down the ridge and then gave way to open country through which, running right to left, was the Warrenton–Washington road.[19]

The Valley regiments spent most of Thursday, August 28, trying to escape from the heat. A majority of the men sprawled out under the trees to rest or sleep. Occasionally a group moved leisurely off to nearby springs to fill canteens with water. By 5 P.M. empty stomachs began to growl.

Suddenly the word came to prepare for battle. The men jumped up in surprise and moved stealthily to the edge of the woods. Brigade pickets, lying on the ground, intently watched a long blue column moving down the road from the west. The size of the force stamped it as a division. That the Federals were unaware of the Rebels was obvious from the casual manner of their march. The

16. *Ibid.*, 107.
17. Casler, *Stonewall Brigade*, 154. A member of the Rockbridge Artillery reported exuberantly to his hometown newspaper: "We destroyed millions of property at Manassas. I counted 45 cars in one train crammed with every imaginable article of use or luxury . . . Alas! Poor Pope. Lee, Jackson & Co. have plucked the wings of this vain butterfly." Lexington *Gazette*, September 11, 1862.
18. Slaughter, *Fairfax*, 38.   19. *Official Records*, XII, Pt. 2, p. 645.

Stonewall Brigade was about to play a new role: it was going to ambush General Rufus King's division.

Slaughter Mountain, sickness, and long marches had depleted the brigade to 635 effectives.[20] But nothing had dulled its confidence. The confiscations at Manassas and a day's rest had invigorated the Valley men. Confident Confederates crouched in the woods and quietly checked their rifles as the van of the Federal columns passed. Jackson stood beside them, calmly watching the ambuscade develop. Old Jack turned to his divisional officers and said, "Bring up your men, gentlemen." This was the signal!

Out of the wood burst the Men of Manassas, filling the air with the loud scream for which Confederates had become famous. Behind them the batteries of Poague, Carpenter, and Harry Wooding began their deep-throated booms. The Stonewall Brigade raced down the hill as the Federal ranks broke to meet the unexpected flank attack. Veering slightly to the west, the Rebels ran toward a farmhouse and orchard to assail the nearest columns. They gained the house and a segment of the orchard, then met a human wall of resistance. They had collided head-on with their Union counterpart: John Gibbon's Iron Brigade, sturdy Midwesterners as tenacious and proud as any unit on either side.[21]

Few battles in the Civil War equalled the one these two brigades waged in the waning afternoon. It was mostly a stand-up fight, with the two lines at times less than seventy yards apart. Like two titans, the opposing brigades struggled back and forth across the rolling field in a battle the Iron Brigade's commander called "the most terrific musketry fire I . . . ever listened to." [22] Lieutenant Colonel Lawson Botts, commanding the Second Regiment, was knocked from his horse by a bullet that entered the left side of his face and came out behind his ear.[23] Colonel Grigsby was twice grazed by

---

20. *Ibid.*, 661, 663–64.
21. This brigade was organized by Rufus King soon after the war began, and was composed initially of the 2nd, 6th, and 7th Wisconsin and the 19th Indiana. Its members wore standard blue uniforms, but soon adopted the distinguished emblem of wide-brimmed, black felt hats turned up on the lefthand side. Consequently, in the first days of the war the unit was known as the "Black Hat Brigade."
22. John Gibbon, *Personal Recollections of the Civil War* (New York, 1928), 54.
23. Botts lingered for two weeks at the home of a Middleburg minister before dying

Lieutenant General
Thomas J. Jackson,
the first commander of the Stonewall Brigade,
from an engraving by A. C. Campbell of New York.

Brigadier General
Richard B. Garnett,
the second
commander of the brigade.

Brigadier General
Charles S. Winder,
the third
brigade commander.

Colonel
William S. H. Baylor,
the fourth
brigade commander.

Brigadier General
E. Franklin Paxton,
the fifth
brigade commander.

Brigadier General
James A. Walker,
the sixth
brigade commander.

Brigadier General
William Terry,
the last commander
of the Stonewall Brigade.

W. S. McClintic

Edward A. Moore

R. T. Barton

William T. Poague

Henry Kyd Douglas

George R. Bedinger

Wesley Culp

John Echols

Robert E. Lee, Jr.

Dr. Hunter H. McGuire

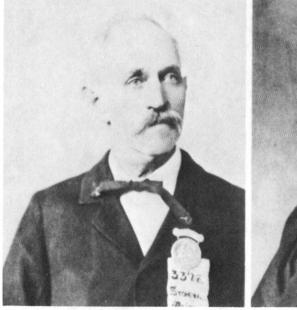

John O. Casler

Frederick W. M. Holliday

John R. Jones

Robert Lewis Dabney

Andrew Jackson Grigsby

William Nelson Pendleton

Minié balls, but stayed in the fight. When part of the Midwestern troops, protected by natural works, began firing at Confederates out in the open, Colonel John Neff's Thirty-third Regiment took cover behind a fence and returned the fire at close range. John Casler of that unit wrote that the men behind the fence "would lie down, load and fire, and it seemed that everyone who would raise up was shot." [24] Twenty-eight-year-old John Neff, a Dunkard who had gone off to war against the wishes of his family, was riddled with bullets before he could complete the disposition of his regiment.[25]

For over two hours both sides fought desperately. In the gathering dusk, a Confederate later recalled, "everything around was lighted up by the blaze of musketry and explosion of balls like a continuous bright flash of lightning." [26] Both sides rushed in reinforcements, but they too took a fearful beating that was not confined solely to the men in the ranks. General William Taliaferro, commanding the Stonewall Division, was shot in the neck, arm, and foot. General Ewell was so seriously wounded that a leg had to be amputated.

At 9 P.M. darkness settled over the blood-smeared field. The Federals slowly backed off. The Confederates held the orchard, but never had such a price been paid for apple trees. Exclusive of the Thirty-third Regiment (whose battle report was lost), the Stonewall Brigade had suffered over two hundred casualties and was down to little more than a good-sized regiment, with the Twenty-seventh Regiment numbering exactly twenty-five men.[27] Writing home two days after the battle, a member of the Rockbridge Artillery lamented: "The old Stonewall Brigade suffered on Thursday . . . Oh, how we suffered in the loss of noble, valuable men and officers." [28]

---

on September 16. Richmond *Examiner*, September 23, 1862; Walker, *VMI Memorial*, 56.

24. Casler, *Stonewall Brigade*, 156.

25. See *ibid.*, 109, 165; Walker, *VMI Memorial*, 396–405.

26. Oates, *Union and the Confederacy*, 142.

27. *Official Records*, XII, Pt. 2, pp. 661, 663–64. Casler noted that Company A of the 33rd Virginia went into the fight with 17 men and lost 5 killed, 5 wounded, and 1 missing. *Stonewall Brigade*, 157.

28. Lexington *Gazette*, September 11, 1862.

But the fighting had just begun. During the night Jackson moved his lines to the left of the Groveton battlefield. The Stonewall Brigade brought up the rear and took a position at the south end of a flat-topped ridge covered with dense undergrowth and scattered trees. Five hundred yards below the hill was a railroad cut of an unfinished spur of the Manassas Gap line. The cut itself ran along a slight hill, with open ground descending sharply to the east. Jackson posted his 18,000 men along a 3,000-yard front and prepared to meet John Pope's 50,000 Federals.

August 29 dawned hot and quiet. Men in the Stonewall Brigade obtained rations and ammunition from the wagons in the rear, then hurried back to the south end of the railroad cut. At 10 A.M. Pope opened the battle with a thundering roar of artillery. Throughout the day Federals assailed Powell Hill's sector far to the left of the brigade's position. The battle was raging furiously when several men in the brigade saw a long column of dust moving in from the west.

If the approaching men were Federals, the day was lost. General William E. Starke, now commanding Jackson's division, rode off to ascertain their identity. Baylor prepared his brigade for action. A few minutes later Starke raced through the woods shouting, "It's Longstreet!" The jubilant cry was repeated up and down the line, and the Stonewall Brigade rent the air with its Rebel yell.[29]

As Longstreet's men filed into position astride the Warrenton–Washington road to the right of the brigade, the Federals made one concerted attempt to crack Baylor's line. A Yankee regiment moved toward the railroad cut and was immediately engaged by the Second Regiment, now under the command of Raleigh T. Colston. The Second was in an advanced position; when it appeared that the Yankees were about to envelop it on both flanks, Baylor ordered it back beyond the cut. The combined fire of the Stonewall Brigade and the units on Longstreet's left soon drove the Federals back down the ridge.

Hardly had the assault been repulsed when Jeb Stuart rode up to Baylor and asked for the aid of the brigade on the far left. Baylor,

---

29. *Confederate Veteran*, XVII (1909), 550.

covered with dust and powder grime, politely refused. "I was posted here for a purpose," he said, "and have positive orders to stay here, which I must obey." [30]

The firing ceased with the coming of night. Trees and dry grass set afire during the battle sent white acrid smoke across the ridge. Behind the lines at brigade headquarters Will Baylor enjoyed a cup of coffee with William Poague of the Rockbridge Artillery and Captain Hugh White of the Liberty Hall Volunteers. Although the men were tired, Baylor suggested that the brigade hold a prayer service. Captain White, a ministerial student, volunteered to make the arrangements. He sought out Chaplain Abner Hopkins of the Second Regiment, then passed the word down the line for all men desiring to worship to meet at Colonel Baylor's tent. Almost the entire brigade turned out for the meeting, "and the service was carried out with great zeal." [31]

The next morning promised no relief from the heat. Soon after dawn members of the Second Regiment on the far right saw blue-coats forming for an attack. Many of the Confederates lay on their stomachs and watched the movements with interest. E. A. Stickley of the Second "saw them massing in the woodland east of us, but keeping pretty well hidden and moving many of their troops directly south, looking to our right." Jackson rode up and watched the deployments silently, then turned to Baylor and said matter-of-factly, "Well, it looks as if there will be no fight today, but keep your men in line and ready for action." [32] Until noon the Stonewall Brigade remained on the alert. An ominous silence hung over the field. The men had just eaten their meager rations when Jackson again rode to their front. No infantry movements were discernible, but Federal batteries had wheeled into view in the distance.

Immediately an order went to Poague and his Rockbridge Artillery, in a field of haystacks three hundred yards in the rear of the brigade, to move quickly to the ridge where Baylor's men were posted. When Poague arrived, Jackson instructed him to drive

---

30. *Official Records,* XII, Pt. 2, p. 740.
31. *Southern Historical Society Papers,* XIV (1886), 370–71; Poague, *Gunner,* 38–39.
32. *Confederate Veteran,* XXII (1914), 231.

an advanced Federal battery to cover. A few quick and well-aimed shots had the desired effect and prompted Jackson to state in admiration: "That was handsomely done, very handsomely done." [33]

The afternoon laziness suddenly vanished in the explosion of Pope's artillery. Waves of bluecoats started forward toward the area held by the Stonewall Brigade. E. A. Stickley wrote: "The Federals came up in front of us suddenly as men rising up out of the ground, showing themselves at the old railroad line opposite our line in double battle phalanx and coming forward in slow time, pouring their shot into our ranks in unmerciful volume." [34]

Three times the Federals hurled themselves against the thin ranks of the Stonewall Brigade; three times they were hurled back in confusion. "The conflict from the woods to the railroad was terrible," Colonel Colston wrote in his official report.[35] Just as the second assault was falling apart, Baylor saw the color-bearer of the Thirty-third fall mortally wounded. Rushing over, the colonel picked up the flag, waved it aloft, and shouted, "Boys, follow me!" Cheering and shouting, a portion of the brigade counterattacked, only to be thrown back with heavy loss. A volley of gunfire almost lifted the charging Baylor off the ground. As his dead body slumped earthward, the colors were seized by Captain Hugh White—with whom Baylor had prayed the evening before. No sooner had White taken a step forward than he was riddled by several bullets and fell lifeless beside his companion in arms.[36]

Colonel Andrew Jackson Grigsby, now the ranking officer in the brigade, quickly assumed command and tried to tighten up the thinning ranks to meet another Federal assault. Summoning Lieutenant Stickley, Grigsby ordered the aide to find Jackson, inform the commander of Baylor's death, and tell him that the weakened Stonewall Brigade could not hold out much longer. Stickley rushed through the woods and soon located Jackson far on the right. In jumbled words the young officer explained the perilous situation.

---

33. Edward A. Moore, *Cannoneer*, 118.
34. *Confederate Veteran*, XXII (1914), 231.
35. *Official Records*, XII, Pt. 2, p. 660.
36. *Ibid.*, XIX, Pt. 2, p. 657; *Confederate Veteran*, XXII (1914), 231; William S. White, *Hugh White*, 117–18, 121.

Jackson did not catch Baylor's name and asked, "What brigade, sir?"

"The Stonewall Brigade, sir," Stickley replied.

"Go back," Jackson answered, "give my compliments to them, and tell the Stonewall Brigade to maintain her reputation." Stickley saluted and started off somewhat bewildered; Jackson stopped him and said that Pender's brigade would be dispatched in ten minutes.[37]

By now the men around the railroad cut were running out of ammunition. But this time there would be no retirement. Some of the men, recalling Jackson's instructions at Kernstown, fastened bayonets to their muskets; others who had no weapons picked up rocks and began hurling them at the advancing Yankees.[38] In some spots hand-to-hand fighting broke out as graycoats fought viciously to preserve their thin line. Sergeant Major John Baldwin of the Thirty-third Regiment rushed up to Captain James Garnett of the brigade staff and shouted, "Mr. Garnett, for God's sake, can't you bring us some reinforcements?" Just as the captain started to the rear, Dorsey Pender's men came double-timing through the woods. But these fresh troops became so hotly engaged that they soon had to retire from the field.[39]

The situation was now desperate; one more effort by the Federals and the Confederate line would collapse from sheer exhaustion. "Just then," wrote Stickley, "we beheld the most beautiful and welcome sight that had as yet ever come before us." [40] Moving in rapidly and obliquely to the left were the massed ranks of Longstreet's corps. "Old Peter" had picked the critical moment to launch the bulldozer-type of counterattack for which he would become famous. The remnants of the brigade leaped up from behind their earthworks with a cheer and dashed out at the Federals, now caught in a cross fire of advancing Confederates. All along the line Lee's army was moving forward to destroy Pope and his Army of Vir-

---

37. *Confederate Veteran*, XXII (1914), 231.
38. *Ibid.*, XV (1907), 85; Riley, *Stonewall Jackson*, 167.
39. *Official Records*, XII, Pt. 2, p. 698; *Southern Historical Society Papers*, XL (1915), 227.
40. *Confederate Veteran*, XXII (1914), 231.

ginia. "As far as the eye could reach the long grey lines of infantry, with the crimson of the colours gleaming like blood in the evening sun, swept with ordered ranks across the Groveton valley." [41] On into the darkness the pursuit continued. Finally, when it was impossible to distinguish friend from foe, the men halted. The Stonewall Brigade encamped near the Groveton crossroads. Its appearance was pitiful: 415 out of 635 men had been lost.[42]

Jackson was returning to the ridge when he saw a soldier painfully trying to crawl out of the railroad cut. Old Jack reined up beside the man and asked if he were injured.

"Yes, General," came the reply, "but have we whipped them?"

Jackson dismounted, told the soldier that the army was victorious, and asked the man's unit.

"I belong to the Fourth Virginia, your old brigade, General. I have been wounded four times but never before as bad as this. I hope I will soon be able to follow you again."

Jackson bent over the tattered and blood-smeared private and replied in a voice shaking with emotion, "You are worthy of the old brigade and I hope with God's blessing, you will soon be well enough to return to it."

Turning to Dr. Hunter McGuire, Jackson directed his personal physician to place the soldier in an ambulance and to attend to the wounds. The soldier could not speak his gratitude; he strained to watch his old commander ride off, but tears had dimmed his vision.[43]

---

41. Henderson, *Stonewall Jackson,* II, 178.
42. Casualties included 67 killed and 348 wounded. *Official Records,* XII, Pt. 2, p. 561. Cf. *Battles and Leaders,* II, 500.
43. Douglas, *I Rode with Stonewall,* 142.

|||||||||||||||||||||||||||||||||||||||||||||||||||||||||||||||||||||||||||||||||||||||||||||||||||

CHAPTER XIII

THE MARYLAND INVASION

For two days rain drenched the weary soldiers. Captain James Garnett of the brigade staff summed up their condition by stating: "The men were so tired and nervous from continual marching and fighting that the pop of a cap would start them off, but they would soon rally." [1] Although most of the brigade served as reserves during the battle of Chantilly (September 1, 1862), some were detailed to bury the hundreds of bodies that lay around the railroad cut. Then, on September 4, Jackson's command, now unofficially called a corps, left the Manassas plains and moved northwestward.

Passing through Leesburg on the fifth, the men crossed the Potomac at White's Ford. The brigade waded across the river in columns of four, laughing, shouting, and singing as the Stonewall

---

1. *Southern Historical Society Papers*, XL (1915), 229.

Brigade Band up front filled the air with strains of "Maryland, My Maryland." Despite their pitiful appearance, the Valley men were reported "in excellent order and high spirits." [2] Why not? They were carrying the war right into Yankee land. At least, they thought so. It was impossible to learn from Jackson where they were going.

By September 7 the regiment halted briefly two miles north of Frederick. Major H. J. Williams of the Fifth Virginia wrote that "our short sojurn in the land of promise wrought a salutary change in the general appearance and condition of the troops. The ragged were clad, the shoeless shod, and the inner man rejoiced by a number and variety of delicacies to which it had been a stranger for long, long weary months before." [3]

After four days of recuperation the men broke camp at sunrise and marched westward over rolling hills to Boonsboro. Then, to the complete surprise of the soldiers, the head of the column turned southward. A puzzled Stonewall Brigade recrossed the Potomac at Williamsport. In spite of their bewilderment at this change of march, the troops were so happy at returning to the Valley that chorus after chorus of "Carry Me Back to Old Virginny" rang across the hillsides.

Jackson had hoped to trap the Federals at the Martinsburg arsenal, but the bluecoats managed to escape to Harpers Ferry. The brigade spent two hours in Martinsburg, where thankful citizens heaped both food and praise upon the men. In the meantime, stragglers who had fallen behind in the march combed the countryside in quest of food. A lady near Shepherdstown told of one of Jackson's men knocking on her door and saying, "I've been a-marchin' an' a-fightin' for six months stiddy, and I ain't had n-a-r-thin' to eat 'cept green apples an' green cawn, an' I wish you'd please to gimme a bite to eat." [4]

---

2. *Official Records,* XIX, Pt. 1, p. 1011.

3. *Ibid.* Longstreet's corps reached Frederick a day later, and a member of the Washington Artillery noted: "Jackson's foot cavalry had been here before us, and had gobbled up all the plunder." William M. Owen, *In Camp and Battle with the Washington Artillery* (Boston, 1885), 131.

4. *Battles and Leaders,* II, 687. The colonel of the 12th South Carolina was placed under arrest by Jackson for allowing his men to break ranks and loot an apple orchard. Both the colonel and his men insisted, however, that the guilty culprits were mem-

In the van of Jackson's army, the brigade bivouacked at Hall-town, then occupied the high bluffs overlooking Harpers Ferry early on September 15. The batteries of Poague and Carpenter were placed on an eminence overlooking Bolivar Heights; from this advantageous position they opened a destructive fire on the Federal garrison.[5] Unable to answer the guns on the bluffs, and with all escape channels closed by Jackson, the Federals soon hoisted a white flag. Colonel Andrew Grigsby, temporarily commanding the Stonewall Brigade, did not see the flag and ordered Poague—who insisted that a truce had been called—to continue firing. A few minutes after Jackson's cease-fire order was given, Poague sent a message to Grigsby that his guns were still loaded. "What shall I do with them?" Poague asked.

"Tell him," Grigsby snorted, "to fire them off the way they are pointed. He won't kill more of the damn Yankees than he ought to!" [6]

Included in the surrender of the arsenal were 11,000 men, 73 pieces of artillery, and 13,000 small arms. As the Valley regiments marched down into the village to replenish their supplies, they passed a long line of Yankee prisoners attired in shiny new uniforms.

"Hello, Johnny," one of the bluecoats called out, "why don't you wear better clothes?"

"These," came an immediate reply, "are good enough to kill hogs in." [7]

At 2 A.M. on September 16 the brigade and the rest of Jackson's force left for Sharpsburg and the rendezvous with Lee's army. The march to Antietam Creek surpassed in severity any hike ever made in the Valley. In three and a half hot, dusty days before the Harpers Ferry action, the men tramped more than sixty miles, crossed two mountain ranges, and twice forded the Potomac. The siege of the Ferry offered no rest, since the men lay on their arms in constant

---

bers of the Stonewall Brigade. Louise H. Daly, *Alexander Cheves Haskell: The Portrait of a Man* (Norwood, Mass., 1934), 77.

5. *Official Records*, XIX, Pt. 1, p. 954.

6. John H. Worsham to R. W. Hunter, June 23, 1904, Confederate Records, 27th Virginia Records, Virginia Archives; Baylor, *Bull Run to Bull Run*, 73.

7. *Ibid.*

expectation of battle. Then, as soon as the fort capitulated, they rushed back to camp, hastily cooked rations, and started a rapid night march toward Sharpsburg, seventeen miles away. Straggling reached critical proportions. Despite the fact that it had replenished its ranks with many new recruits from the Valley, the Stonewall Brigade arrived at Sharpsburg with barely 250 men. Even Jackson felt compelled to term the march "severe." [8]

In mid-afternoon of September 16 the long gray columns sneaked around to the west of Sharpsburg and took battle positions on Longstreet's left near a Dunkard church. Jackson's line faced north and northeast. The Stonewall Brigade and Jackson's division were posted in the center of his line and at the northern edge of a large cornfield seven hundred yards north of the little white church. The brigade assumed a line perpendicular to, and on the immediate left of, the Sharpsburg–Hagerstown turnpike. Its position was in advance of what came to be known as the West Wood.

Until sundown that Tuesday, Poague's battery contested hotly with Federal guns partially concealed across the road in the East Wood.[9] That night troops slept on their arms while regimental officers carefully checked final dispositions.[10] Occasionally the uneasy silence was broken by picket fire, causing nervous men to jump from their blankets into battle position. Around Confederate campfires, those who could gain no rest from sleep mumbled premonitions of Death reaping a harvest on the morrow.

As the gray light of dawn washed away the night, an annoying drizzle began to fall that turned woolen uniforms into smelly and itching sacks. The downpour turned out to be little more than a shower; with sunrise came a heavy mist that shrouded the land and masked all movement. Yet the men in the Stonewall Brigade knew that the initial assault would be made against their position, and the close sound of boots splashing through muddy fields was

---

8. Henderson, *Stonewall Jackson*, II, 271. The figure for the brigade's strength does not include the 2nd Virginia, which was left at Martinsburg as provost guard. *Official Records*, XIX, Pt. 1, p. 1013.
9. Poague's casualties were 6 men and 14 horses killed or wounded. *Ibid.*, 1009–10.
10. Regimental commanders at this battle were: 2nd—Captain Raleigh T. Colston; 4th—Lieutenant Colonel R. D. Gardner; 5th—Major H. J. Williams; 27th—Captain F. C. Wilson; 33rd—Captain Jacob B. Golladay.

indication enough that the attack was forming.[11] At 6 A.M. the countryside seemed to explode as sixteen Federal batteries loosed a barrage against the Confederate left. Young Sandie Pendleton of Jackson's staff was aghast at the intensity of the bombardment. "Such a storm of bullets I never conceived it possible for men to live through," he later wrote.[12] As the sun burned away the damp mist and revealed the glistening woods and fields, the batteries of Poague and Carpenter tried gamely to answer the Federal cannon. But advancing Federal infantry soon sent men, horses, and guns scurrying to the safety of the woods to the rear.

From the outset it was apparent that McClellan hoped to turn Jackson's left. With 12,000 men poised to assail Jackson's 3,500 defenders, the Federals had every reason to anticipate success. Near 6:30 A.M. line after line of blueclad soldiers moved out of the East Wood in one of the grandest displays ever witnessed by the Valley troops. "In apparent double battle line," wrote Lieutenant Stickley of the brigade staff, "the Federals were moving toward us at charge bayonets, common time, and the sunbeams falling on their well-polished guns and bayonets gave a glamour and a show at once fearful and entrancing." (Stickley would be more than an observer that day. A few moments after witnessing the Federal advance, he started to mount his horse. Suddenly a shell ripped through the belly of his mount. Completely covered with the animal's blood, Stickley rushed on foot to join the Stonewall Brigade, and he must have presented a horrible sight in the subsequent fighting—in which he lost an arm and suffered painful bruises.) [13]

At long range Jackson's batteries poured volley after volley into the approaching Federal ranks. Canister chewed large holes in the column; each time the blue ranks staggered, then closed quickly, and continued their advance. The Stonewall and Second Brigades, two hundred yards in advance of the main Confederate line, were concealed behind a fence and a slight rise in the ground. Just as the

---

11. This was Major General Joseph Hooker's I Corps, which opened the battle. The Stonewall Brigade was attacked by Brigadier General Abner Doubleday's division of four brigades, composed mostly of New Yorkers.
12. Lee (ed.), *Pendleton*, 216.
13. *Confederate Veteran*, XXII (1914), 66.

first line of Federals swept forward to gain the fence, the four hundred Southerners jumped up and delivered a point-blank fire that shattered the first wave and caused the succeeding lines to fall back in confusion.

But the Federals were only stunned; regrouping rapidly, they started again. For forty-five minutes Grigsby and his Stonewall Brigade kept up the contest against overwhelming odds. Yankee reinforcements continued pouring in, but each Confederate that fell left an unfilled gap in the line. Soon the Valley regiments were forced to fall back to the edge of the woods and on the reserve brigades. From this secondary position Jackson's men stunted repeated Federal assaults in a wild thirty minutes of fighting "during which the Rebels were subjected to a heavy bombardment of canister." [14] A momentary lull broke the action; then the Confederates surged across the field in a desperate effort to regain the lost ground.

Blue and gray lines slammed together out in the open, and for several minutes the number of men who slumped dead and dying to the ground gave the impression that both sides were determined to fight to the last soldier. Finally, wrote Major H. J. Williams of the Fifth Virginia, the blue line buckled, "unable to withstand the resolute valor of our troops," and withdrew across the cornfield and into the East Wood.[15] Yet the Confederate ranks, reduced to fragments by the fighting, could not push their advantage. William Starke, commanding Jackson's division, was dead; General John Jones of the Second Brigade had been borne bleeding to the rear. Colonel Grigsby, entrusting command of the Valley brigade to the Fourth Virginia's Charles Ronald, had taken over the Stonewall Division. To hold the advanced position was impossible for, according to one brigade officer, "the heavy loss sustained, the confusion unavoidably arising from the change of commanders, and the protracted nature of the contest, rendered necessary the withdrawal of our weary troops to the West Wood from which they had advanced." [16]

---

14. Major Williams erroneously reported that the brigade was subjected to grapeshot. *Official Records*, XIX, Pt. 1, p. 1012.
15. *Ibid.*   16. *Ibid.*

The men had just taken a position in the cover of the woods when Jubal Early arrived with his fresh brigade. Valley units formed on his right as the whole line started forth into the field again; yet the gray advance immediately stalled when hordes of Federals were seen trampling down cornstalks as they raced toward the ridge on which the Dunkard church was located. The Stonewall Brigade rapidly moved to Early's left and formed a diagonal line with its left occupying a hollow in the edge of the wood. The sound of musketry rose to a deafening blast. Bodies piled up all around the shell-wracked church. Foot by foot the Confederates were pushed through the woods and out into an open plain. General Alpheus Williams' division of Joseph Mansfield's XII Corps had reinforced Hooker in an effort to break Jackson's line, which had now bent roughly into a large L. Early's men still faced northward, but the Stonewall Brigade and the remnants of Jackson's division had swung around almost perpendicular to their original position to meet the new onslaught.

The brigade took cover behind a ledge of rocks, and for over an hour the Virginians hurled back assault after assault with heavy loss. Though their own casualties were slight, the continual hammering of the Federals taxed both nerves and endurance. Jackson soon rushed in the last of his reserves; reinforcements could not have arrived more opportunely, for the Yankees had just launched a last do-or-die attempt to pierce the Southern line. For several minutes the West Wood appeared on fire from the countless flashes of musketry that erupted from both sides.

The Federal line wavered; suddenly it broke, and as bluecoats again raced back through the East Wood, shouting Confederates pursued them. According to Major Williams, the Yankees were driven "in confusion for half a mile, leaving scores of killed, wounded, and prisoners in our hands." [17] With the woods cleared and the battle shifting to the east toward Harvey Hill's front, the Stonewall Brigade was ordered to the south edge of the woods. Here the men remained until noon, when they marched to the rear to rearm and eat. This was a welcome order, as some had not eaten since leaving Harpers Ferry two days before. Salt bacon was tho

---

17. *Ibid.*, 1013.

only available fare and the troops had to cook it on forked sticks, but they enjoyed it as much as if it had been a full-course dinner.[18]

Throughout the remainder of the day the weakened Stonewall Brigade listened to the battle as it shifted to the south. Although the men stood by their arms to move out at the first call, their day's work was done. Of the 250 men in the ranks that morning, 11 were dead and 77 were wounded.[19] What remained did not equal two full companies. Jackson's division, commanded by Colonel Grigsby, had lost 700 of its 1,800 members.

The Rockbridge Artillery had also suffered heavily, losing three of its six guns in the early-morning contest. At the critical moment of the battle, the gunners witnessed a tender scene. Poague was moving the remnants of his battery back to a new position when General Robert E. Lee rode up on his way to the Dunkard church area. Poague saluted the commander and informed him of the state of affairs in the West Wood. Lee ordered the battery to give every assistance in checking the Federal tide. Just then, one of the powder-begrimed gunners walked up to the General and saluted. Lee returned the salute unconsciously and prepared to ride off when the soldier identified himself as the General's son "Rob."

Lee congratulated the youth on being unhurt. Then Rob asked, "General, are you going to send us in again?"

"Yes, my son," came the gentle reply. "You all must do what you can to help drive these people back." [20]

That night proved fearful to the Confederates. The Potomac River lay dangerously close to the back of their thin line. Thousands of Federals were still massed in their front. Kyd Douglas said that not one soldier in Jackson's army slept half an hour. Moreover, he added, "nearly all of them were wandering over the field, looking for their wounded comrades, and some of them, doubtless, plundering the dead bodies of the enemy left on the field. Half of Lee's army was hunting the other half." [21] The following day, wrote Ned Moore, "the two armies lay face to face, like two exhausted

---

18. *Southern Historical Society Papers*, XXV (1897), 35–36.

19. *Official Records*, XIX, Pt. 1, p. 812, 1012–13.

20. Edward A. Moore, *Cannoneer*, 153–54. Variations of the same story appear in Poague, *Gunner*, 48; *Confederate Veteran*, XXVII (1919), 294, XXVIII (1920), 417.

21. Douglas, *I Rode with Stonewall*, 174.

monsters, each waiting for the other to strike." [22] On Friday, September 19, the Confederate columns moved off warily for the Potomac.

One Federal attempt was made to prevent the river crossing, but it was thrown back by Powell Hill's light division, which turned like a wounded tiger and fought tenaciously enough to permit Lee's army to return to Virginia. No one in the brigade bothered to sing "Carry Me Back to Old Virginny" on this occasion. As John S. Sawyers of the Rockbridge Artillery wrote: "The yankees slitely got the best of the fight in Maryland. You ought to have Seen us Skeedadling across the Potomac River and the yankees close in our rear." [23]

The Stonewall Brigade halted between Bunker Hill and Winchester to guard against a possible Federal thrust at Lee's crippled army. Wagonloads of wounded from all brigades clogged the road into Winchester. Inside, the town was a picture of horror. "I saw such fearful sights in town today that I turned sick," Mrs. Cornelia McDonald noted in her diary. "Long rows of wounded men sitting on the curbstones waiting for some shelter to be offered them, the wagons still unloading more. Ah! their pitiful faces, so haggard with suffering. Some with torn and bloody clothes, and others with scarcely anything to keep their wounds from the hot sun, their shirts having been torn partly off in dressing the wounds." [24]

Those in the Valley regiments who escaped wounds at Sharpsburg limped about their camp, barefooted and unarmed. Every uniform was in tatters. The ranks were pitifully depleted: one soldier wrote home that only twelve men composed the once-proud Twenty-seventh Virginia.[25] Reorganization on every level was necessary. While a comprehensive recruiting program got underway, changes were also made in high command. On September 18 Lee's army was officially divided into corps, with Jackson placed at the head of the Second Corps.[26] And one of the first duties confronting Old Jack was to find a new commander for his Stonewall Brigade.

---

22. Edward A. Moore, *Cannoneer*, 156.
23. John S. Sawyers to W. M. McAllister, September 26, 1862, McAllister Papers. See also Casler, *Stonewall Brigade*, 169.
24. McDonald, *Diary*, 88–89.
25. John Garibaldi to his wife, October 24, 1862, Garibaldi Letters.
26. *Official Records*, Ser. IV, Vol. II, 198.

The logical choice seemed to be Colonel Andrew Jackson Grigsby of the Twenty-seventh Virginia, who was the ranking officer in the brigade and, as far as the Valley fighters were concerned, the only man deserving of the post. Born in Rockbridge County on November 2, 1819, Grigsby was one of the older officers in the Stonewall Brigade. He entered West Point in July, 1837, but was expelled a year later for academic deficiencies. Nevertheless, his meritorious conduct in the Mexican War as a member of the Virginia Regiment stamped him as a soldier of great potential. Grigsby was farming in Giles County when civil war broke out; at the first shot, he left his plow, grabbed his shotgun, and joined the Valley forces with an enthusiasm characteristic of his entire war career.

Commissioned a major in the Twenty-seventh Virginia by Governor Letcher, Grigsby quickly rose to lieutenant colonel and then colonel and commander of the regiment. He was popular, impetuous, and profane. In appearance and personality he bore a marked resemblance to his namesake. Tall, lanky, hawk-nosed, and heavily bearded, he proved as outspoken as he was reckless, as caustic as he was daring. On several occasions he narrowly escaped death; so consistently were his troops in the middle of actions that the regiment became known in the army as "The Bloody Twenty-seventh." Yet to his men he was ever "the gallant Grigsby, who knew no fear." [27]

He assumed command of the Stonewall Brigade in the closing stages of the Second Manassas fight. When Lee struck northward, there was no time to make an official appointment, but the other regimental commanders were pleased to have Grigsby at the head of the five Valley regiments. During the blood-drenched Wednesday along Antietam Creek, Grigsby gallantly demonstrated his capacity for command; by day's end, with all other brigadiers dead or wounded, he was commanding Jackson's entire division. In less than a month he had jumped from regimental colonel to divisional command normally occupied by a major general. Small wonder that

---

27. *Confederate Veteran*, XV (1896), 69; *Southern Historical Society Papers*, XL (1915), 228. For commendations on Grigsby's conduct in battle, see *Official Records*, XII, Pt. 2, p. 381, XI, Pt. 2, p. 572; Casler, *Stonewall Brigade*, 87; Howard, *Recollections*, 180.

Grigsby returned to Virginia with the army quite proud of his achievements. Loyal service, laudatory recommendations from fellow officers, two wounds, and proved ability in high command all convinced him that he would be the next commander of the Stonewall Brigade. For six weeks he waited impatiently for the announcement.

Early in November he learned through indirect but reliable sources that Jackson's choice for the position was not himself but Major Frank Paxton of Jackson's staff. A staff officer! A personal friend of Jackson's and a fellow Presbyterian! A man who, the preceding spring, had lost the election in his bid for a commission in Grigsby's own Twenty-seventh Virginia! [28]

This was more than the rankled warrior could take. On November 12, 1862, Grigsby resigned as colonel of the Twenty-seventh Virginia, stating that he could no longer "hold the position with honor." [29] Cognizance of the affection and outspoken praise of the Stonewall Brigade made him even more determined that he should command the unit. After swearing to a staff officer "As soon as the war ends, I will challenge Jackson to a duel," Grigsby struck out for Richmond to plead his cause and the unwarranted affront to his record.[30] He finally secured an audience with President Davis— a meeting that degenerated into a shouting interchange between the two men. At one point Davis jumped to his feet in anger and stammered, "Do you know who I am? I am President of the Confederacy!"

Raging like a bull, Grigsby shot out of his chair and roared, "And do you know who I am? I am Andrew Jackson Grigsby of Rockbridge County, Virginia, late colonel of the Bloody Twenty-seventh Virginia of the Stonewall Brigade, and as good a man as you or anyone else, by God!" [31]

Needless to say, Grigsby's pilgrimage to Richmond was unfruitful. He returned to civilian life in Lexington, an embittered and

28. *Southern Historical Society Papers*, XXXVIII (1913), 281.
29. Andrew J. Grigsby to George W. Randolph, November 12, 1862, Grigsby's personal file, National Archives.
30. Howard, *Recollections*, 180–81.
31. Bean, "A House Divided," *loc. cit.*, 404.

broken man, seething with resentment at what he regarded as Jackson's grave injustice.

The real reasons for Jackson's bypassing Grigsby as brigade commander are unknown. Popular rumor had it that the pious Jackson did not like Grigsby's constant use of profanity. Yet Old Jack disliked the same trait in his outspoken quartermaster, Major Harman, and he not only retained him but trusted him implicitly.[32] If Grigsby's failure to make the grade at West Point created a question of his ability as a soldier, the same suspicions would have applied to Major Paxton, who did not even attend the academy. Perhaps Jackson felt Grigsby too impetuous and reckless, especially when compared to the calm and orderly Paxton. After all, the Twenty-seventh was the only regiment that buckled during the fight at Slaughter Mountain. And perhaps the extraordinarily high casualties in that unit created some doubt in Jackson's mind as to the competence of its leadership. Jackson's only reference concerning a successor to the dead Baylor was the laconic statement that he considered none of the five regimental colonels capable of brigade command at that time.[33] Whatever the sources of Jackson's displeasure with Grigsby, unknown personal reasons must have been involved.

Nevertheless, Grigsby was not easily forgotten. In March, 1863, more than forty officers of the Stonewall Brigade signed a petition asking for his promotion to brigadier general and an appropriate command. "No bolder or more daring officer," the document read, "ever led troops into a fight, or managed them better when actually engaged." The petition was endorsed by Grigsby's successor, General Paxton, and by divisional commanders Powell Hill and Jubal Early. Paxton, who went out of his way to plead Grigsby's cause, concluded his recommendation by stating: "I have no idea that there is any officer of this rank in the Confederate army who has seen and survived as much." Powell Hill called him "the bravest of the brave," and Early spoke in superlatives of his conduct at Sharpsburg.[34]

---

32. Although this was not his own opinion, McHenry Howard reported the rumor in his *Recollections*, 181.
33. *Official Records*, XXV, Pt. 2, p. 645.
34. The petition is in Grigsby's personal file, National Archives.

The petition was of no avail. By December of that year "the old fellow was chafing," one officer commented.[35] Soon afterward Grigsby concluded that the Confederacy had no further use for him in the field, and for the remainder of the war he contented himself as much as possible with organizing local militia companies to defend the Valley.

In submitting Frank Paxton's name for command of the Stonewall Brigade, Jackson stated emphatically: "There is no officer under the grade proposed whom I can recommend with such confidence for promotion to a Brigadier-Generalcy." [36] The War Department confirmed the appointment on November 1, 1862; and, like Winder, Paxton assumed command of a hostile Stonewall Brigade. The men, particularly the handful of survivors in the Twenty-seventh Virginia, received him with unmasked disapproval. It was due to Paxton's remarkable talents and warm personality that he soon won the affections of the seasoned veterans under him.

In many respects, Elisha Franklin Paxton was a human paradox. A native of Rockbridge County and descended on both sides from the Valley's earliest settlers, he was born on March 4, 1828. His grandfather had commanded a Rockbridge company during Washington's siege of Yorktown; his father was a veteran of the War of 1812; and Paxton could easily trace his lineage back to the Presbyterian fighters of Oliver Cromwell. If young Paxton himself ever envisioned a West Point education, the dream vanished with a boyhood injury that blinded him in one eye. He was graduated from Washington College in 1845, took another degree from Yale two years later, and, in 1849, received a law degree at the head of his class from the University of Virginia. A year later he began practicing law in Lexington, although in the succeeding four years he concerned himself primarily with locating land claims in Ohio for interested Virginians.[37]

In 1854 he married Elizabeth H. White of Lexington, and by 1856 his successes were such that he established and became presi-

---

35. L. B. French to Custis Lee, December 30, 1863, *ibid.*
36. *Official Records,* XXV, Pt. 2, p. 645; Paxton (ed.), *Memoir,* 65.
37. The exact nature of the claims and the resultant cases is vague. When Jed Hotchkiss was compiling data on Paxton's career, he was never able to ascertain precisely what Paxton was seeking in behalf of his clients.

dent of the Bank of Rockbridge, the first such institution in the county. By 1860, however, failing vision in his one good eye forced an abandonment of the legal profession. He purchased a large and beautiful estate just outside Lexington, named it "Thorn Hill," and began a successful career as a gentleman farmer.

Lincoln's election late in 1860 infuriated Paxton. "Ordinarily a man of calm temperament," his son wrote, "he was a man of powerful emotions and when they were excited he was at times violent . . . Policy had little influence with him. He was a man of outspoken conviction always and of great energy of purpose." [38] Paxton was a steadfast and uncompromising Democrat of extreme states' rights leanings. As early as November, 1860, he advocated the immediate secession of Virginia. Throughout the Valley, debates for and against secession were frequent and heated. Lexington became a center of controversy, and Paxton was one of the most vehement protagonists of disunion. Consequently, he alienated many of the city's leading citizens, including Dr. George Junkin (president of Washington College) and Colonel J. T. L. Preston, father-in-law and brother-in-law respectively of Professor Thomas J. Jackson of the Virginia Military Institute. Jackson himself replied angrily on more than one occasion to Paxton's outspoken arguments over several issues. Although both Paxton and the man under whom he was to serve until his death mingled in the same Lexington social circles, at the outbreak of the war they were not even on speaking terms.[39]

"At the first tap of the drum" in April, 1861, Paxton joined the Rockbridge Rifles and was promptly elected first lieutenant. The unit was dispatched to Harpers Ferry, made a temporary part of the Fourth Regiment, and attached to Jackson's First Brigade. It appears that Paxton and Jackson, as companions in arms, soon forgot their prewar political differences, for Paxton became one of Old Jack's most trusted lieutenants.

In facial features Paxton bore a faint resemblance to Jackson. He had a high forehead, cold and penetrating blue eyes, and a black mustache and beard. Of stocky build, he stood five feet, ten inches tall. Unusual physical strength and a loud, deep voice quickly

---

38. M. W. Paxton to Jed Hotchkiss, November 6, 1897, Hotchkiss Papers.
39. *Ibid.*; Bean (ed.), "A House Divided," *loc. cit.*, 404–405.

earned him the name of "Bull" Paxton.[40] Although without any formal military training, and lacking in the ability to win the collective devotion of troops over whom he served, Paxton displayed a loyalty to the Southern cause and an obedience to Jackson's orders as much as any man who wore the tattered uniform of the Stonewall Brigade.

On August 7, 1861, having proved himself at the Manassas baptism, he was named to Jackson's staff. Two months later he became major in the Twenty-seventh Virginia and held that post until defeated for re-election the following spring. He went home dejected but was promptly recalled by Jackson and served as a volunteer aide to the General through the Slaughter Mountain–Cedar Run Campaign. Following the resignation of the Reverend Mr. Dabney as Jackson's chief of staff, Paxton moved up to that post and apparently served well in staff capacity. Three days after Sharpsburg, unknown to every officer and man in the Stonewall Brigade, Jackson recommended Paxton for brigadier and assignment as commander of the five Valley regiments. The appointment was announced to the brigade on November 6, 1862.[41]

The modest Paxton was not enthusiastic about his new assignment. He accepted it, he wrote his wife, "with much reluctance . . . I go where there is much thankless work to be done and much responsibility to be incurred. I am free to admit that I don't like the change. If my duty be done to the best of my ability, it will not, I fear, be with such result as to give entire satisfaction." [42]

Yet he did an amazing job of reorganizing the Stonewall Brigade. Within two months, recruiting and the return of absentees had swelled the ranks of the five regiments from 200 to 1,200 men. On October 20, before Paxton assumed command of the brigade, the Rockbridge Artillery was transferred to the reserve batteries of Jackson's corps. This dissolved a connection that had existed since the war began and was lamented by both brigade and battery.[43] Further reorganization occurred with the appointment of four regi-

---

40. Paxton (ed.), *Memoir*, 2. A veteran of the 4th Virginia said Paxton won the nickname because "when he took hold at any point along the line, like the bull dog he would hold fast." R. M. Harris to J. G. Paxton, October 1, 1906, Paxton Family Papers, Alderman Library, University of Virginia.
41. *Official Records*, XIX, Pt. 2, p. 699.   42. Paxton (ed.), *Memoir*, 71.
43. For example, see Slaughter, *Fairfax*, 40.

mental colonels. H. J. Williams continued at the head of the Fifth Virginia; J. Q. A. Nadenbousch took over the Second, R. D. Gardner succeeded Colonel Ronald at the head of the Fourth, J. K. Edmondson assumed command of the Twenty-seventh, and Edwin G. Lee was promoted to colonel of the Thirty-third.[44]

44. *Official Records*, XXI, 543. Only Lee was a full colonel. Gardner, Williams, and Edmondson were lieutenant colonels; Nadenbousch was a captain. Their promotions did not come through until after the Fredericksburg Campaign.

⁞⁞

CHAPTER XIV

LIFE IN WINTER QUARTERS

For two months the brigade relaxed in camps near Winchester. Three of the regiments were north of town; the remainder were at Camp Allen near Berryville. The men did spend the early part of October tearing up railroad tracks in the Martinsburg–Shepherdstown area. Only one encounter with Federals took place, and that was on October 17, when portions of the Second, Fifth, and Twenty-seventh Regiments "ran into a nest of Yankees" near Kearneysville. A two-hour skirmish followed between the Confederates and the lead elements of General Andrew A. Humphreys' Corps. Federal reinforcements in large numbers caused the graycoats to retire to Winchester with a loss of three men killed and twenty-one wounded.[1]

---

1. Jim P. Charlton to Oliver P. Charlton, October 20, 1862, Charlton Letters; *Official Records*, XIX, Pt. 2, pp. 86, 89.

During these idle months brigade members spent most of their time on picket duty. As Private John Garibaldi stated, the first weeks were pleasant and peaceful. "The boys here are as lively as crickets, just as lively as if it was in time of peace, or as if they were at home." [2] But the loneliness of picket duty, the monotony of camp life, and the constant exposure to the elements soon combined to transform the outward joy of the men into moody grumblings. In November, Garibaldi again wrote his wife, but by then the tone of his letters had changed. It was "peaceable in camp," he declared, but "I intend to take a French furlow and [come] home myself if I can." [3] When a smallpox epidemic confined the Fourth Regiment to its quarters and thus cancelled all pending furloughs, the men heaped abuse on their sick comrades—as if they had purposely contracted the disease.[4]

The brigade soon moved to "Camp Baylor" near Bunker Hill. The men were growing increasingly anxious to go into winter quarters, for that would enable them to construct wooden huts, lean-tos, and other similar structures as protection from the cold. But no order came, and the troops huddled in their blankets around campfires and made the most of the few tents that were available. Urgent appeals went home for food and clothing; many in the Stonewall Brigade even volunteered to spend their leaves collecting provisions for their comrades.[5] The Valley folk responded to the calls with patriotic sacrifices. In one week Rockbridge County contributed 175 blankets, 75 pairs of socks, 50 pairs of shoes, leather for an additional 50 pairs, and no less than $750 in cash.[6]

In the leisure of camp the men thought more and more of home, peace, and better quarters. Their yearnings were reflected in a letter from Private Garibaldi to his wife. After bemoaning his failure to receive more letters from home, he wrote:

There is some talk about us going back to Camp Zollicoffer where we made our winter quarters last winter, and we will, then, be stationed in our old shanties that we built last winter.

2. John Garibaldi to his wife, October 24, 1862, Garibaldi Letters.
3. Ibid., November 2, 1862.
4. Jim P. Charlton to Oliver P. Charlton, November 20, 1862, Charlton Letters.
5. Ibid., November 21, 1862.
6. Staunton Spectator and General Advertiser, December 2, 1862.

Dear, there is some little talk of peace about the camp some thinks that next spring will bring peace and we shall all then come home and rejoin our wifes once more.[7]

Many of the men were cheered by a great religious revival that broke out in the brigade camp that fall. One regimental chaplain was elated. "Thirty-five soldiers have professed to be converted," he wrote. "Daily meetings are being held, and the numbers are manifesting a deep interest in reference to spiritual things." [8]

Although many members of the brigade were sincere in their religious fervor, others participated as much to please Old Jack as themselves. One night Jackson started across a field toward Camp Baylor to attend a prayer meeting. A soldier saw him approaching and ran ahead to pass the news of the unexpected visitor. Many of the troops were in their tents playing cards by the light of a candle stuck in the socket of a bayonet. Hearing the "messenger," they bolted from the tents and raced for the meeting site. Jackson shortly arrived, visibly pleased that the entire brigade had turned out for the religious services. With heads bowed and hats in hands, the men stood reverently while Jackson led them in prayer.[9]

On Saturday morning, November 22, the citizens of Winchester watched with sorrow as the army filed southward out of town. Only after the troops had crossed the Blue Ridge at Luray Gap did they learn their destination. They were moving to the vicinity of Fredericksburg, where Lee was holding at bay the Army of the Potomac, now under the affable but inept Major General Ambrose E. Burnside. Many of the Valley men were in high spirits at the prospect of "a new Sharpsburg" with their old antagonists. "Our corps musters thirty thousand men for duty," Sandie Pendleton wrote, "in as fine trim and as eager for another fight as I have seen men during the war. We are confident that we can handle any sixty thousand Burnside has, and, if Longstreet can do his part, we'll finish this army for them this winter." [10]

7. John Garibaldi to his wife, November 20, 1862, Garibaldi Letters.
8. Bennett, *The Great Revival*, 210.   9. Douglas, *I Rode with Stonewall*, 197.
10. Like his father, General Pendleton, Sandie had little respect for conservative James Longstreet, who now commanded the Army of Northern Virginia's 1st Corps. Lee (ed.), *Pendleton*, 238–39. Jackson's 2nd Corps actually numbered 34,000 men and 98 guns. Vandiver, *Mighty Stonewall*, 417.

The weather was clear and cold. The hardship of the long march was intensified by the shortage of clothing. In spite of liberal contributions from Valley folk, many members of the Stonewall Brigade remained barefooted and without overcoats.[11] Both troops and wagons moved slowly over the Piedmont through Orange and Madison Court Houses, Gordonsville, and a tangled wilderness broken only by the little road junction of Chancellorsville. As Lieutenant Randolph Barton of the brigade staff wrote in later years: "Doubtless, on that march, with the merry jest that always enlivened a marching column, many a brave fellow trod ground which in a few months became his grave." [12]

On December 2 the weary regiments encamped at Guiney's Station, ten miles south of Fredericksburg on the Richmond, Fredericksburg and Potomac Railroad. For a week they remained in position, anxiously awaiting some order or movement. In the meantime, soldiers chopped wood daily to exercise and keep warm, and dirt was piled against tent sides as an added buffer against the cold. Frank Paxton was agreeably surprised by the cheerfulness and apparent contentment of the men in the face of their hardships. Caught up in their enthusiasm, he wrote his wife: "I begin to feel that my highest ambition is to make my brigade the best in the army, to merit and enjoy the affection of my men." [13]

Orders came before daylight on December 12, directing Paxton to bring the Stonewall Brigade to Fredericksburg and rejoin the remainder of the Second Corps. The columns marched out of Guiney's Station at 6 A.M. A heavy fog blanketed the ground; breath turned white in the icy air. As a part of Taliaferro's division, the Valley brigade reached the vicinity of Hamilton's Crossing early that afternoon. The men shifted positions several times before reaching a large wooded area on the crest of a hill. They were four hundred yards behind Maxcy Gregg's brigade which, with the rest of Powell Hill's division, formed Jackson's first line. Paxton's orders

11. Paxton (ed.), Memoir, 73; Bean (ed.), "A House Divided," loc. cit., 406.
12. Barton, Recollections, 37.
13. Paxton (ed.), Memoir, 74–75. The brigadier also stated that on the march from the Valley to Guiney's Station, only two men straggled from his brigade.

were "to support General Gregg, and be governed in my action by his movements." [14]

Fog again covered the Virginia countryside at dawn on Saturday, December 13. The men in the Stonewall Brigade spent three hours lying on their arms in anticipation of a Federal assault. At 10 A.M. the sun broke through the mist. Across the plain and clearly visible stood the massed ranks of General W. B. Franklin's "Left Grand Division"—half the Army of the Potomac. The dazzling sun reflecting off the snow on the ground and the thousands of poised bayonets almost blinded the Confederates who stood confidently in their hastily constructed earthworks.

Although not engaged in repelling the first two assaults on Jackson's line, the Stonewall Brigade was subjected to an intense artillery bombardment from Federal batteries atop Stafford Heights. Near eleven o'clock the third Union onslaught rammed across the field and broke Gregg's line. Paxton received word of the penetration and immediately rushed his brigade forward. In battle columns the men struck for the works around the railroad. The Second and Fourth Virginia were on the right, with the Fifth in the center and the Twenty-seventh and Thirty-third Regiments to the left.

In a thick clump of woods the Second and Fourth Regiments made initial contact with the Federals. The Twenty-seventh and Thirty-third Regiments swerved to support their sister units; they collided instead with stationary Confederate troops who refused to part and let the Virginians pass.[15] By the time the supporting regiments plunged into the dark forest, the Second and Fourth Virginia had driven the Federals back and restored the line. For the Stonewall Brigade this was the battle of Fredericksburg. Casualties, confined almost exclusively to Winchester's Second and the upper Valley's Fourth Regiments, had been slight: three killed and sixty-seven wounded, with many of the losses incurred during the Federal bombardment earlier in the day.[16]

---

14. *Official Records*, XXI, 677.
15. In his official report Colonel Edmondson told of his 27th Virginia passing "over troops which, to all appearances, seemed to be doubting as to their duty." *Ibid.*, 684.
16. E. F. Paxton to F. W. M. Holliday, December 27, 1862, Frederick W. M. Holliday Papers, Duke University Library.

Although the losses were small, two of them created great sorrow in the Stonewall Brigade. Youthful Randolph Fairfax, one of the most beloved gunners in the Rockbridge Artillery, was killed during an artillery exchange. And while leading his Fourth Virginia against the Federals, Colonel R. D. Gardner was hit twice by Federal shrapnel. One piece imbedded in his face, making a hideous wound; the other went in below the shoulder blade and so worked itself downward that eleven years later it was removed by surgery. These injuries ended Gardner's military career. The personable colonel who had led the Stonewall Brigade at Cedar Run retired from service with the high regard of the Valley men.[17]

Late in the afternoon of December 13, the battle having reaped a full, horrible harvest, Paxton shifted his brigade three hundred yards to the right in order to protect the railroad at Hamilton's Crossing. That night was extremely cold, but the men did not seem to show it. After constructing new earthworks the soldiers gathered around campfires, told jokes, and related incidents in the day's fighting. As the hour grew late, several choruses of "Annie Laurie" rang out across the Fredericksburg plain, covered with thousands of Union dead and dying.[18]

For four days the Valley troops withstood extremely cold weather, all the while keeping a wary eye on Burnside's army across the Rappahannock. The men appeared "cool, firm, eager & manly," Colonel Edwin G. Lee wrote of his Thirty-third Virginia, and Captain George Bedinger of the rowdy Emerald Guards expressed a similar opinion: "I never saw men in more glorious fighting condition . . . Our sufferings, preceding and following the battle, were considerable. Marching and camping or lying upon the frozen earth, but not a man deserted his post." [19]

The long-awaited orders to go into winter quarters came a week before Christmas. The Stonewall Brigade accompanied Jackson to Moss Neck, the home of Mr. and Mrs. Richard Corbin three miles

---

17. *Official Records*, XXI, 682–83; *Confederate Veteran*, XIV (1906), 419.
18. Douglas, *I Rode with Stonewall*, 203–204; *The Land We Love*, I (1866), 116.
19. Edwin G. Lee to F. W. M. Holliday, December 22, 1862, Holliday Papers; George R. Bedinger to his mother, December 23, 1862. Dandridge Papers. Bedinger added: "I am very much pleased with the conduct of my Irishmen; they are enthusiastic and have at the same time obedience."

from Guiney's Station. As the men began settling down for the winter months, Paxton took stock of his unit. "The Brigade is not what I would like it to be," he wrote. "The severe campaign through which it has passed has reduced it to a mere skeleton." After listing the number of men in each regiment (411 in the Second, 367 in the Fourth, 430 in the Fifth, 208 in the Twenty-seventh, and 260 in the Thirty-third), he concluded sadly: "A very bad exhibit I am sure, & as there is no prospect of filling up with conscripts, we begin the next campaign with this very small establishment." [20]

To his wife, Paxton painted an equally gloomy picture. Brigade losses in 1862 had totaled 1,220 men—"more than we could turn out for a fight to-day. Out of fifteen field officers elected last spring, five have been killed and six others wounded, leaving only four that have been unhurt." [21]

At this time the men of the Stonewall Brigade did not share Paxton's pessimism, for they were busy constructing "Camp Winder," their winter quarters. A site had been chosen that offered good drainage, adequate wood and water supplies, proximity to the Yankees, and access to the Richmond, Fredericksburg and Potomac Railroad. Then, Roberta Corbin wrote, "the great forests surrounding Moss Neck were literally mowed down" as the men chopped down trees and dragged them to the spots selected for their huts. [22]

In building their shelters, many of the soldiers dug holes three to five feet deep and then erected log cabins over the excavations. After the logs had been chinked and daubed, dirt was packed against the sides to shut out freezing winds. Fireplaces and chimneys were generally built opposite the entrances. Flooring was rarely used; the men seemed content simply to pack the earth. Four to ten soldiers usually occupied each hut, which normally was about eight feet high. [23]

Furnishings were crude. Most of the beds were double and triple-deck bunks, with hay, leaves, and other soft materials used for mat-

20. E. F. Paxton to F. W. M. Holliday, December 27, 1862, Holliday Papers.
21. Paxton (ed.), *Memoir*, 82.
22. *Confederate Veteran*, XX (1912), 25.
23. Jim P. Charlton to Oliver P. Charlton, December 28, 1862, Charlton Letters. Much of the material on winter quarters was gleaned from Bell Irvin Wiley, *The Life of Johnny Reb* (Indianapolis, 1943), 59–67.

tresses. Chairs were made of boxes and logs. Many soldiers converted barrels into curved-back seats. Desks were easily constructed by fastening boards atop boxes or on logs imbedded in the ground.

Men fortunate enough to have tents often reinforced them with wooden sides and added a fireplace and chimney at one end. Requiring less effort to build, these smaller structures afforded warmth and coziness to the inhabitants. Captain George Bedinger of the Thirty-third wrote after constructing one of these barricaded tents: "I am extremely comfortably fixed, have an excellent tent and stove and would rather prefer bad weather, as it reduces the possibility of our marching until a more favourable season." [24]

Picket duty and laziness prevented many soldiers from enjoying the comfort of these crude shelters. Some made "gopher holes" by digging down deep into the snow or the ground, wrapped themselves in blankets, and buried themselves for the night. Evidently this type of bed did provide warmth. When reveille sounded one morning, a member of the Fourth refused to get up, stating that he intended to stay in his gopher hole until the rains washed him away.[25]

In the daytime soldiers passed the idle hours clustered around campfires. According to a popular story of the time, Jackson and a divisional commander were riding through the camp one day when they saw a group shivering around an open fire. The subordinate officer shook his head and said, "Poor devils, poor devils."

Jackson instantly corrected him: "Call them suffering angels." [26]

Quagmire was a constant source of irritation. Sandie Pendleton wrote his mother of mud being "so intense that no one ever thinks of moving from camp except under the pressure of duty. Its depth is appalling to us uncivilized beings from the mountains. The whole bottom of the earth seems to have sunk about three feet." The Stonewall Brigade soon "paved" its streets by cutting down pine trees, placing the trunks across the paths, piling brush on the logs, and covering the whole with dirt.[27]

---

24. George R. Bedinger to his sister, February 8, 1863, Dandridge Papers.
25. Jim P. Charlton to Oliver P. Charlton, November 11, 1862, Charlton Letters. See also Douglas, *I Rode with Stonewall*, 22–23.
26. *The Land We Love*, V (1868), 278.
27. Lee (ed.), *Pendleton*, 252–53; Casler, *Stonewall Brigade*, 207–208.

Obtaining a well-balanced diet was an acute problem in every winter camp. Late in December, Captain John Welsh of the Twenty-seventh Virginia wrote optimistically to his wife: "As to eating, we still do very well; we have bread, none of your flat cakes but nice light rolls, beef rather poor but makes good hash, salt pork, none of the best but makes good shortening and rye coffee well sugared." He added that green apples could be purchased at a dollar a bushel.[28] Because of bad bread and a lack of fruits and vegetables, General Paxton was ill throughout most of that winter, and he noted an improvement in his health only after securing half a bushel of dried peaches.[29]

Generally speaking, the first months in winter quarters were pleasant. Private Jim P. Charlton wrote near year's end that the men were "all in fine spirits and know they will have a little rest for awhile." Captain Welsh, writing at the same time, stated: "I think that we will get through safe if the Yankees let us alone and the prospects are very good for that; I think they got enough of it at Fredericksburg." Captain Bedinger agreed with Welsh: "As to 'Mr Fighting Joe Hooker's' advancing, I do not fear it at this present time; he comes to his destruction and he knows it." [30]

The Valley units evidenced their happy feeling with wild choruses of Rebel yells at almost any hour of the day. At night the popular Stonewall Brigade Band entertained with concerts. Until the weather grew unbearable, the men often passed the early evening hours sitting around their fires singing "Lorena," "Home Sweet Home," "Her Bright Smile Haunts Me Still," "Ever of Thee," and other camp favorites.[31] The first heavy snowfall was always a time of merrymaking. Sledding, building snowmen, and staging regimental snowball battles were common diversions. When severe weather persisted, the men generally spent their time talking, reading, writing letters, or sleeping.

---

28. Bean (ed.), "A House Divided," *loc. cit.*, 407, 410.
29. Paxton (ed.), *Memoir*, 87–94.
30. Jim P. Charlton to Oliver P. Charlton, December 28, 1862, Charlton Letters; Bean (ed.), "A House Divided," *loc. cit.*, 407; George R. Bedinger to his sister, February 8, 1863, Dandridge Papers. See also John Garibaldi to his wife, January 27, 1863, Garibaldi Letters.
31. *Confederate Veteran*, XX (1912), 25.

Religion helped to alleviate the miseries of war. Early in January, 1863, "by a multitude of willing hands," the Valley men began construction of the first log chapel at Moss Neck. The V-shaped building, with the pulpit at the intersection of the two wings, was completed on February 1. On the following Sunday, Jackson rode over to attend morning services, but he found the chapel so packed that he had to go elsewhere and return in the evening.[32]

Prayer meetings were held almost nightly that winter. Jackson's presence at the services initially caused some embarrassment. The ragged and dirty privates, unaccustomed to the presence of a general, shied away when Jackson sat down among them for fear of contaminating him with their uncleanliness.[33] When it became obvious that Old Jack was going to be a regular attender at the services, the men took more care with their toilet. "I was much pleased by the appearance of my men," Paxton once wrote after a Sunday service. "They looked clean and comfortably dressed, and were attentive to the sermon. We have, it is true, many bad men in the army; but, as a whole, I would not expect to find better men in any community than I have in my brigade." [34]

As the weeks passed slowly by and the weather became more severe, boredom and discomfort increased. Pleasantries were forgotten, tempers grew short, and camp fights became daily activities. Men who earlier had written hopefully of approaching peace now envisioned the war as a long, drawn-out struggle. To his wife Private Garibaldi confided: "There is a heap talk of peace now in the north, but I wouldn't put no dependence on them, but after awhile I think they'll get tire[d] to get whipt and they will then give us up for a bad job, but that may not be for a good while." [35]

In their pessimism many soldiers vehemently denounced the male civilians who remained at home while they fought the war. Captain Welsh of the Twenty-seventh Virginia, for example, felt that "if

---

32. Dabney, *Jackson*, 650; Douglas, *I Rode with Stonewall*, 212; *Southern Historical Society Papers*, XXXVIII (1910), 282–83.

33. Yet, according to Jackson's chaplain, he "was never so well satisfied as when he had an unkempt soldier touching his elbow on either hand, and all the room about him compactly filled." Dabney, *Jackson*, 650–51.

34. Paxton (ed.), *Memoir*, 90.

35. John Garibaldi to his wife, January 4, 1863, Garibaldi Letters.

Charge of Federal troops
against the Stonewall Brigade
in the battle of Cedar Mountain, Virginia,
August 9, 1862.
A heretofore unpublished drawing by Edwin Forbes.

Custer's cavalry
routing Confederate soldiers
in the battle of Winchester, Virginia,
September 19, 1864.
Drawing by Alfred A. Waud.

Battle of Gettysburg, July 3, 1863.

This Edwin Forbes drawing, published here for the first time, contains Forbes's marginal notes:
"The rebels made a most desperate attack on this position,
for six hours and a half they hurled the veterans of Jackson's old corp's
against the breastworks, they were defeated in every attempt with terrible slaughter."

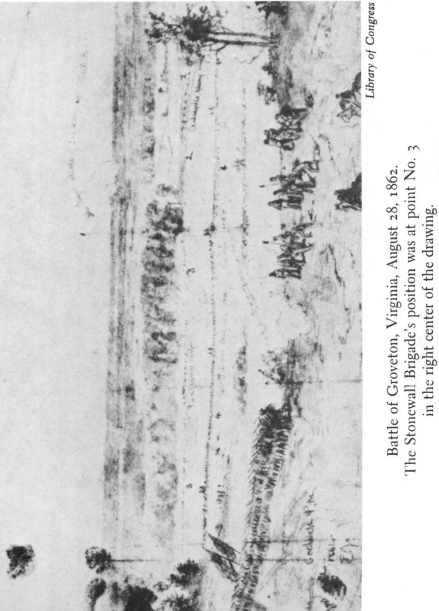

Battle of Groveton, Virginia, August 28, 1862.
The Stonewall Brigade's position was at point No. 3
in the right center of the drawing.
From a heretofore unpublished sketch by Edwin Forbes.

Battle of White Oak Swamp, Virginia, June 30, 1862.
Jackson's men are in the background.
From an oil canvas by an unknown artist,
painted probably in 1862.

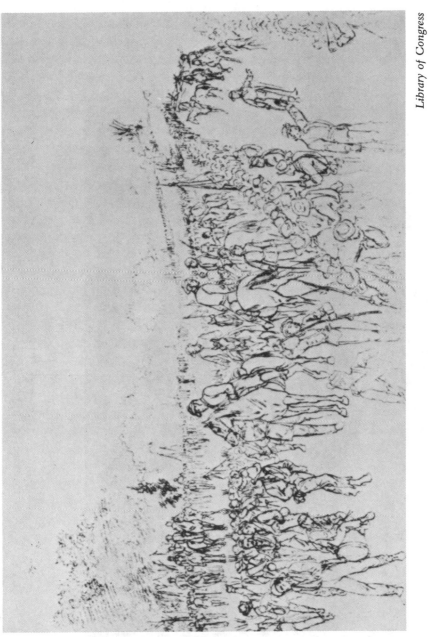

The surrender
of the Army of Northern Virginia.
Pen-sketch by John R. Chapin.

Stonewall Jackson
and his men,
from a painting by Haddon Sundblom.

Courtesy of *The Coca-Cola Company*

Battle of Spotsylvania, May 12, 1864.
Wrote one of the men of the Stonewall-Brigade:
"All that human courage and endurance would effect
was done by these men on this frightful morning, but all was of no avail."
From an original by American Lithographing Company.

FOLLOWING STONEWALL

Confederate Museum

This sketch,
drawn by the noted Confederate artist William L. Sheppard,
apparently depicts the Romney Campaign.

some of these abominable speculators and cowardly scamps about home would turn out as they ought to we would make short work of the Yankees; but I hope they will get their deserts yet; if they don't, I am mistaken." [36]

Favorite targets for expressions of ill-feeling in winter quarters were the officers. Beloved and obeyed in battle and on marches, commanders in camp were often criticized by bored and frustrated privates for their harsh discipline. Although many of the officers were doubtless innocent of the brutality attributed to them, Jackson proved relentless in his enforcement of discipline. This was particularly true where his old brigade was concerned; if any offenders were found within its ranks, an example was made of them to deter similar actions by other units of the Second Corps.

In February, 1863, six members of the Stonewall Brigade were tried and convicted by court-martial for desertion. The punishments were severe: one culprit was given six months' labor with ball and chain; two were ordered flogged; the remaining three were condemned to the firing squads. Paxton bitterly protested the decisions. Only one of the three men should be shot, he said in an appeal to General Lee, and that one should be chosen by lot among the condemned trio. Jackson promptly disagreed. In his endorsement of the appeal, he wrote his first criticism of the new commander of the Stonewall Brigade: "With the exception of this application, General Paxton's management of this brigade has given me great satisfaction. One great difficulty in the army results from over lenient Courts and it appears to me that when a Court Martial faithfully discharges its duty that its decisions should be sustained." Lee upheld Jackson's opinion; however, on the day that the three men were to die, President Davis commuted the sentences.[37]

This was not the only instance of unrest and misbehavior in the Stonewall Brigade that winter. When John Casler of the Thirty-third Virginia was jailed for another in a long line of minor offenses, he observed: "I found two or three hundred in the guard house, and the court martial in full blast. Punishments of all kinds were being inflicted on the prisoners, such as shot to death, whipped,

---

36. Bean (ed.), "A House Divided," *loc. cit.*, 409.
37. Douglas, *I Rode with Stonewall*, 213–14.

heads shaved and drummed out of service, riding wooden horses, wearing barrel shirts, and all other punishments in the catalogue of court martials." [38]

In the meantime, up at brigade headquarters Frank Paxton had mastered the duties of a brigadier and had also demonstrated a marked improvement in character. Initially, his ignorance of the minute aspects of high field command caused him some rough sledding. For example, in December a mild disagreement with his divisional commander, General Taliaferro, over the proper manner to endorse a communiqué resulted in Paxton's arrest for ten days. On receiving the order, Paxton curbed his anger and replied simply: "The offense of Genl. Taliaferro, in abusing his power as my superior officer, I think he will find, in the opinion of all disinterested gentlemen, is a much graver offense than any I have committed." A week later, probably due to the personal intervention of Jackson, Paxton was restored to command. (The rank-conscious Taliaferro, chafing that he was not promoted to the major generalcy which his position warranted, soon asked for and received transfer from Lee's army.) [39]

With the exception of this incident, Paxton never gave Jackson any cause to regret his assignment. And both before and after the Fredericksburg Campaign, he won the friendship of his troops by his fatherly attention to their comfort and problems. He toiled unceasingly to ease the plight of the men in their quarters that bitter winter. As many furloughs were granted as military expediency would permit; and when plans were laid for a brigade chapel at Camp Winder, Paxton exempted all men from military duty who wished to help in the construction of the building.[40]

In the seven months that he commanded the Stonewall Brigade, the profane, hot-tempered, and somewhat agnostic general became —almost miraculously—a quiet and humble Christian. This transformation may have been due to the danger of battles which he now had to direct, the awe of his new position, the influence of Jackson

---

38. Casler, Stonewall Brigade, 206. On April 13, 1863, flogging was prohibited by an act of the Confederate Congress. Official Records, Ser. IV, Vol. II, 476.
39. Douglas, I Rode with Stonewall, 209; Freeman, Lee's Lieutenants, II, 504–505.
40. Charles F. Pitts, Chaplains in Gray (Nashville, 1957), 12–13.

—or a combination of these things. He became an ardent reader of the Bible, and, like Jackson, he began to write more and more of the beauty of Providence and Eternity. In the field he was never without his Testament; and from the number of conversions recorded in the camp of the Old Brigade that winter, Paxton's new-found piety must have been contagious.

:|:|:|:|:|:|:|:|:|:|:|:|:|:|:|:|:|:|:|:|:|:|:|:|:|:|:|:|:|:|:|:|:|:|:|:|:|:|:|:|:|:|:|:|:|:|:|:|:|:|:|:|:|:|:|:|:|

CHAPTER XV

CHANCELLORSVILLE HEARTACHE

The approach of spring signaled the resumption of fighting. As the men began to gather their meager possessions together in anticipation of a march, John Garibaldi of the Twenty-seventh Virginia speculated on the future in a letter to his wife:

Allthough there is a heap of talk about fighting, I think that there wouldn't be as much fighting this summer as there was last summer. there may be a fight or two here and if we whip them I think we shall [have] some tall fighting to do. . . . The furloughs have been suspended for the present and it is very likely that there will not be anymore granted untill next winter, but I hope that by that time we shall have peace and that we shall all come home to stay with our families, never to be devided any more unless by death.[1]

---

1. John Garibaldi to his wife, March 29, 1863, Garibaldi Letters. See also James A. Kibler, 33rd Regiment, to his sister, March 30, 1863, Confederate Accessions, Virginia Archives.

For a month the Valley fighters waited expectantly for the order to move forward against the Federal army, now commanded by Major General Joseph Hooker. Grim determination, with a sprinkling of forebodings, was the prevailing sentiment at Camp Winder. "Though sound in health and strength," Frank Paxton confided to his wife, "I feel that life to many of us hangs upon a slender thread." The camp grew unusually quiet, but a brigade officer assured his hometown newspaper that the men were ready for battle. "I have never seen this army so devoted to the cause as now," he said. And he added: "Originally much enthusiasm was mingled with our patriotism, and many mistook love of adventure for love of country; but the transient passions having long subsided, the pure flame of devotion to our Country, Liberty, and Honor, burns brightly upon almost every heart." [2]

In that spirit the Stonewall Brigade marched to Hamilton's Crossing on April 28, 1863. For two days it remained there under a steady rain that forced Paxton to set up his headquarters in an ambulance wagon.[3] Soon after midnight on Friday morning, May 1, the gray columns moved out in a heavy fog toward a small hamlet known as Chancellorsville. On through the night the men tramped silently, each lost in his own thoughts. At dawn the still mist that hung over the countryside parted to usher in a cloudless day. All was quiet— too quiet—and the sun beating down on the four-abreast ranks soon brought a trail of discarded overcoats and blankets. At twilight the Valley regiments bivouacked astride the plank road that ran northeastward toward dense forests and the Chancellorsville road junction. Orders to remain quiet were superfluous; the Men of Manassas knew when Jackson was planning to execute another of his stealthy flank assaults.

Throughout the morning of a cloudless May 2 the Stonewall Brigade, with the remainder of the Second Corps, eased around the right of the Union lines. Only the occasional snap of a twig or bark of a startled squirrel gave any indication that the woods were swarm-

---

2. Paxton (ed.), *Memoir*, 101; E. F. Paxton to his brother, April 13, 1863, William W. Moss Papers, Alderman Library, University of Virginia; Lexington *Gazette*, April 22, 1863.
3. Douglas, *I Rode with Stonewall*, 218.

ing with Confederates. At 3 P.M. Jackson's divisions were in position almost touching the exposed right flank of General Oliver O. Howard's XI Corps. Having been detached from the main force to guard the plank road, the Stonewall Brigade was placed in the "novel sensation of watching a running fight without taking part in it." [4]

At five o'clock Jackson struck. The woods in front of the deployed Valley units seemed to ring with the sound of cannon, musketry, and shouting men. Paxton's troops formed Jackson's anchor on the extreme right of the flanking force, and it was on them that the army pivoted for battle. For half an hour men in the brigade squirmed impatiently. When the order came to move forward and keep pace with the rest of the assaulting line, the foot cavalry raced down the dusty road and moved through abandoned Federal camps. The impoverished troops wanted badly to stop and confiscate the rich stores scattered about, but they were afraid nearby officers "might whack them over the head with their swords if they saw them plundering." [5]

By dusk the Stonewall Brigade had moved across the turnpike, taken position on the far left of Jackson's line, and faced east toward Chancellorsville, where Hooker was frantically collecting his troops to counteract this Rebel thrust. Until midnight the brigade shifted from one sector to another in an effort to solidify the left of the Confederate line. Confusion prevailed: officers tried to keep the ranks together in the underbrush and darkness, but their commands were lost in the loud shouts of men trying to find their units. At the same time, Federal cannon were firing in their direction, causing Private Casler to term it "the most terrible and destructive shelling that we were subjected to during the war." [6]

When the brigade lines were finally established, as Colonel J. H.

---

4. *Ibid.*, 221. Although the Stonewall Brigade was not engaged at this time, Randolph Barton wrote that it "was under some hot fire of shells" that slowed down the men, already weary from "a long and trying march." *Recollections*, 41.

5. Casler, *Stonewall Brigade*, 219–20. Casler added that temptation nevertheless got the best of many of the men, "and they would run their hands in some of the dead men's pockets as they hurried along, but seldom procured anything of value." On the other hand, Captain Welsh of the 27th Virginia once wrote his wife: "I can't bring myself to plundering, yet I can fight them & kill them." Bean (ed.), "A House Divided," *loc. cit.*, 414.

6. Casler, *Stonewall Brigade*, 221.

S. Funk later wrote in his report, "the men, worried and worn out by the rapid detour made that day and by a want of rations, were permitted to rest for a few brief hours." [7] But the men got little rest. Scattered volleys throughout the night made sleep impossible; moreover, Lieutenant Barton of the Thirty-third Virginia wrote, "we all knew that day-break would usher in an awful conflict." [8] Even more disturbing than the enemy guns was the shocking news that Jackson had been seriously wounded by accidental fire from one of his own regiments. This report, first heard at 9 P.M., spread through the ranks "with amazing rapidity" and created great concern among the members of the Old Brigade. [9]

The report of Jackson's wounding seemed to confirm Frank Paxton's growing apprehensions about his own safety. For several days prior to this battle, he had thought increasingly of death and had spoken of it often to his staff officers. During the lull on the night of May 2, Lieutenant Douglas went to Paxton's tent, where he found the general slumped in his chair reading his Bible with almost feverish intent. "He did not seem morbid or superstitious," Douglas later recalled, "but he spoke with earnest conviction." In unusually calm tones, Paxton asked Douglas to insure that, after the next day's fighting, his body, personal belongings, and papers were sent to his wife in Lexington. The young aide added, after leaving the commander's tent: "I was never so impressed by a conversation in my life . . . I need not say my night was a sleepless, cheerless vigil." [10]

Throughout that night Federals were heard felling trees for new earthworks. At 6 A.M. on May 3 Union batteries began pounding the Confederate positions. Shells splintered trees, ripped gaping holes in the ground, and filled the air with sulfurous fumes that half choked the crouching graycoats. Private Finley Curtis wrote dramatically: "With nerves and muscles taut, hearts wildly pounding, guns loaded, yet with not a qualm of fear, not a thought of death, we waited impatiently for orders." [11]

---

7. *Official Records*, XXV, Pt. 1, p. 1013.

8. Randolph Barton to J. G. Paxton, September 14, 1885, Paxton Papers.

9. *Southern Historical Society Papers*, XXX (1902), 117.

10. Douglas, *I Rode with Stonewall*, 224.

11. *Confederate Veteran*, XXV (1917), 304. See also *Official Records*, XXV, Pt. 1, p. 1018.

While the men stood poised, Paxton used the early morning light to read intently from his small gilded Bible. The sound of approaching conflict increased; Paxton carefully placed the Testament in his left pocket and began making last-minute inspections. He was wearing a new gray uniform that had arrived from Richmond a few days before—a gift from his wife. On his collar were the three stars of a colonel. Soon an aide from General Jeb Stuart, now commanding Jackson's corps, rode up and repeated urgent orders for Paxton to send his men forward. The Stonewall Brigade promptly moved out in battle line, with the Thirty-third and Twenty-seventh Regiments on the left, the Fifth in the center, and Fourth and Second Virginia on the right. Three hundred yards across the plank road the men came to their first obstacle: some log defenses that the Federals had hastily thrown up.

Here too the Valley troops found General Samuel McGowan's leaderless South Carolina Brigade, lying behind the logs and refusing to budge. The intensity of the Federal fire was too much even for this renowned Palmetto unit. The Virginians passed through, "saying, with no very pleasant levity," according to one of the South Carolinians, "that they would show us how to clear away a Federal line." [12] But the Virginians proceeded only one hundred yards when they became entangled in dense underbrush and swamps. Federals concealed on solid ground in their immediate front suddenly loosed a withering fire into the semi-helpless men.

For a short time it seemed as if Mother Nature had collaborated with the Yankees in the sector south of the plank road. "Nothing but the hand of God could save a man," one officer swore.[13] Confederates by the score were shot as they tried to free themselves from the boggy ground and endless vines. Colonel Edmondson of the Twenty-seventh Virginia was knocked from his horse by a shell

12. J. F. J. Caldwell, *The History of a Brigade of South Carolinians Known First as "Gregg's" and Subsequently as "McGowan's" Brigade* (Philadelphia, 1866), 80. General Dodson Ramseur, whose brigade was to the left of Paxton's, mistakenly accused the Valley men of this cowardice. *Official Records*, XXV, Pt. 1, p. 996. Although Ramseur later corrected his error (*Ibid.*, 1015), Colonel William Terry of the Stonewall Brigade went to some length to erase the temporary stigma placed on his unit. See *Southern Historical Society Papers*, XIV (1886), 364–70.
13. Bean (ed.), "A House Divided," *loc. cit.*, 413.

that mangled his left arm.[14] All the while, Paxton and Lieutenant Barton were on foot, trying desperately to reform the brigade lines. The two men were running toward another sector when Barton heard a thud. Looking back, he saw Paxton reel and fall, face down, to the ground. The general tried to raise himself with extended arms; Barton turned him over on his back. Now oblivious to the fury of battle around him, the commander groped for the breast pocket where he kept his Bible and pictures of his wife and children. Barton thought he heard him mumble "Tie up my arm," but he never was able to know for certain, for in a moment Paxton was dead.[15]

By the time Colonel Funk of the Fifth Virginia received orders from Stuart to take command of the brigade, the men had freed themselves from their entanglement and were rushing forward. For forty-five minutes they battled at close range with Federals lying behind fallen trees and in earthworks. Funk wanted to deliver a co-ordinated assault, but it was impossible. Four of the regiments were without commanders. The Second Regiment on the far right had become detached and was too far back in the woods to be of immediate use. The Fourth Virginia, which now formed the right of the brigade, could give no aid, for it had lost 160 men in the ten minutes' fighting in the swamp.[16]

As Federal reinforcements piled into the area, Funk ordered the Virginia regiments back to the breastworks where stragglers still crouched. Soon after reaching the log defenses, the brigade was reinforced by the remaining units of General George H. Anderson's division. Troops were standing in massed battle formation when the colorful Stuart rode up "in his usual happy manner." Orders were issued to fix bayonets; then came a shout from the officers: "Charge, and remember Jackson!" [17] Graycoats, oblivious to the

---

14. John Garibaldi to his wife, May 11, 1863, Garibaldi Letters. See also *Official Records*, XXV, Pt. 1, p. 1021.
15. Randolph Barton to J. G. Paxton, September 14, 1885, Paxton Papers. The assertion in Paxton (ed.), *Memoir*, 102, that the general lived for an hour is erroneous. Both Barton and Douglas, in *I Rode with Stonewall*, 225, stated that death was almost instantaneous. Paxton was interred in Lexington Cemetery, where he now rests scant yards from the tomb of his chief, Stonewall Jackson.
16. *Southern Historical Society Papers*, XIV (1886), 366.
17. *Official Records*, XXV, Pt. 1, p. 1017; Dabney, *Jackson*, 703.

perspiration streaming down dirty bodies and collecting on tattered uniforms, leaped forward and filled the smoky air with their famous Rebel yell. Two hundred yards away Federals opened up again with canister and musketry. In no time the Stonewall Brigade was chopped to pieces, yet the fragments swept forward through the dense woods. The lead elements leaped atop the breastworks and clubbed defiant Federals with musket butts as they fought their way into the trenches. By the time the main body—what was left of it —reached the works, the Federals had fled to the rear.

For three-quarters of a mile, through a storm of shot and shell, Confederates pursued Hooker's army. Many of the Southerners were so weary that they were fighting largely by instinct. "Reason lurched drunkenly," the Second Virginia's Finley Curtis later recalled. "I was worn in body, sweat-soaked, smoke-begrimed. Pungent cartridge powder plastered my lips and teeth. But my Enfield was not yet red-hot." [18]

The Stonewall Brigade soon swarmed around the Chancellor House, which had been Hooker's headquarters at the opening of the battle. Colonel Funk saw a Federal column in the rear of the house moving to flank his forces. He called quickly for a concentration against the bluecoats; yet before the Confederates could form a tight battle line, the Yankees retreated. Then, wrote Funk, "Our ranks having been greatly reduced by the severe conflict of the day, one-third of their number having fallen, entirely out of ammunition and unsupported, the brigade was of necessity forced to retire, which they did like veterans." [19]

The depleted ranks reformed behind the earthworks that they had recently captured. Details of men were sent to the ordnance wagons in the rear to bring up ammunition. At 3 P.M. the regiments moved northward again, this time on the road leading to the United States Ford. They had advanced only a short distance when Federal artillery opened fire on their ranks with canister. The men halted; Funk sent out skirmishers who reported Yankees in strength near the ford. At Funk's orders the troops wearily set up camp and remained in this forward position for the next three days.

18. *Confederate Veteran*, XXV (1917), 305.
19. *Official Records*, XXV, Pt. 1, p. 1014.

It was fortunate for the Stonewall Brigade that the battle of Chancellorsville did not last longer. In no other engagement of the war did this unit suffer as many casualties: 493 men, including the principal officers. The survivors did not aggregate a full-sized regiment.[20] Regimental losses were:

	Killed	Wounded	Missing	Total
2nd Virginia	8	58		66
4th Virginia	18	148	3	169
5th Virginia	9	111	5	125
27th Virginia	9	63	1	73
33rd Virginia	10	50		60

While it was true, as one newspaper reported, that "the old Stonewall Brigade surpassed itself and added fresh laurels to those heretofore so nobly won," equally true was the terse comment made many years later by Douglas Southall Freeman that the brigade "never was itself in full might after that battle." [21]

On the night of May 3 Lieutenant Kyd Douglas visited the wounded Jackson and recounted the events of the day's battle. Jackson wept at the report of Paxton's death; and when told of the gallant charge of the Stonewall Brigade against the Federal breastworks, the Calvinist warrior, his eyes moist, his voice quavering, replied, "It was just like them, just like them. They are a noble set of men. The name of Stonewall belongs to that brigade, not to me." [22] As the stricken Jackson was being moved to the safety of Guiney's Station, another officer mentioned the valor of the Valley fighters. Again Jackson spoke of their worthiness to share his sobriquet: "The name 'Stonewall' ought to be attached wholly to the men of the Brigade, and not to me; for it was their steadfast heroism which had earned it at First Manassas." [23]

---

20. *Ibid.*, 1015. The 4th Virginia lost 48.4 per cent of its membership. Fox, *Regimental Losses*, 557.
21. Lexington *Gazette*, May 13, 1863; Freeman, *Lee's Lieutenants*, II, 650.
22. John L. Johnson, *The University Memorial*, 349; Douglas, *I Rode with Stonewall*, 227. Dr. Hunter McGuire reported hearing Jackson say later: "The men of that brigade will be someday proud to say to their children, 'I was one of the Stonewall Brigade.' " *Southern Historical Society Papers*, XIV (1886), 158. A more dramatic account of Jackson's praise is in the Leesburg *Washingtonian*, September 29, 1865.
23. Dabney, *Jackson*, 713.

In the meantime, the remnants of the five Valley regiments spent uneasy hours at their forward position. On May 4 Captain George Bedinger of the Thirty-third Virginia wrote his wife: "To-day we are in line and throwing up breastworks. Whether we will attack or the enemy retreat further, I cannot say. I am pretty certain of more fighting. Thank God I am spared to write you this note, tho half of my little company were killed or wounded." [24] On that same day, details were sent out to bury the dead. John Casler stated that he "witnessed the most horrible sight my eyes ever beheld." In many places the shelling had been so intense that leaves on the ground caught fire. Wounded soldiers unable to crawl to safety were cremated along with their dead comrades.[25]

On May 7 the Stonewall Brigade moved back to its Hamilton's Crossing encampment. Pickets soon called truces, swapped coffee and tobacco, and even enjoyed swims together in the Rappahannock.[26] Most of the brigade lay in the open without tents, "in anticipation of anything." [27] All of the men were concerned about Jackson. Reports from Guiney's Station grew more unfavorable with each passing day. But, the soldiers reassured each other, Old Jack would pull through all right; nothing could daunt his spirit.

On Sunday morning, May 10, prayer services were held in the Stonewall Brigade camp. Divine blessings were sought for the prostrate general. Toward dusk of that warm and sunny day a courier galloped into camp; seconds later, a terse message went up and down the line. It was a short communiqué, but never in the history of the Stonewall Brigade did three words strike with such impact:

Jackson is dead.

"There is a great deal of gloom in our Brigade on account of Gen. Jackson's death," Captain Welsh of the Twenty-seventh Virginia laconically wrote his mother.[28] Many of the men expressed the con-

---

24. George R. Bedinger to his sister, May 4, 1863, Dandridge Papers.
25. Casler, *Stonewall Brigade*, 229.   26. *Ibid.*, 230.
27. John Garibaldi to his wife, May 9, 1863, Garibaldi Letters.
28. Bean (ed.), "A House Divided," *loc. cit.*, 414.

viction that the Southern cause was now lost.[29] On the day after Jackson's death, and at the request of the regimental officers, Captain Kyd Douglas went to Robert E. Lee and asked that the Old Brigade be appointed honor guard for the remains. Lee listened attentively as the young officer described in detail the great love the members of the Valley brigade had for their first commander. Then Lee, grief-stricken himself at the loss, replied painfully:

I am confident that no one can feel the loss of General Jackson as deeply as I do; for no one has the same reason. I feel the loss of a good friend and a valuable officer. So far as I can see it personally, the death of General Jackson has been to us an irreparable loss; to himself, without doubt, it is an equal gain. I can fully appreciate the feelings of the members of his Brigade. They have reason to be proud of him, as he was proud of them. To the tried men of the Brigade, he was not only a General but a friend. They have been with him and true to him from the beginning of the war.

I should be glad, if practicable, to grant any request they might make which had for its object to show their regard for their lost General; and I am only sorry that the situation of affairs will not justify me in permitting them to go not only to Richmond with the corpse but to his home in Lexington that they might see it deposited in its last resting place. But it may not be. I have people over the river who are again showing signs of movement, and it is so necessary for me to be on hand, that I cannot leave my headquarters long enough to ride to Guiney's depot to pay to my dear friend and General the poor tribute of seeing his body placed upon the cars.

I do not see that I can let a Brigade of tried men leave the army at such a time. I have directed that a detail discretionary with Major General A. P. Hill be made from each Regiment of the Brigade to escort the body from the house in which he died to the cars, and, also have telegraphed to General Elzy at Richmond to receive the corpse with the military, and to show all the respect due his rank and character. His friends of the Stonewall Brigade may be assured that their General will receive all the honor practicable.

General Jackson, when living, never allowed his feelings for friends or home to interfere with his duty; so now he would not rest the quieter in his grave could he know that even his old Brigade had left the presence of the enemy for the purpose of seeing him buried. Go back to them, Captain, and tell them what I have said. Tell them how I sympathize with them and appreciate the honorable feelings which prompted their

---

29. See, for example, Opie, *Rebel Cavalryman*, 138; Casler, *Stonewall Brigade*, 231.

request; and say to them, deeply as we all lament the death of their General, and our friend, yet, if his body only is to be buried, and if his spirit still remains to actuate his old Brigade, his Corps, and the whole army, and to make us more watchful and determined in our cause, we have reason to hope that his loss may be to us in the end, as it is to himself now, a great gain.[30]

The Stonewall Brigade as a whole was disheartened by Lee's denial of their request, but those members designated as a funeral escort hastily cleaned themselves up and waited for the order to leave for Guiney's Station. For hours they stood impatiently; then the order was mysteriously countermanded and they were told to remain in camp. Years later, and still embittered, John Casler of the Thirty-third Virginia expressed the reaction of the brigade: "We all thought very hard of it, for we wished to show our respect for our beloved commander, and gaze on his face once more; but that privilege was denied us. His only escort were some doctors and officials who never saw him in battle, while the men who had followed him from Harper's Ferry to Chancellorsville had to lay idly in camp." [31]

Yet, by various and questionable means, Stonewall Brigade members got to Richmond. A Confederate soldier who witnessed the funeral procession recorded a moving scene: "To the slow wail of the dead march Jackson's old veterans who were in the city at the time followed the battle-steed as they had done so many times before; and as they walked they wept like children, strong men as they were. We watched them as they passed, wondering at the

---

30. Lee's remarks are a compilation from the journals of two Stonewall Brigade members. One version is in the autograph book of Lieutenant Andrew W. Varner, 27th Virginia, in the Alderman Library of the University of Virginia. Varner penned his account while imprisoned at Johnson's Island, Ohio. The other account, also in an autograph book, was written by Lieutenant Charles C. Burks of the 4th Virginia during his stay at Fort Delaware. This journal is in the possession of Mrs. A. D. DePriest, Buena Vista, Va. Both men may have received their versions from Kyd Douglas, who was imprisoned at Johnson's Island and Fort Delaware. His shorter account of Lee's remarks is in *I Rode with Stonewall*, 228–29. For the sake of clarity, necessary spelling and punctuation have been added to the quotation.
31. Casler, *Stonewall Brigade*, 223. In the second edition of this study (Girard, Kan., 1906), Casler's grammar is much more polished.

devotion, the indescribable enthusiasm with which this great soldier inspired his troops." [32]

In the brigade camp at Hamilton's Crossing a collection was taken to finance the construction of a monument over Jackson's grave. Less than two weeks later, $5,688 had been obtained; by month's end the figure had reached $6,000.[33] On May 16 the brigade officers also adopted resolutions bemoaning Jackson's loss and dedicating themselves anew to the Confederate cause. And in closing they petitioned the President officially to designate their unit as the Stonewall Brigade.[34] On May 30, 1863, the War Department granted their request, and the Stonewall Brigade thus became the only large unit in the Confederate Army to have a sanctioned nickname.[35]

---

32. Hunter, *Johnny Reb and Billy Yank*, 364.
33. Douglas, *I Rode with Stonewall*, 239; Staunton *Vindicator*, May 6, 1864. See also *Confederate Veteran*, XXVIII (1920), 47.
34. Freeman, in *Lee's Lieutenants*, II, 638, erroneously stated that the petition was drawn up before Jackson's death. The original document, clearly dated May 16, 1863, is in the Robert L. Dabney Papers, Virginia Archives. The committee named to draw up the petition was composed of Colonel Funk of the 5th Virginia, Lieutenant Colonel Colston of the 2nd, Major Terry of the 4th, Captain Frazer of the 27th, and Captain Bedinger of the 33rd. Lexington *Gazette*, June 3, 1863.
35. *Official Records*, XXV, Pt. 2, p. 840; Staunton *Vindicator*, June 5, 1863.

CHAPTER XVI

"THE WHOLE CAMPAIGN
WAS A BLUNDER"

Jackson's death stirred a reaffirmation of faith among the members of the Old Brigade. On May 19, 1863, at "Camp Paxton" near Hamilton's Crossing, 151 Valley veterans formed a Christian association "for the promotion of vital godliness in the brigade." Headed by Chaplain L. C. Vass of the Twenty-seventh Virginia, the group met every other Saturday night for worship and meditation. Each man swore to be a member in good standing of some recognized church, to be of high moral character, and to refrain from drinking, gambling, and all sins enumerated in the Ten Commandments.[1]

---

1. W. Harrison Daniel, "The Christian Association: A Religious Society in the Army of Northern Virginia," *Virginia Magazine of History and Biography*, LXIX (1961), 94–100.

While the majority of the Stonewall Brigade rededicated themselves to the principles by which Jackson had lived, a complete reorganization took place in the Second Corps of the Army of Northern Virginia. Appointed to fill the large gap in corps command left by the death of Old Jack was General Richard S. Ewell. He too had succumbed to Jackson's piety and had changed from a caustic, godless officer into a subdued, God-fearing commander. Yet he was ever a character, and the men loved him for his lisp and unpredictable eccentricities. The new divisional commander was a Virginian, General Edward Johnson. Large and rough-looking, with a personality as fiery as his speech, he was known affectionately to Confederate soldiers as "Old Allegheny." The name originated at the battle of McDowell where, rushing forward and roaring like a bull, Johnson stopped a bullet that shattered his ankle. He still hobbled badly on a cane, and he became adept at using it to emphasize a point. A rather uncouth manner, plus an affection in one eye that made him wink unceasingly, tended to have an adverse effect on women—particularly those to whom he was first introduced. Nevertheless, Jackson thought highly of Johnson, which was enough to facilitate promotion to major general and command of a division.

Replacing Frank Paxton, however, proved a difficult task. In his official report Lee praised Paxton's "conspicuous conduct" and leadership at Chancellorsville. A member of the Rockbridge Artillery expressed the opinion of many Valley soldiers when he called him "the best specimen of Scotch-Irish soldier given by Rockbridge [County] to our cause," and Valley newspapers went to great lengths to emphasize his virtues of character and leadership.[2] Despite its skeleton ranks, the Stonewall Brigade was a proud unit and would not settle for anything less than a first-rate commander. Moreover, both officers and men in the five Valley regiments felt that Paxton's successor should come from the eligible officers of the brigade, all of whom had more than demonstrated proficiency in leadership.

When the appointment went instead to Colonel James A.

---

2. *Official Records,* XXV, Pt. 1, p. 803; Poague, *Gunner,* 66; Lexington *Gazette,* May 14, June 3, 1863.

Walker, commanding Jubal Early's brigade, indignation and hostility poured forth to Lee and Walker (particularly the former, since the brigade still smoldered at being denied permission to act as escort for Jackson's body). Outraged—in spite of the fact that Walker's first military service was with the Old Brigade—all five regimental commanders promptly resigned. In their collective resignations they stated that any of three men, including Sandie Pendleton of the brigade staff, would have been acceptable.[3] Lee, with characteristic tact and calm, declined to accept the resignations and persuaded the five officers to remain with the brigade, and under Walker.

Sturdy and doughty James Alexander Walker was born in Augusta County, Virginia, September 27, 1833, of good Scotch-Irish stock. He entered the Virginia Military Institute in 1848 and quickly showed great promise as a future army officer. However, in his senior year the impetuous youth became involved in a classroom disturbance and was ordered from the room by none other than Professor T. J. Jackson. Feeling himself wronged and insulted, Walker retorted hotly, was shouted down by Jackson, and then brashly asked the professor for satisfaction on the field of honor. Jackson debated the question for a while; before he could render his decision, Walker was court-martialed and expelled.[4]

For eighteen months Walker served as a terrain engineer, principally for the Chesapeake & Ohio Railroad. He then began the study of law, first under the noted John B. Baldwin of Staunton and then under John R. Minor at the University of Virginia. A law degree and marriage to Sarah A. Poague both came in 1854. Walker then moved to Newborn in Pulaski County and resided there until the outbreak of war. He was elected county commonwealth attorney in 1857.

Following John Brown's raid, Walker raised a militia company

---

3. The identity of the other two preferences is unknown. Lee (ed.), *Pendleton*, 273. William Couper, in his *One Hundred Years at V. M. I.*, III, 178–79, attributed the resignations of the officers to a reorganization of the army that took place after Chancellorsville.

4. J. William Jones stated that Walker was at the head of his class when dismissed. *Southern Historical Society Papers*, IX (1881), 92. By order of VMI's Board of Visitors, a degree was presented to Walker after the war.

which assumed the name Pulaski Guards. As their captain he molded the men into such an efficient unit that they were one of the first companies summoned to duty when Virginia seceded. The Pulaski Guards were designated Company C, Fourth Virginia—and assigned to Walker's old nemesis, Professor Jackson. Apparently no animosity existed between the two men after April, 1861. Walker served obediently and displayed such conspicuous gallantry in the opening campaigns that he was soon promoted to lieutenant colonel and transferred in June, 1861, to A. P. Hill's Thirteenth Virginia. The following March, when Hill was promoted to brigadier general, Walker was elevated to colonel and given command of the regiment.

Walker's reputation soared in the ensuing months. He and his regiment seemed to be in the thick of every fight of which they were a part. At Gaines' Mill his triumphant assault was so violent that when informed of the losses in his regiment, Walker slumped to the ground and wept openly. He was credited with saving the day when Jackson's line cracked at Cedar Run.[5] At Sharpsburg, while commanding Trimble's brigade temporarily, Walker was wounded, his horse was killed, and his brigade suffered a loss of 280 men (including three of the four regimental colonels) out of less than 700 men engaged.[6] Small wonder that both Early and Ewell strongly recommended his promotion to brigadier. Early called attention to Walker's "most conspicuous gallantry and good conduct" in battle and added that his bravery gave him more claims for promotion than any other colonel in the Confederate armies.[7]

Command of the Stonewall Brigade came to Walker on May 19, 1863.[8] If he was disturbed by the cold reception accorded him by this famous unit, Walker gave no outward sign of it. Indeed, it was hard to discern anything about him save the air of a determined fighter. Bismarckian in appearance, he had a large mustache that compensated well for his lack of beard and sparsity of hair. He was

---

5. See *Confederate Veteran*, X (1902), 36.
6. *Official Records*, XIX, Pt. 1, pp. 806, 968.
7. J. A. Early to James A. Seddon, January 23, 1863, Walker's personal file, War Records Group, National Archives. Lee, in his endorsement of the recommendation, said he knew of no one more deserving of brigadiership.
8. *Official Records*, XXV, Pt. 2, p. 809.

tall and muscular, with small, penetrating eyes that peered out from beneath bushy brows. An extrovert in almost every sense, he relished a good-sized drink, liked to play practical jokes, and enjoyed life in general, especially if a fight of some kind seemed likely. Brigade members soon warmed to him, and by the end of the first month in command he was affectionately called "Stonewall Jim." [9]

In spite of grief over the death of Jackson and loss of so many comrades at Chancellorsville, the Valley veterans enjoyed a pleasant stay at Camp Paxton. "We are getting rations at present," the Twenty-seventh Virginia's John Welsh wrote. "They have increased our ration of meat to half a pound. Everything is quiet here, but I can't say how long it will be." [10] Speculation was widespread as to when and where the enemy would next move. One private ventured the opinion: "That we are going to commence an active campaign is the belief of every body in the army, and it may be that we will take another trip into Maryland before the summer shall end." [11]

On June 8 Lee's army started for Culpeper. Ewell's corps led the way, with the Stonewall Brigade fourth in line. The men reached Culpeper late on the ninth and encamped there for two days. Except in a brief cavalry skirmish, no Federals had been encountered. On Thursday, June 11, with Ewell's corps still in the van, the army filed through Chester Gap and down to Front Royal. The Stonewall Brigade bivouacked north of town on the night of the twelfth. The men hastily began preparing three days' rations, for they now knew their destination. They were making a second invasion of the North via the Valley turnpike. One major obstacle blocked their path: General Robert Milroy had an estimated 6,000 to 8,000 Federal troops in the vicinity of Winchester. Ewell planned to envelop this division before it could escape and rejoin Hooker's army.

Johnson and Early left for Winchester with their eight brigades at four o'clock the following morning. Moving northwestward, the two divisions reached the outskirts of town at noon. Early continued moving to the left to get in battle position west of the city.

9. *Southern Historical Society Papers*, XX (1892), 309.
10. Bean (ed.), "A House Divided," *loc. cit.*, 415.
11. John Garibaldi to his wife, June 3, 1863, Garibaldi Letters.

Walker, after dispatching the Second Virginia as skirmishers, posted the remainder of the Stonewall Brigade astride the Front Royal road to await the arrival of Ewell's corps. The Valley regiments stacked arms and spent a restless night in a clover field just to the north of the road.

On the following morning, while Early broke a surprised Milroy's defenses west of Winchester, Walker's and General George Steuart's brigades eased forward from the east. The Fifth Virginia scaled a range of hills overlooking Winchester and secured the ridges after a brief skirmish with Federal pickets. The chief casualty of this contest was Colonel H. J. Williams, the commander of the Fifth, who fell seriously wounded from a badly gashed thigh.[12] That night Walker ordered his brigade to continue moving slowly toward the town. In the meantime, Ewell, aware that Milroy's only chance of escape was by the turnpike north of town, had laid plans to sever that route. He ordered Johnson to take his division to Stephenson's Depot, four miles from Winchester, and to block Milroy from retiring to either Martinsburg or Harpers Ferry. At 9 P.M. Old Allegheny wrote a rash of letters and left promptly—too promptly, for the courier sent to order Walker's men into motion got lost in the darkness trying to follow the hastily written directions. Consequently, the Stonewall Brigade did not leave for Stephenson's Depot until midnight.

The sky was just beginning to gray when the Valley troops approached the road junction. Suddenly the sharp crack of musketry split the early morning air. Walker ordered his men forward in quick-time, and the troops began jogging in columns of four toward the sound of firing. Soon Captain Kyd Douglas rode up and informed Walker of the situation: Johnson had fallen upon Milroy's whole division in retreat. The Confederates, however, were out of ammunition and were being flanked on both sides. Help was urgently needed.[13] Walker's response was to hasten his men onward. The Men of Manassas gave a tremendous Rebel yell, and the whole column sped forward. With the Second and Fifth Virginia in the

---

12. Major James W. Newton then assumed temporary command of the regiment. *Official Records,* XXVII, Pt. 2, pp. 516, 524.

13. *Ibid.,* 502, 517; *Confederate Veteran,* XXIX (1921), 44.

lead, the brigade pushed across open fields, past the woods where Steuart's troops were holding on tenaciously, and then advanced northward across the Valley Pike.

Smoke and fog restricted visibility to a few feet. As Walker led the men farther, he saw a large group of soldiers half hidden in the mist ahead. The lead columns of the Stonewall Brigade immediately opened fire, but Walker shouted for them to stop. He then rode forward and inquired in a loud voice to what unit the soldiers belonged. When no answer came, he was certain that they were Federals. He quickly rode back to his men and ordered them to open fire. The Confederates delivered a close-range volley into the Federals, then leaped forward with another Rebel yell. This broke Milroy's flank movement and "saved the position," one soldier wrote. General Johnson himself stated that "nothing could have been more timely than the arrival of the Stonewall Brigade." [14]

Walker's men pushed the Federals back into the woods as Johnson's whole division now rushed forward. The blue defenses collapsed; Federals began surrendering in companies and squads. When it became apparent that all escape routes were closed, Milroy's whole division, with the exception of the General himself and 300 cavalrymen, laid down their arms. The Stonewall Brigade captured parts of six regiments, many of whom had stacked their muskets and were awaiting their captors. Over 800 Federals surrendered to the brigade; more than 2,000 fell into Johnson's hands. All this was accomplished by the Valley brigade at a loss of 3 killed, 16 wounded, and 19 missing. Private Garibaldi of the Twenty-seventh Virginia boasted: "This was the cheapest victory [that] ever was achieved," and Captain John Welsh of the same regiment added: "We took more prisoners than we had men in our Brigade." [15]

A fatigued and dusty Confederate army bivouacked in the fields

---

14. McKim, A Soldier's Recollections, 150; Official Records, XXVII, Pt. 2, p. 502.
15. John Garibaldi to his wife, June 16, 1863, Garibaldi Letters; Bean (ed.), "A House Divided," loc. cit., 417. The Stonewall Brigade captured six stands of colors. Walker gave each regiment one flag and kept one for himself. Casler, Stonewall Brigade, 240. The Federal regiments that surrendered to Walker's troops were the 5th Maryland, 12th West Virginia, 18th Connecticut, 87th Pennsylvania, 122nd Ohio, and 123rd Ohio. Official Records, XXVII, Pt. 2, pp. 503, 518, 520.

surrounding Winchester. Several of the regiments, including those in the Stonewall Brigade, were permitted to march into the town where, since dawn, townspeople had lined the streets in anticipation of seeing friends and relatives. As the marching column swung down the main street of Winchester, Mrs. McDonald recorded joyfully in her diary that "with one accord" the civilians broke into a lusty chorus of "The Bonnie Blue Flag." "The [regimental] bands all stopped, and the troops stood still till they had finished, and then their shouts rent the air, caps were waved, and hurrahs resounded." [16]

Winchester was the scene of wild celebrations that night as townspeople reveled in their "liberation" from the Federals and troops rejoiced "in another 'glorious Victory,' which, to use our good old chieftain's expression, God has given us." [17] At eleven o'clock the following morning the rejuvenated foot cavalry started northward with Ewell's Second Corps. Crossing the Potomac at Shepherdstown, the men moved slowly on Sharpsburg. On the twenty-third the Stonewall Brigade bivouacked near the riddled Dunkard church so familiar to most of the Valley men. The troops filed through Hagerstown the following day and were subjected there to loud jeers from the citizenry. One woman, leaning precariously from her upstairs window, taunted the Rebels for their shabby uniforms. As the Thirty-third Virginia passed, one large Irishman (probably of the Emerald Guards) squinted up at her and replied with a familiar retort: "Bejabbers, lady, we always put on our dirty clothes when we go hog-killing!" [18]

Slowly the long gray lines moved into Pennsylvania and through Greencastle and Chambersburg. Many of the soldiers wanted to take advantage of the slow pace to plunder nearby farms, but watchful officers managed to keep most of them in place. Nevertheless, John Casler wrote, the graycoats stripped ripe cherries from trees alongside the road to such an extent that nothing remained "but the trunks." [19] On June 27 the Stonewall Brigade reached Carlisle Barracks, its northernmost point of thrust; three days later it doubled

---

16. McDonald, *Diary*, 174–75.
17. George Bedinger to his sister, June 16, 1863, Dandridge Papers.
18. Casler, *Stonewall Brigade*, 247.   19. *Ibid.*

back to Fayetteville and bivouacked in anticipation of an eastward march on the following morning. So far no Federals had been encountered, but the Valley men sensed that they were gathering somewhere to the east, perhaps at Frederick, Emmitsburg—or Gettysburg.

At noon on Wednesday, July 1, the brigade moved eastward with the Stonewall Division. The Confederates marched down the road at a rapid pace, now that many of them had confiscated new shoes from Federal prisoners whom a part of Early's brigade was escorting to Virginia. (When the prisoners passed his troops, General Johnson personally ordered the Federals to remove their shoes. They could get shoes easier than could his men, he said; besides, his Confederates had work to do.) [20]

Just as the gray columns were trudging through South Mountain, Colonel Sir Arthur J. L. Fremantle rode up beside the Valley regiments. Members of the Stonewall Brigade called out to this noted British officer and inquired if the general they saw up front was really "Old Peter" Longstreet. When Fremantle replied in the affirmative, many of the men ran ahead to get a better look at the famous general. Fremantle himself was a little surprised at Jackson's famous infantrymen. In writing of Johnson's division he commented: "Among them I saw, for the first time, the celebrated 'Stonewall' Brigade, formerly commanded by Jackson. In appearance the men differ little from other Confederate soldiers, except, perhaps, that the brigade contains more elderly men and fewer boys." [21]

Throughout the hot afternoon the brigade struggled with the rest of the Second Corps to get through the dust to Gettysburg, where intense firing indicated that a great battle had developed. Longstreet's wagons, and the slow marching of the columns in front, subjected the Stonewall Brigade and other units in the rear to severe dust. [22] Night was descending when the Valley regiments finally passed through Gettysburg and reached their stopping point a mile

---

20. *Ibid.*, 253.
21. Arthur J. L. Fremantle, *Three Months in the Southern States* (New York, 1864), 252.
22. *Official Records*, XXVII, Pt. 2, pp. 503, 518, 530.

to the east of town on the Hanover road. They had marched twenty-five miles that day, but, a member of the Twenty-seventh Virginia wrote, they were "eager for the fray." [23]

Instead of going into action in true "Jackson fashion," the troops were ordered to bivouac on the extreme Confederate left astride the Hanover road and near a commanding eminence known as Culp's Hill. Grumbling in the Stonewall Brigade was unconcealed. As Private J. N. Small of the Second Virginia put it, "Jackson would have kept us going until we reached the heights." Throughout the night, around every campfire, the Valley men asked the same questions: "What are we doing here?" "What is the delay?" "Why not keep going, as we used to do when Old Jack was with us?" [24]

The following morning the Valley troops lay impatiently in position on the left of the line. Hour after hour passed without the signal to assault what Old Allegheny termed "a rugged and rocky mountain, heavily timbered and difficult of ascent." [25] One man in the Second Virginia was very familiar with Culp's Hill. Certainly he should have been, for his name was Wesley Culp, the hill was part of his family's estate, and he had grown up playing among the trees and boulders of the ridge.

Desultory firing continued until 4 P.M. Several Stonewall Brigade members made the most of the inactivity by plundering food from abandoned farmhouses nearby. [26] By six o'clock, however, the men of the brigade had taken such a pounding from sharp-shooters concealed in the woods to their front that Walker dispatched the Second Virginia to clear the area. Colonel John Nadenbousch led his spirited regiment in a dash that routed the bluecoats from the timber and sent them running back

---

23. Edward M. Daniel (ed.), *Speeches and Orations of John Warwick Daniel* (Lynchburg, Va., 1911), 82.
24. Charlestown *Spirit of Jefferson*, July 9, 1913. As the Stonewall Brigade's actions that day were in no way responsible for Ewell's failure to assault Culp's Hill late in the afternoon, no discussion is given to the long-standing controversy of whether or not his lack of aggressiveness pre-doomed the Gettysburg campaign. Examples of the various opinions of his conduct may be found in Freeman, *Lee's Lieutenants*, III, 171–72; Kenneth P. Williams, *Lincoln Finds A General* (New York, 1949–59), II, 724–29.
25. *Official Records*, XXVII, Pt. 2, p. 504.
26. Casler, *Stonewall Brigade*, 255, 257.

across an open field. Three men were wounded when Federal artillery, covering the withdrawal of their infantry, opened fire on the Confederates and drove them back into the cover of the woods.[27]

While the Second Regiment was busily engaged in dislodging the Federals from the woods, General Johnson received an order for his whole division to advance against Culp's Hill. As it was nearly sundown, the assault had to be made quickly. Johnson immediately directed the three brigades of George Steuart, J. M. Jones, and Francis Nicholls (under Colonel J. M. Williams) to move out against the wooded and rocky hill. Walker was ordered to bring the Stonewall Brigade into action as soon as possible.

Although he had been expelled from the Virginia Military Institute, Walker possessed a keen military mind. He reasoned quickly that if he joined the division in the assault, he would expose the Confederate left flank and rear to attack. Moreover, Walker wrote, "as our movement must have been made in full view of the enemy, I deemed it prudent to hold my position until after dark, which I did." At 8 P.M. he withdrew his skirmishers, left a picket to guard the Hanover road, and rejoined Johnson.[28]

Johnson is often criticized for the seemingly haphazard way in which he assaulted the hill on the evening of July 2. Rather than launch an attack all along the eastern face of the hill, he fell prey to McClellan's "Sharpsburg disease" and sent his men in one brigade after another. In reality, General George G. Meade had almost stripped the hill of its defenders to counteract Longstreet's assault at the Round Tops. Johnson did not know this, of course, and stopped the assault largely because of darkness and ignorance of the terrain. One Confederate soldier wrote of Johnson's action: "This was certainly a case of a wrong man in the wrong place." [29]

In any event, by the time the Stonewall Brigade reached Johnson, his three brigades were valiantly trying to hold a line at the base of the hill. Flashes of musketry split the darkness; rocks tumbled down from the Federal position atop the ridge. But the graycoats hung on doggedly. Walker posted his brigade behind George Steuart's unit

27. *Official Records*, XXVII, Pt. 2, p. 521.   28. *Ibid.*, 518–19.
29. Hunter, *Johnny Reb and Billy Yank*, 405.

on the extreme left. Jones's men composed Johnson's center, and Nicholls' brigade formed the right, facing southward.

At 4 A.M., just as daylight of July 3 began to creep over the eastern hills, the battle resumed. Johnson's whole line swept up the slope, was checked and then thrown back. The Federals counter-attacked in an effort to turn the Confederate left. At this point Walker answered Steuart's plea for help. The Stonewall Brigade rushed into action with its Rebel yell, but found itself confronting the bulk of General Henry Slocum's XII Corps, reinforced by General James Wadsworth's division of Abner Doubleday's I Corps. For five hours the Valley men tried desperately to break the Federal line on Culp's Hill, but to no avail. Sheer weight of numbers and a penetrating fire from above tore the gallant regiments to pieces. The famous student company of the Fourth Regiment, the Liberty Hall Volunteers, ran out of ammunition far up the hill as bluecoats assailed it on three sides. Of its twenty-one members, only three escaped; the remainder surrendered rather than die uselessly.[30]

Other members of the Stonewall Brigade picked up muskets and cartridge boxes from fallen comrades in order to continue the struggle. The Fourth Virginia fell back for lack of bullets; the Fifth Regiment, now under Colonel Funk, raced over to its aid, but their small numbers were no match for the hordes of Yankees who poured a destructive fire into graycoats as they inched up the rocky slope. The Second Virginia far on the left was pinned down among the rocks. The Twenty-seventh met a similar fate, and a portion of the Thirty-third, to its right, was cut off and forced to surrender.

At 9 A.M. Walker ordered the brigade to retire to the cover of Benner's Hill, one hundred yards to the northeast. There the men cleaned their guns, ate what rations they had, and refilled cartridge boxes from nearby ordnance wagons. An hour later Johnson directed the Stonewall Brigade to move to the right of the line between the units of Jones and Nicholls, both of which were still fighting desperately. The result, Walker wrote, was "equally bad success." Hardly had his regiments reached their position when Federal guns delivered "a murderous and enfilading fire" into their

---

30. *Official Records*, XXVII, Pt. 1, p. 468; Lexington *Gazette*, July 15, 1863.

ranks. For forty-five minutes the troops were raked by canister and musketry; Walker, seeing "it was a useless sacrifice of life to keep them longer under so galling a fire," ordered the shattered units back to Benner's Hill.[31]

Again Stonewall Jim reformed the pitiful remnant of his brigade. Just before noon Johnson sent the order for a third assault. In a mass display of courage, the Valley men swept forward across the field, reached the base of the hill, and broke through the first line of Federal earthworks. For a moment the men wavered, as Yankees loosed a hail of bullets into their ranks. Captain William Randolph of the Second Virginia suddenly leaped atop the earthen works and shouted for the Stonewall Brigade to follow him. A handful of brave men answered his call and were shot down only a few feet from the trenches from which they advanced.[32]

The entire brigade made one final effort to rush the hilltop. It was valiant but vain. Several companies of the Thirty-third Virginia were trapped by counterattacking Federals. Captain George Bedinger was among those killed; the remainder were captured. Major William Terry of the Fourth Virginia, Walker wrote, "gallantly led his regiment almost to the second breastwork of the enemy, and only retired after losing three-fourths of his command." [33] The Second, Fifth, and Twenty-seventh Regiments could make no headway, and were butchered for trying to do so.

General John Geary, commanding one of the divisions in the Federal XII Corps, wrote: "Large numbers of Confederates crawled under our breastworks and begged to be taken as prisoners. Among these were many of the celebrated 'Stonewall Brigade,' who, when ordered for the last time to charge upon General [George] Greene's breastworks, advanced until they met our terrible fire, and then, throwing down their arms, rushed in with white flags, handkerchiefs, and even pieces of white paper, in preference to meeting again that fire which was certain destruction." [34]

For the third time in seven hours, Walker was forced to order a

---

31. *Official Records*, XXVII, Pt. 2, pp. 519, 526.
32. Walker, *VMI Memorial*, 553–54.
33. *Official Records*, XXVII, Pt. 2, p. 519.
34. *Confederate Veteran*, XXXII (1924), 17.

withdrawal. The Stonewall Brigade fell back to Benner's Hill, too exhausted and too depleted to continue. The fight for Culp's Hill ended. Johnson's division had suffered over 1,820 casualties. Of 1,450 men in the Stonewall Brigade, 35 were dead, 208 were wounded, and 87 were missing and presumably prisoners.[35] The Twenty-seventh Regiment lost 47 of 129 members, including Captain John Welsh, who died after the battle from a gangrenous leg wound.[36]

And somewhere amid the dead sprawled on the rocky slopes of Culp's Hill was a youth who died within sight of his home: Private Wesley Culp, Company B, Second Virginia.[37]

That afternoon, during the inactivity on the Confederate left, two officers in the First Maryland visited the Stonewall Brigade in quest of food. From Walker they were able to procure two stale biscuits, which was all the food he had. While the officers were conversing, a Dutch prisoner from a Pennsylvania unit was brought to the headquarters tent. The only reply that he would give to questions was that he belonged to the "Oonan" army. Walker turned to one of the Maryland officers and said angrily, "It is too bad to think that such men as we have around us should be butchered by the miserable mercenary devils of which this is a fair specimen. Sometimes I am half inclined to show the wretches no quarter. Take the creature to the rear." [38]

That night was warm and still. No campfires were permitted, so the troops lay on the grass atop Seminary Ridge northwest of town

---

35. *Official Records*, XXVII, Pt. 2, p. 506; Battlefield Marker: "Walker's Brigade," Culp's Hill; *Battles and Leaders*, III, 438. Cf. *Official Records*, XXVII, Pt. 2, p. 286. The total number of men given for the Stonewall Brigade is probably too high, since barely 300 of its members survived the hell of Chancellorsville.

36. Bean (ed.), "A House Divided," *loc. cit.*, 418. Even in the ferociousness of the assaults that day, blue and gray found time for compassion. At Spangler's Spring— declared an unofficial truce area by thirsty soldiers of both sides—a badly wounded Virginian was given a cup of water by bluecoats. As he sipped the refreshing liqud, the Confederate soldier looked up at his enemy befrienders and said with feeling: "You uns have been right kind to we uns." *Sketches of War History, 1861–1865: Papers Read before the Ohio Commandery . . .* (Cincinnati, 1888–90), II, 40.

37. Douglas, in *I Rode with Stonewall*, 251, erred in stating that Private Culp was subsequently borne a short distance to the family cemetery. His body was never found. Testimony of Joseph Rosentcll, Gettysburg National Museum.

38. Goldsborough, *Maryland Line*, 142–44.

and discussed their condition. Word had reached them of the failure of Pickett's charge. Doubtless they had also heard of the death
of General Richard Garnett, their second commander, who fell a
few feet from the Union breastworks. Dejection clouded all conversation. Many of the men felt that defeat came from lost op-
portunities. A former member of the Fifth Virginia stated bluntly:
"The plain truth and incontestable solution of the matter is this:
Lee blundered; Stuart blundered; Longstreet, Ewell and Pickett
blundered; the whole difference being, some of them blundered
forward and others blundered backwards. The whole campaign was
a blunder." [39]

Throughout the following day the men stood in readiness for a
Federal counterattack. According to Johnson, the troops hoped
"that the enemy would give us battle on ground of our own selec-
tion." [40] This was probably a reflective boast, since Lee's whole
army had taken a severe pounding in the three-day struggle. Moreover, the retreat to Virginia began at ten o'clock on the night of
July 4. The columns moved slowly toward Hagerstown "in a violent
storm of rain and for two days suffered on account of the inclem-
ency of the weather." [41] On July 14 the Stonewall Brigade crossed
the Potomac at Martinsburg and encamped for a short period at
Darkesville, near the scene of its first victory at Falling Waters, long
long ago.

---

39. Opie, *Rebel Cavalryman*, 167.   40. *Official Records*, XXVII, Pt. 2, p. 505.
41. Regimental Returns, 5th Virginia, Company I, July–August, 1863, War Record
Group 109, National Archives.

CHAPTER XVII

SLAUGHTER AT SPOTSYLVANIA

Many of the men took the opportunity during this rest period to write the homefolk of their experiences. Private Garibaldi, for example, gave the following report on Northern farmers:

The people of Pennsylvania treated us very kindly but I think it was only from their teeth out. When we went to their houses they gave us plenty to eat of everything they had . . . The generality of the people haven't got more than eighty acres of land and they have it in highest state of cultivation and living like princes almost. They seem to be very much unconcerned about the war. Very seldom they see a soldier, and they hardly know what war is, but if the war was to be careed on there as long as it was careed on in Virginia they would learn the effects of it, and perhaps would be willing to make peace like we are.[1]

---

1. John Garibaldi to his wife, July 19, 1863, Garibaldi Letters.

The Stonewall Brigade crossed the Blue Ridge through Thomason's Gap on July 18 and moved to Orange Court House, where, early in August, it encamped astride the Plank Road near President James Madison's home, "Montpelier." The weather continued hot and dry, yet the Gettysburg survivors had little to do but serve on picket duty, lie idly in camp, and wait for recruits to fill some of the gaps in the ranks. Newspapers throughout the Valley were urging men to join the brigade and "help continue its reputation." [2] The veterans of the Valley regiments, on the other hand, had little enthusiasm for a continuation of the war. As John Garibaldi wrote to his wife: "It is the general belief that the war will be over by next spring and that we shall come home. I wish I was at home now and [could] be with you for I am getting tired of this war and would like to come home to see you!" [3]

The Valley regiments left camp on September 7 and marched to Morton's Ford, where they remained on guard duty for three weeks. Many of the companies had to build earthworks along the Rapidan, and few of the men appreciated this duty. "I don't expect that it will do much good," Garibaldi philosophized, "for the yankees never did attack us in our fortifications yet. Wherever we fortify in one place, they go and attack us in another." [4] Early in October, Walker took part of his men on a 160-mile expedition to Bristoe Station to tear up the Orange and Alexandria Railroad from Bristoe to the Rappahannock. When the task was accomplished, the detachment encamped in the vicinity of Brandy Station.

During this period the Stonewall Brigade was involved in but one small engagement. On October 26, while carrying off a large quantity of railroad iron from Bealton Station, portions of the Fourth and Fifth Regiments were surprised by Federal cavalry. The Confederates "whipped superior numbers and carried off the iron," one newspaper reported, but at a cost of two killed, twelve wounded and fourteen missing. [5] Colonel John Funk of the Fifth Virginia was in command of the Confederate raiding force. According to one

2. Lexington *Gazette*, August 12, 1863.
3. John Garibaldi to his wife, August 4, 1863, Garibaldi Letters.
4. *Ibid.*, September 25, 1863.
5. Staunton *Vindicator*, October 30, 1863; *Official Records*, XXIX, Pt. 1, p. 616. Dejection within the Stonewall Brigade at this time can be seen in a letter from

source, he "played the part of the hero" by emerging unharmed from the skirmish with five bullet holes in his clothing.[6]

These months of picket duty were boring and gloomy. Early in September the Valley men were forced to witness the execution of several convicted deserters.[7] This only heightened the restlessness of military inactivity. Despite the fact that the regimental colonels were perhaps the best that the brigade would have at one time, the men in the ranks began their usual grumblings against officers.[8] General Walker's conduct so incensed Private Jim Charlton that he wrote:

I have enough to make me low-spirited . . . We are not allowed any privileges at all. We have a guard that we can't get out unless we have a pass from *Walker* and when we want to go from the Brigade we must have a pass from Johnson. The officers had a pictnick the other day and that night when the guard was going around they found *Genl* Walker Drunk in the road. If it had been a private he would have had him put in the guard house and linched. Such a man is not worth living.

I would rather be marching all the time than to be in camp and do the guard duty but I see no way to git from under him.[9]

Harsh feelings of a similar nature were expressed toward Johnson and such "outside" officers as Generals A. P. Hill and Henry Heth.[10]

The dissatisfaction that Captain Welsh voiced against army exempts the previous winter came forth again in one of Private Garibaldi's letters: "I believe that if all these bushwackers and deserters would come into the army, we could whip the yankees thoroughly and have peace by next winter." [11]

Private Garibaldi in which he stated that the Confederates lost "four hundred killed, wounded and missing." John Garibaldi to his wife, November 1, 1863, Garibaldi Letters.

6. Staunton *Spectator*, November 3, 1863.

7. Barton, *Recollections*, 47–48; Casler, *Stonewall Brigade*, 281. Casler added that just after the battle of Mine Run, two Louisiana soldiers were taken out to be shot. When they broke and ran away, the firing squad fired into the air. *Ibid.*, 297.

8. The regimental officers were: J. Q. A. Nadenbousch, 2nd; Charles A. Ronald, 4th; John H. S. Funk, 5th; James K. Edmondson, 27th; and Frederick W. M. Holliday, 33rd. *Official Records*, XXIX, Pt. 2, pp. 339, 684.

9. Jim P. Charlton to Oliver P. Charlton, August 31, 1863, Charlton Letters.

10. See John Garibaldi to his wife, October 21, 1863, Garibaldi Letters. The semi-literate Garibaldi told his wife that the brigade was encamped "near Caul Pepper," meaning, of course, Culpeper.

11. *Ibid.*, September 25, 1863.

As at Fredericksburg in the second winter of the war, the men began to think more of a cessation of hostilities. When cold weather set in, rations grew short and monotony increased. Garibaldi expressed a sentiment that must have been widespread: "I think if fighting will settle the matter, there has been enough now, and if fighting wouldn't settle it, there is no use of any more blood shed, for it is the general belief among the soldiers and in foreign countries that fighting can't settle it." [12]

Picket duty continued to be a cold and thankless chore. "Everything seems all quiet all along the line," Private Charlton wrote. "I was on guard and I like to froze." [13] As had almost become customary, opposing pickets struck a truce, swapped commodities, ate together, and "were always in sight of one another, but never shot." [14]

A few events alleviated the misery of camp life. In the Stonewall Brigade another religious revival broke out—although not as fervent as in the days of Jackson. Meetings were nevertheless earnest and prolonged. Private Garibaldi wrote that the brigade was having "preaching here every day and three times on holy days." [15] On several occasions grateful citizens of the Valley sent money, food, and clothing to the soldiers. Garibaldi expressed his appreciation by writing: "I must tell you now that there was sent here from Staunton a whole lot of clothes, especially for this Brigade, and that we all had [a] chance to anything we want in the way of shoes, drawers, shirts, pants and jackets . . . This was by far the best clothing for winter we drew for a long time, so that we are all of this Brigade supplied of good warm clothing." [16]

Except for a seeming overfondness for the battle, "Stonewall Jim" Walker had in preceding weeks endeared himself to the Valley veterans. He "was bold in battle and everywhere else," Lieutenant Barton later recalled. "He was nervously constituted and could not help dodging bullets, but he was a splendid soldier and leader." [17]

---

12. *Ibid.*, September 30, 1863.
13. Jim P. Charlton to Oliver P. Charlton, September [n.d.], 1863, Charlton Letters.
14. John Garibaldi to his wife, October 6, 1863, Garibaldi Letters.
15. *Ibid.*, October [n.d.], 1863.   16. *Ibid.*, November 21, 1863.
17. Barton, *Recollections*, 48, 53.

That Walker went to extreme—and sometimes humorous—lengths to see that his troops were well provided for made him one of the most beloved commanders of the Stonewall Brigade. In mid-November, for example, the brigade was ordered to encamp in a downpour of rain with no protective covering. Walker saw no reason to subject his ragged men to the cold dampness of late fall. He secretly dispatched an orderly to the quartermaster wagons a mile to the rear, and the teamsters were ordered in blunt terms to bring up a supply of tents and food. After insuring that his men were dry and well fed, Walker retired for the night to his own tent. The following morning he appeared wet and disgruntled before the divisional commander, "Old Allegheny" Johnson, and sighed, "Well, General, we had a rough time in the rain last night." [18]

The monotony of camp routine was broken when on November 26 orders came to prepare for action. The Stonewall Brigade moved to the Rapidan earthworks and bivouacked, then resumed the march the following day for Mine Run, one of the tributaries of the river. Johnson's objective was to form his division to the left of Lee's main force, already at the Run awaiting attack by General Meade's Army of the Potomac. On that cold and windy November 27 the Stonewall Brigade was third in the divisional line of march. At 3 P.M. General Steuart's lead brigade was suddenly assailed by Federals pouring from woods to the left of the road.

As Steuart veered to meet the attack, the other brigades moved into battle position on his right. Without waiting for orders, the men in the Stonewall Brigade began constructing earthworks in anticipation of an assault on their front.[19] Walker detailed the Second Virginia as skirmishers to ascertain the position of the Federals. The Winchester companies had barely entered a thick wood before they became hotly engaged with massed bluecoats of William French's III Corps and John Sedgwick's VI Corps. Valiantly the Confederates maintained their forward posts until Walker could get the remainder of his brigade up in support. Just before the reinforcements arrived, Lieutenant Colonel Colston was

18. *Ibid.*, 48–49. For another instance of Walker's humor, see *Southern Historical Society Papers*, IX (1881), 364–65.
19. *Official Records*, XXIX, Pt. 1, pp. 854–55.

riding up and down the line of the Second Virginia reassuring his men and making alignments. Suddenly he shouted, "Oh my God, I am shot!" and toppled from his horse, mortally wounded with a shattered left leg.[20]

At 4 P.M. Johnson ordered a general advance to break the Federal line. The Stonewall Brigade moved forward, "at first in quick time, and then in double-time, and with a shout, it appearing that the enemy with a heavy line of battle was driving our skirmishers back." [21] Slowly and stubbornly, amid a din of musketry and yells, the bluecoats were forced back through the woods. At the edge of the timber the Yankees broke and raced across an open field to the cover of a fence at the far end. By the time the Confederates reached the end of the grove, brigades and regiments were so disorganized that they "discreetly stopped at the fence" on their end of the field.[22]

The Valley fighters seemed content to remain in their positions, but Walker was not satisfied with that small taste of victory. He seized the colors, jumped his horse over the fence into the field, and waved his men on in pursuit, while Federals no more than eighty yards away delivered a concentrated fire in a vain attempt to kill him. The men rushed after him, as much amazed by his reckless courage as his apparent immunity to Federal bullets.[23] For half an hour the battle swung back and forth across the field. Rebels would charge, break up against the taut Yankee line, and scurry back to safety in small groups. Major William Terry, leading the Fourth Virginia, fell in the middle of the field from a deep shoulder wound. As Federals moved around to enfilade the Confederate left, Walker's men began running out of ammunition; yet with darkness fast approaching Johnson deemed it expedient to withdraw the troops from the field. The men fell back in orderly fashion, Colonel Funk of the Fifth Virginia wrote, "carrying our dead and wounded

---

20. Colston was borne to the rear and the fractured limb amputated. He died a few weeks later of pneumonia and was buried on Christmas Day in Charlottesville. See Walker, VMI Memorial, 128–29; Judith W. McGuire, Diary of a Refugee, 246, 248–49.

21. Lieutenant Colonel Abram Spengler, 33rd Regiment in Official Records, XXIX, Pt. 1, p. 854.

22. Barton, Recollections, 49.

23. Ibid.; Official Records, XXIX, Pt. 1, p. 848.

with us." [24] Meade's attempt to crush Lee's left had failed, with heavy loss. In stopping the flanking movement, the Stonewall Brigade suffered casualties of 20 killed, 124 wounded, and 10 missing.[25]

For three days thereafter the Valley regiments stood in earthworks awaiting another Federal attack that never came. Meade shortly retreated across the Rapidan, ending the long and costly campaigns of 1863. The Stonewall Brigade wearily went into winter quarters near Pisgah Church. The men were ordered to guard the numerous fords of the Rapidan in that area. In the meantime, "comfortable" quarters were built at "Camp Stonewall Jackson" and, Randolph Barton added, "the winter was passed in drilling the men and preparing for the campaign of 1864, which promised to be as vigorous as any we had passed through." [26]

The officers of the brigade seemed to enjoy a happy Christmas season, however. After a hearty meal in a nearby private home, Walker invited his lieutenants to his tent for some liquid refreshment. Randolph Barton wrote that he consumed several cups from "a bucketful of vile stuff, which we called egg-nog, and which sent me to bed with my boots on." [27]

For most of the foot cavalry, the winter months passed slowly and painfully. The shortage of food became a critical problem. Early in January, 1864, John Garibaldi wrote his wife Sarah that daily meat rations had been reduced to four ounces of bacon and twelve ounces of beef. He added that most of the bacon was actually lard and that the beef was often tainted. Flour rations had been cut from eighteen to ten ounces a day, and probably would be reduced even more, he said. On occasion the men were able to draw a little sugar, rice, coffee, and dried fruit; but soap, which had sold for four dollars a pound the preceding fall, had doubled in price. By the end of March, officers were eating the same rations as the men and were glad to get it.[28]

The troops built their customary log cabins; or, lacking energy

---

24. *Ibid.*, 853. General French, on the other hand, stated that the Confederate dead and wounded were left on the field. *Ibid.*, 736.
25. Federal losses were 927 men, including 127 killed. *Ibid.*, 20, 837.
26. Regimental Returns, 5th Virginia, Company H, November–December, 1863, War Record Group 109, National Archives; Barton, *Recollections*, 50.
27. *Ibid.*
28. John Garibaldi to his wife, January 9, April 5, 1864, Garibaldi Letters.

and initiative, they simply boarded the sides of their tents. Yet that winter of 1863–64 was particularly severe to the survivors of the Stonewall Brigade. Most of the men were shoeless; many lacked even socks. Although some comfort could be obtained by huddling together around campfires, pickets found it necessary to wrap clothing around their numb and swollen feet as protection from the cold. In January, Private Garibaldi wrote that he had not had any socks for the past two months and did not expect to get any in the foreseeable future. By the first of February one Valley newspaper reported that there were two hundred men in the brigade without shoes and socks. A Waynesboro shoemaker hastily contributed fifty pairs; his wife knitted a similar number of socks, but the situation remained acute.[29]

The commanding general of the Army of Northern Virginia finally came to the aid of Jackson's old brigade. For a month Lee forwarded every pair of socks sent to him by sympathetic homefolk to Walker's brigade. Many of the pairs were knitted by his own wife and cousins. In a letter to Mrs. Lee early in April, the beloved commander stated: "I have sent to that brigade [a total of] 263 prs. Still there are about 140 men in that brigade whose homes are within the enemy lines & who are without socks. I shall continue to furnish them untill all are supplied. Tell the young women to work hard for the brave Stonewallers." [30]

Enduring their misery as best they could, the Valley troops found several diversions to offset the monotony of the winter. Several members of the Thirty-third Virginia got together with a part of Leroy Stafford's Louisiana Brigade and staged an amateur minstrel show. They built a log hut for a theater and charged admission for their production. All proceeds were given to widows and orphans of Confederate soldiers. The shows were a series of satirical skits on officers, quartermasters, politicians, and others rating low in soldier esteem. A skit enjoyed highly by both actors and audiences was a spoof on doctors and their alleged treatment of the wounded. As the

---

29. *Ibid.*, January 9, 1864; Staunton *Vindicator*, February 4, 1864.
30. R. E. Lee to his wife, April 2, 1864, Robert E. Lee Papers, Library of Congress. Other references to the Stonewall Brigade's destitute condition are contained in letters of March 18, 20, and 24, 1864.

men cheered and applauded, the actors portrayed the army surgeons drinking medicinal spirits, playing cards while the wounded suffered, and assigning amputees to ambulance and wagon duty.[31]

On March 23, 1864, after a heavy snowfall, there occurred probably the most famous snowball fight in the history of the war. The Stonewall Brigade and Stafford's Louisiana Brigade challenged George Doles's Georgians and Dodson Ramseur's North Carolinians to battle. The Georgians at first declined on the grounds that they were not familiar with snow, but brigade pride soon got the best of them and they entered the fray. After some light skirmishing, the fight began in earnest. The Louisianians were soon routed and driven back across a field to the line of the Stonewall Brigade. A "cavalry charge" against Walker's right was hurled back in confusion. Walker then became flushed with battle fever. In a voice that must have carried all the way back to the camps, he shouted for the Stonewall Brigade to charge. The Valley men leaped forward, some molding "bullets" as they ran, others "firing" with both hands.

The Georgians centered their attack on Walker and literally transformed horse and rider into a white mass. The Valley regiments were forced back; the Georgians pushed forward to press their advantage—only to run into a surprise flank attack from Stafford's brigade concealed in the woods. The Georgians and Carolinians were pursued hotly over the rolling, snowbound countryside until darkness ended the five-hour struggle, and in the flush of victory the Stonewall Brigade gave its famous Rebel yell.[32]

Only one brush with Federals broke the serenity of that winter. On February 8 Walker's and Steuart's brigades were called out to repulse a raid across the Rapidan. The Yankees were quickly driven back over the river with a loss of "17 dead Dutchmen and 42 prisoners," Sandie Pendleton contemptuously reported.[33] Yet by April the men knew that heavy action was soon to begin. A general by the name of Ulysses S. Grant had taken over supreme command

31. Casler, *Stonewall Brigade*, 307–309.

32. LaBree (ed.), *Camp Fires of the Confederacy*, 55–58. Casler closed his account of the snowball battle by commenting: "If all battles would terminate that way it would be a great improvement on the old slaughtering plan." Casler, *Stonewall Brigade*, 307.

33. Bean, *Stonewall's Man*, 187.

of the Federal army, and he had a very impressive record for win-
ning battles. But John Garibaldi of the Twenty-seventh Virginia
was confident that Grant, like most of his predecessors in the Eastern theater, would be "badly whipped." That Garibaldi was hoping
more than speculating was evident in the closing lines of his letter:
"I am pretty tire[d] of this war by this time but there is no chance
for us unless the war stops, for we all have [to] keep fighting untill
the yankees gives up or untill we shall be subjugated." Ten days
later Colonel William Randolph of the Second Virginia wrote his
mother: "The sweet bright days are gone, and now the stern work
of war is about to begin." ³⁴

At midnight on May 4 the Stonewall Brigade stuffed its gear into
wagons and left the winter quarters. With Ewell's Second Corps
it passed through the Mine Run breastworks and bivouacked below
Locust Grove on the Orange–Fredericksburg Turnpike. The troops
were on the edge of the Wilderness, a large tangled thicket of pine,
scrub oak, and cedar made even more dense by thick underbrush of
briars and honeysuckle. Somewhere in that almost impassable jun-
gle was the advancing Federal army, heavily reinforced and under
new command.

General John B. Gordon, commanding a brigade in Early's division, wrote that "a more beautiful day never dawned" than Thursday, May 5.³⁵ Under a cloudless sky the Old Brigade marched with
Ewell's corps toward Chancellorsville and Grant's army. Near the
intersection of the turnpike and the Germanna plank road, Ewell
ordered his brigades into a heavy oak timber on the left. Skirmishers
were sent out, and at 12:20 P.M. they encountered Federals. After
twenty minutes of scattered musket fire, loud explosions were heard
ahead and to the right of the turnpike. Leaving a line of skirmishers
at this position, Walker faced his men to the right and double-
timed them across the road toward the sound of battle. When his
new skirmishers had advanced only thirty yards into the dense
wood, they stumbled into massed Federals.³⁶

34. John Garibaldi to his wife, April 22, 1864, Garibaldi Letters; John L. Johnson,
The University Memorial, 559.
35. John B. Gordon, *Reminiscences of the Civil War* (New York, 1903), 235.
36. Lieutenant J. S. Dozle, 33rd Regiment, "Reminiscences of the Wilderness," pp.
2, 4, typescript, Hotchkiss Papers.

To meet the approaching assault, Walker about-faced his men and wheeled to the left into a position at right angles to the Germanna plank road. The troops were almost hidden in the thick underbrush; some confusion prevailed as companies and even regiments became momentarily separated. Walker suddenly realized that his right (the Fifth Virginia) was not resting on Stafford's left; as at Cedar Run, this gap could be fatal. Just as he turned his Valley men to close the hole, his skirmishers came racing through the woods with Federals close behind them and only forty yards away from the main body of the Stonewall Brigade.

Before the Rebels could turn to meet the onslaught, they received a point-blank volley that added chaos to confusion. The Fifth Virginia was the most exposed to the fire and it fell back "in some confusion" on the Twenty-seventh, which in turn began to give way.[37] Colonel Terry's Fourth Regiment was next in line, but that officer, seeing the flank attack developing and acting on his own responsibility, formed his regiment perpendicular to the Valley brigade's line. Instead of striking the flank of the Fourth, the charging Federals ran into a murderous fire from the entire regiment in battle position.

Walker quickly adjusted his brigade lines to meet the assault. In the next few minutes no less than eight attempts were made to crack the Confederate positions.[38] The Federal commander, "Uncle John" Sedgwick, tried to break the Stonewall Brigade's left by a heavy flank attack. For two hours the Second and Thirty-third Regiments held on doggedly. Boyish Colonel William Randolph was reassuring members of his Second Virginia when he was struck by bullets and toppled dead from his horse. (Randolph was the seventh and last colonel to command the lower Valley regiment. Of the other six, only John Nadenbousch escaped death on the field, and then because he was so mutilated from wounds that he had to leave the army.)[39]

The Federals "failed to force back the men who had learned

---

37. *Ibid.* Dozle added that the disorder "was so great & unexpected that there was fear lest the brigade could not sustain its position." See also *Official Records*, XXXVI, Pt. 1, p. 1070.
38. Staunton *Spectator*, May 17, 1864.   39. Dunlop, *Lee's Sharpshooters*, 390.

heroic constancy from Jackson," one Confederate boasted. Still, the Yankees soon were in a position to deliver so "galling" a fire into the front and flank of Walker's position that Stonewall Jim ordered his ranks to retire seventy-five yards to the rear. Federals who quickly occupied the abandoned earthworks "seemed indisposed to advance further." For the remainder of the day the two sides maintained a severe skirmishing rendered ineffectual by visibility, which was no more than fifty yards in the smoke-filled Wilderness. At five o'clock Walker's men, relieved by Harry Hays's Louisiana Brigade, marched back to the rear to reorganize and rearm. Although no casualty figures for the whole Stonewall Brigade are available, losses were reported as "heavy." The Fourth Virginia, for example, had five killed and forty-five wounded out of less than a hundred engaged.[40]

That night was one of comparative quiet, made more so by a welcome rain that came soon ofter midnight. At dawn Federals began probing the Confederate positions but decided against a full-scale attack. Throughout the day sharpshooters stayed busy, taking a heavy toll on both sides. The greatly revered Captain John Hall of the Fifth Virginia was walking toward his earthworks when he received a fatal shot in the stomach. As the Twenty-seventh Virginia was shifting its position late in the afternoon, Lieutenant Colonel Philip Frazer was killed by a bullet wound in the head. Only nineteen years old, Frazer had been promoted to a colonelcy that morning.[41]

On May 7 skirmishers reported the Federal works abandoned. Countless tents, blankets, canteens, guns, and other accoutrements that were lying about were picked up eagerly by tattered Valley soldiers. The remainder of the day was spent cleaning guns, making use of new possessions, and preparing for another battle. After dark the regiments moved off slowly to the right. At first the men were disposed to laugh and cheer, until orders came through the ranks to maintain silence, as Grant's army was moving parallel to the Confederates.[42]

40. Bosang, Memoirs, 11–12; Dozle, "Reminiscences," 5; Howard, Recollections, 274; Battles and Leaders, IV, 154. See also Diary of Joseph McMurran, 4th Regiment Virginia Archives, entry of May 5, 1864.
41. Walker, VMI Memorial, 209–10.   42. Dozle, "Reminiscences," 8.

The Stonewall Brigade marched through the night, stopping frequently but never long enough for sleep. At dawn the columns halted and the men were allowed two hours to eat and clean up. Then the march continued at an accelerated, uncomfortable pace through the woods. Sergeant Joe McMurran of the Fourth Virginia wrote: "The weather was very hot, water scarce & the road thro' the Wilderness thick set with undergrowth which had been set on fire & was so warm that the troops almost suffocated." Many of the men fell out of ranks long enough to vomit, then returned to the marching columns. Others simply collapsed along the road.[43]

Late in the afternoon the Valley regiments reached Spotsylvania Court House. The men were wearily making their way north of town to form battle positions with the rest of the Second Corps when General Ewell rode up, told them that Federals were threatening to break the Confederate line, and ordered them forward at double-quick time. "In spite of a forced march of more than sixteen hours," wrote Percy G. Hamlin, the Stonewall Brigade "responded with a yell and passed to the front under artillery fire." [44] By 11 P.M. Walker had his brigade in its assigned position, but he did not like the location. On the left the Second, Twenty-seventh and Thirty-third Regiments were atop a dry, chalky hill; the Fourth and Fifth Virginia were at the bottom of the ridge in an ankle-deep swamp. On his own initiative Walker ordered the five regiments back to ground more adaptable for defense. "Profiting by their experience of the last few days in the Wilderness," Lieutenant J. S. Dozle of the Thirty-third Virginia wrote, "the men went to work with great alacrity (in spite of their broken-down condition) and by daylight were sleeping comfortably behind a strong breast-work of rails and earth." [45]

Soldiers in the Old Brigade awoke on May 9 to find themselves occupying the most important point along the Confederate line. As part of Johnson's division, they were posted in a parabola atop a ridge and facing northward. The Valley brigade defended the left-center portion. In front of them was a rolling and open field that

43. McMurran Diary, entry of May 8, 1864; Dozle, "Reminiscences," 8.
44. Percy G. Hamlin, *Old Bald Head* (Strasburg, Va., 1940), 175.
45. Dozle, "Reminiscences," 8. See also *Southern Historical Society Papers*, XXI (1893), 233.

ended one hundred yards away in a grove. Spasmodic firing from the trees gave ample indication that Federals were concealed among the foliage. Control of "The Salient" was important, the Rebels knew, for if the Federals gained control of that high ground, their artillery could and would rake Lee's entire line.[46]

For two days the men worked on their breastworks, making them so impregnable in their own eyes that they "lay waiting and wishing for the enemy." [47] Artillery was posted immediately behind the parapets and earthworks so as to pour close-range fire across the field at any Federal advance. In the midst of these activities, on the afternoon of May 10, a probe in force by the Federals attempted to break The Salient at the position of Doles's brigade, posted on Walker's immediate left. Yankees raced across the field and over- ran the earthworks so quickly that many of Doles's men were cap- tured while still seated around their cook fires. After gaining the Confederate works, the bluecoats swerved toward the Stonewall Brigade and sent the Second and Thirty-third Virginia on the left falling back on the other regiments. Walker rode up, instantly stopped the near rout, and began a concentrated fire into the blue ranks. The arrival of Steuart's brigade caused the Federals to scurry back across the field to cover. Confederates poured a heavy fire of canister and musketry after the fleeing enemy until "the ground was covered with their dead and wounded." [48]

That night the Thirty-third Virginia voluntarily went out and chopped down a large number of pine trees to use them for abatis. By the following day the brigade's entrenchments were a solid wall of felled trees and earth that extended for one hundred yards. Ten traverses (logs placed at right angles to earthworks to protect against flank attacks) strengthened the sector's defenses—and gave them a cattle-pen appearance.

May 11 proved to be a day of comparative calm. Federals again probed the front of Johnson's line in mid-morning, but were handily flung back by accurate shooting from the Stonewall Brigade. At the

---

46. *Official Records*, XXXVI, Pt. 1, p. 1071.
47. Dozle, "Reminiscences," 9.
48. *Southern Historical Society Papers*, XXI (1893), 234. See also Barton, *Recollec- tions*, 51–52.

height of the engagement Walker was heard to exclaim excitedly to Colonel Terry: "If this be war, may it be eternal!" [49]

Soon after dark that night a steady rain began pelting the newly turned earth, "but thanks to the excellent tent-flies so abundantly supplied by the 6th Federal Corps in the Wilderness, the men were able to keep tolerably dry." [50] Occasionally, when the rain slackened, men in the Stonewall Brigade could hear the jingling of caissons and artillery—and the heavy tramp of infantry columns moving into the wood in their front. Colonel Terry, with his Fourth Virginia on the extreme right, said that his line was so close to the Federal position he could hear the talk of the massed troops.[51] The Valley units were experienced enough to know that daylight would bring fighting—even in the rain. But the officers were so convinced that Grant again was shifting his front that the artillery was accordingly ordered to the rear and hitched to the horses preparatory to moving out the next morning. Only two smoothbores remained behind the Stonewall Brigade's earthworks.

A light rain was still falling at dawn on Friday, May 12, and a blanket of fog obscured the whole area. In the grayness of early day, Confederate skirmishers suddenly fell back, shooting as they retired and shouting warnings to the main line. A courier raced up to Walker's headquarters and awoke the commander with cries of "General! They are coming!" Walker bounded half-clothed from his tent and bellowed, "Fall in!" [52] He raced to his brigade's entrenchments, where troops were apprehensively squinting through the fog, trying desperately to perceive some kind of movement. Sounds were coming closer and closer, but the heavy mist shrouded everything.

All at once the fog lifted, and one-third of the way across the field was General Winfield Hancock's II Corps—three full divisions —moving toward the Confederate works. The Federals stopped, as if the formidable defenses ahead of them were too much of an obstacle. While Yankee officers rode up and down the line shouting at the men to continue forward, the Confederates rose above their

---

49. *Ibid.*, 53.   50. Dozle, "Reminiscences," 9.
51. *Southern Historical Society Papers*, XXXIII (1905), 337.
52. Barton, *Recollections*, 54.

earthworks, took careful aim, and pulled countless triggers. But no ear-shattering explosions filled the air, only weak "pops" as hammers struck firing caps. The powder was wet and would not fire; except for the two cannon behind them, the Southerners were without firearms.

The Federals took heart from this turn of fate. A Pennsylvania soldier recorded that they "took up the double-quick, and with . . . flags unfurled rushed up to the works, tore away the obstructions in front, and, quickly clambering over the defenses, sprang among the guns." [53] For a short time, determined Confederates fought wildly, using muskets as clubs, but the blue avalanche soon poured into the works and swerved both right and left. The Confederate brigades of John B. Gordon and John Pegram rushed into the breach to stem the tide, but they were overwhelmed in short order by Hancock's endless lines. The Stonewall Brigade held its position, with eyes turned northward to the approaching action. As Lieutenant Dozle wrote:

The atmosphere was obscured by a thick fog which was increased in density by the smoke of the battle that, in the absence of any breeze, hung in heavy masses in the wood. The scene was terrible. The figures of the men seen dimly through the smoke and fog seemed almost gigantic, while the woods were lighted by the flashing of the guns and the sparkling of the musketry. The din was tremendous and increasing every instant. Men in crowds with bleeding limbs, and pale, pain-stricken faces, were hurrying to the rear, and, mingled with these could be seen many unwounded who had escaped from the wrecks of their comrades. [54]

The Stonewall Brigade stood firm as hundreds of mangled and demoralized men swept through on their way to the rear. Several men in the Valley units saw "Old Allegheny" Johnson, eyes ablaze with fury, rush up into the midst of the fight, swatting at Yankees with his hickory cane as if they were a pack of wild dogs. [55] He was quickly captured by Federals pouring down the breastworks toward the brigade's position. To meet the threat, Colonel Terry turned his Fourth Virginia at right angles to the rest of the brigade. The Valley men waged a severe struggle until they were overcome by sheer

---

53. Charles H. Bane, *History of the Philadelphia Brigade* (Philadelphia, 1876), 245.
54. Dozle, "Reminiscences," 9.
55. *Southern Historical Society Papers*, XXXIII (1905), 338.

weight of numbers. Traverses became the battle lines as Federals pounded Terry's regiment. Rain began to fall and added to the misery. Bodies of blue and gray now hung on the works or lay in the water within the trenches, the dying struggling to get out from under the dead. Beneath the explosion of musketry and cannon could be heard moans from the injured and pleas for mercy from mangled soldiers with but seconds left to live. The rain pelted everything, turning the earth to slime and filling holes with red puddles of water and blood. But the fighting in The Salient continued—and with such intensity that an oak twenty-two inches in diameter was chopped down solely by musket balls and crashed into the works of the nearby First North Carolina.[56]

All the while, "Stonewall Jim" Walker rode back and forth along the trenches, encouraging his men by voice and example. Suddenly he plunged from his saddle, his left elbow shattered.[57] Colonel William Terry fell to the ground, dripping blood. The Stonewall Brigade had now lost its leader and half of the unit commanders, but stubbornly it fought on, hoping for some assistance to stop the Federal assault. As Lieutenant Dozle stated gloomily: "All that human courage and endurance would effect was done by these men on this frightful morning, but all was of no avail." [58] Near 6 A.M., droves of Federals struck the Old Brigade in front, flank, and rear. The Fourth, Fifth, Twenty-seventh, and Thirty-third Regiments were trapped almost to the man. Those who escaped "had to run for it," Casler stated, and the remnants of the four regiments joined the Second Virginia and fell back to the cover of Hays's Louisiana Brigade.[59]

56. In the midst of the fighting, and seeing that he was surrounded, General George H. Steuart walked up to Colonel James Beaver of the 148th Pennsylvania and offered his surrender. "I will accept your surrender," the Federal officer replied. "Where is your sword, sir?" With a tinge of sarcasm Steuart allegedly replied, "Well, suh, you all waked us up so early this mawnin' that I didn't have time to get it on." J. W. Muffly (ed.), *The Story of Our Regiment* (Des Moines, 1904), 123, 857–58; Barnes, *History of the Philadelphia Brigade*, 861.
57. *Official Records*, XXXVI, Pt. 2, pp. 993, 1030. For a short period Walker was reported as captured. Staunton *Vindicator*, May 20, 1864.
58. Dozle, "Reminiscences," 10.
59. Casler, *Stonewall Brigade*, 320. See also *Official Records*, XXXVI, Pt. 1, p. 337; Dunlop, *Lee's Sharpshooters*, 459–60.

Throughout the day, as rain continued to fall, Confederates fought desperately to hold a second line. At sundown the twelve-hour engagement ended. Lee's line was preserved, but the cost had been staggering. Casualties in Johnson's division were so great that Lee's headquarters did not even know the name of the ranking officer. At the outset of the campaign, the division had numbered 6,800 men. Not enough remained to make a normal-sized brigade. The shattered Stonewall Brigade had less than 200 members, no commander, and only two of its five regimental officers.[60]

Consolidation was imperative. On May 14 Walker's, Jones's, and Steuart's brigades were combined into a small brigade under the command of Colonel Terry of the Fourth Virginia, who was still recovering from a wound.[61] Even after the merger, the units remained pitifully small. The Thirty-third Virginia, for example, now consisted of a captain and three privates, one of whom was a horse-less cavalryman.[62]

After the battle of Spotsylvania, and three years of gallant sacrifices, the Stonewall Brigade officially ceased to exist.

---

60. *Official Records*, XXXVI, Pt. 2, p. 1001; *Southern Historical Society Papers*, XXI (1893), 237.
61. *Official Records*, XXXVI, Pt. 2, p. 1001, Pt. 3, p. 813.
62. Casler, *Stonewall Brigade*, 331.

!!!

CHAPTER XVIII

THE BITTER END

As Lee's army continued to shift eastward as a buffer between Grant and Richmond, only 249 men formed the residue of a once-mighty and effective brigade of 2,600 effectives.[1] The number of men in the five Valley regiments was so small that they were barely discernible among the fourteen regiments consolidated into a pint-sized brigade.[2] But there was one consolation: their last commander appropriately came from the battered ranks of the Stonewall Brigade.

Little is known of William Terry, who was less colorful and less conspicuous than any of his six predecessors at the head of the

---

1. Humphreys, *Heroes and Spies*, 191. That a few recruits came in after Spotsylvania to swell its ranks to over 200 men is in itself a tribute to the Stonewall Brigade.
2. This 600-man brigade was composed of the following Virginia regiments: 2nd, 4th, 5th, 10th, 21st, 23rd, 25th, 27th, 33rd, 37th, 42nd, 44th, 48th, and 50th. *Battles and Leaders*, IV, 499.

Old Brigade. He was born in central Virginia's Amherst County on August 14, 1824, and graduated from the University of Virginia in 1848. Admitted to the bar three years later, he settled in Wytheville and in time founded and edited the Wytheville *Telegraph*. John Brown's raid spurred him into joining the Wythe Grays; he was a lieutenant in the company when it left for Harpers Ferry and assignment to the Fourth Virginia. By a constant display of dependability and valor, Terry rose steadily through the hierarchy of this upper Valley regiment. He was a major when wounded at Second Manassas; he was acting colonel of the Fourth after its commander, Colonel R. D. Gardner, was shot down at Fredericksburg; and at Chancellorsville, still at the head of the regiment, he led 350 men into the fight and in the short space of ten minutes saw 160 of them fall.[3] At Gettysburg he was singled out for praise by Walker, who wrote that Terry "gallantly led his regiment almost to the breastworks of the enemy, and only retired after losing three-fourths of his command." [4] On Lee's return to Virginia, Terry was promoted to colonel and officially given command of the Fourth Virginia. He received two slight wounds at Spotsylvania, but managed to escape the Federal envelopment of his troops. On May 21, 1864, after General John B. Gordon's recommendation and Lee's hearty endorsement, he was elevated to brigadier general and given the scraps of the fourteen regiments shattered in and about The Salient.[5]

Terry was an unimpressive-looking officer, of medium height and with hair and beard heavily sprinkled with gray. Thin stature, drooping eyebrows, and quiet manner made him an unobtrusive contrast to such former brigade commanders as Jackson, Winder, Baylor, and Walker. But his battle-scarred body—with more serious wounds yet to come—stamped him as a first-rate fighter, and that was enough to gain him the respect of those members of the Stonewall Brigade still around.

Throughout the hot month of May the jockeying for position

3. Terry's own statement, in *Southern Historical Society Papers*, XIV (1886), 366.
4. *Official Records*, XXVII, Pt. 2, p. 519.
5. John B. Gordon to Samuel Cooper, May 16, 1864, Terry's personal file, National Archives.

between Lee and Grant continued. Terry's men were not engaged in the fight along the North Anna (May 17) or in the bloody massacre of the Federal II Corps at Cold Harbor (June 3). From Richmond defenses the Valley veterans kept a watchful vigil on Grant's maneuvering army. Prayer services were held regularly by the regimental chaplains and a "great interest" in religion was "manifested" again by the Men of Manassas.[6]

On Monday, June 13, the small brigade left the Richmond lines and started westward with the remainder of the Second Corps, now under the command of General Early. Thoughts of returning to the mountains rejuvenated the men; they marched briskly past the Mechanicsville battlefield and continued toward Charlottesville "in cheerful spirits."[7] On the fifteenth the dusty columns wearily bivouacked at Louisa Court House, having marched sixty-four miles in two days. Local citizens gave the troops what water and food they could spare, Sergeant McMurran of the Fourth Virginia wrote, "and were very sad at the thinned ranks of the Stonewall Brigade."[8]

The following day, Early drove the men at a rapid pace toward Charlottesville, twenty-eight miles away. Many of the troops wondered at the necessity of such speed until informed that Lynchburg, their destination and Early's hometown, was besieged by Federals under General David Hunter. Several hours after dark the columns stumbled to a halt at Charlottesville. John Casler wrote—certainly with exaggeration—that his feet were so sore from marching he could gather firewood only by crawling about the camp on his hands and knees.[9]

The troops were overjoyed the next morning to find a train waiting to transport them to Lynchburg. Men scampered gleefully into and atop the boxcars, the engine started forward—then promptly broke down. Disgruntled Confederates had to proceed on foot, but by the time they got to Lynchburg, Hunter's Federals had retreated west of town. Early pursued the Yankees as far as Salem. Convinced that Hunter was heading for the mountains, and cognizant of the run-down condition of his own troops, Early halted

6. McMurran Diary, entry of June 12, 1864.   7. *Ibid.*, entry of June 15, 1864.
8. *Ibid.*   9. Casler, *Stonewall Brigade*, 342–43.

his brigades. On June 21 the Valley troops received their first rations in two days. Each man was given a quarter-pound of bacon and a pound of three-day-old cornbread. Although this was not the kind of fare the men would have liked, Hunter had so devastated the Valley that hundreds of his own Federal soldiers were captured while begging food.[10]

General Hunter's withdrawal into West Virginia virtually stripped the Valley of Federals. Early then decided to take the offensive in order to relieve the pressure on Lee at Richmond. "Old Jube's" plan was bold: He would hasten down the Shenandoah corridor, ford the Potomac, and deliver an assault on the Northern capital. The Second Corps moved off down the Valley pike on June 23. Two days later, long gray lines filed silently into Lexington. The columns halted and, with the remnants of the Stonewall Brigade in front, the men walked past Jackson's grave, where a Confederate flag hung limply. "Every officer and soldier saluted it, and went slowly by the grave of their Hero uncovered." Solemn thoughts indeed must have filled the minds of the Valley soldiers as they gazed for the first time on their old commander's resting place. Too soon the order came to resume the march.[11]

With Gordon's division, of which the consolidated brigade was a part, in the van, Early's corps continued down the Valley at a brisk pace. On July 2 the troops reached Winchester, where joyful citizens again lined the streets to cheer the passing Confederates. Three days later the army crossed the Potomac at Williamsport. Limbs ached as the Rebels marched through Boonsboro and over South Mountain into the rolling country of central Maryland. Near noon on Saturday, July 9, the columns reached Frederick, which had been occupied earlier by Confederate cavalry under General John McCausland, a former commander of the Rockbridge Artillery.

McCausland informed Early that approximately 10,000 Federal

---

10. McMurran Diary, entries of June 20–21, 1864.
11. Humphreys, *Heroes and Spies*, 191–92; Walter Clark (ed.), *Histories of the Several Regiments and Battalions from North Carolina in the Great War, 1861–65* (Raleigh and Goldsboro, 1901), I, 153–54, 275; McDonald, *Diary*, 221. For a description of the tattered and barefooted condition of the soldiers, see Jubal A. Early, *Autobiographical Sketch and Narrative of the War between the States* (Philadelphia, 1912), 381–82.

militia under General Lew Wallace were blocking the crossings of the Monocacy River south of Frederick. Early replied by heading for the river. The divisions of Robert Rodes and Dodson Ramseur were thrown forward on the Baltimore and Washington roads, while Gordon and John C. Breckinridge were directed to move to the right, cross over the fords a mile or two south of the main bridge, and assail the Federal left. Gordon's division waded across the waist-deep river, then met McCausland's dismounted cavalry, which had been beaten back by Federals posted in strength behind a snake-rail fence atop a commanding ridge. Open ground from the river to the hilltop gave the Federals a decided advantage.

Clement Evans' brigade moved off through a small clump of woods to the right in an attempt to turn the Federal left. Stafford's brigade was ordered across the field with Terry's men behind the Louisianians and to their left. Soon Evans' men were hurled back, but they counterattacked with such ferocity that the Yankees were forced to concentrate on this flank, thus leaving the way clear for Stafford and Terry to move their men across the field. When only 125 yards from the fence which protected the Federals, the Stonewall Brigade broke into its customary jog. But Terry shouted, "Stop running and walk, or you will break yourselves down and will not be able to fight the enemy when you get to them!" The men slowed down their advance, while Federals continued "shooting at us for all they knew how." [12]

The Confederates reached the fence, stuck their muskets through the openings, and fired a volley at the retreating Federals. No sooner had Terry's men reformed their ranks than they were ordered by Gordon to veer to the right and strike the Federal right flank, while Stafford assailed the center. Terry's movement, according to Gordon's official report, was "promptly executed, with a simultaneous attack from the front, [and] resulted in the dislodging of this line and the complete rout of the enemy's forces." General A. L. Long wrote that the Federals "fled in wild confusion, spreading dismay for miles in every direction by the terrible accounts they gave of the tremendous forces Early was leading through the country." [13]

---

12. James A. Hutcheson, 5th Regiment in *Confederate Veteran*, XXIII (1915), 77.
13. *Official Records*, XXXVII, Pt. 1, p. 352; *Southern Historical Society Papers*, III (1877), 115.

The Confederates spent the night on the battlefield, enjoying large quantities of coffee, sugar, pork, beans, and crackers left behind by the Federals. While the soldiers of the Stonewall Brigade eagerly devoured these rare luxuries, they were saddened by the fact that the battle of Monocacy had removed 59 of their 253 members. The five Valley regiments now totaled 194 men, which would have been less than two full companies in normal times.[14]

"Every one of Old Stonewall's men felt sure that they would soon file through the streets of the National Capital," one Rebel soldier later wrote. "They marched, rather than dog-trotted, and ran from Monocacy Bridge eastward, and on the eleventh of July drew up before Washington." [15] When the Second Corps halted on the outskirts of the city, they were certain that only old men and convalescents were manning the defenses. "A volley, a Rebel yell, and a vigorous charge, would have given us Washington," a former member of the Fifth Virginia stated.[16]

But Early refused to assault the works and fell victim to the many rumors of Federal corps from Grant's army moving rapidly to Washington. When he ordered the Confederates to retreat, indignation swept through the ranks. "The game was not worth the sacrifice of life," John McMurran cynically noted in his diary. John Opie stated: "Early lost the golden opportunity afforded him of immortalizing himself by capturing the capitol of the nation; but he, himself, was about the only man in that army who believed it impossible of accomplishment." [17]

Alexander Hunter reported that morale among the men dropped drastically on the march back to Virginia. "From that day the grim veterans fought well, but never with dash, and firm determination to do or die, the spirit which had heretofore made them victorious on a bloody field." [18] In reality, few men were left in the Stonewall Brigade to fight. After their return to the Valley by way of Snicker's Gap, the men must have been saddened by their own appearance. The famous Liberty Hall Volunteers of the Fourth

14. *Confederate Veteran*, XXIII (1915), 77.
15. Hunter, *Johnny Reb and Billy Yank*, 650.
16. Opie, *Rebel Cavalryman*, 246.
17. McMurran Diary, entry of July 18, 1864; Opie, *Rebel Cavalryman*, 247.
18. Hunter, *Johnny Reb and Billy Yank*, 651.

Virginia consisted of Lieutenant J. B. Jones and two privates. Company A of the Thirty-third Regiment was down to one man—and he was on sick leave.[19] The five regiments each had an average of about forty-five men. Moreover, a saddened Mrs. McDonald noted, "the old spirit no longer seemed to animate them."[20]

Yet this was a proud remnant. That the men were too fond of the Stonewall Brigade to relish loss of its identity in a brigade of little units was borne out by an inspecting officer who wrote in mid-August: "Both officers and men object to their consolidation into one brigade. Strange officers command strange troops, and the difficulties of fusing this incongruous mass are enhanced by constant marching and frequent engagements."[21]

Prior to this report, Early had given up Winchester when General Philip Sheridan moved into the Valley with a force too large for the Confederates to combat. While the Federal commander plundered and destroyed the lower end of the Valley, Early retired to the shadows of the Massanutten Mountains and awaited reinforcements from Lee. After the arrival of General J. B. Kershaw's division of South Carolinians and Fitzhugh Lee's cavalry, Early moved back down the Valley and forced Sheridan to relinquish the town before overwhelming numbers. Terry's brigade now numbered 963 men, and a Lexington newspaper assured its readers that "our troops are in fine spirits and confident of thrashing the Yankees."[22]

A month later Sheridan was back with 40,000 soldiers, and Early's corps of half that size was dispersed at several villages and mountain passes. Accordingly, Sheridan struck Early's depleted brigades at Winchester on the morning of September 19. Terry's brigade was posted in an open field three miles northeast of town when the Federals assaulted. The Confederates fought tenaciously, but were no match for the endless blue waves surging against them. Barely had the graycoats retired to a new position when Terry heard a shout. Turning, he saw Federal cavalry swooping down upon the Confederate left. Before he could give an order, Terry was shot down, seriously wounded.

---

19. Casler, *Stonewall Brigade*, 350–51.   20. McDonald, *Diary*, 226.
21. *Official Records*, XLIII, Pt. 1, pp. 609–610.
22. *Ibid.*, 1002; Lexington *Gazette*, August 19, 1864.

The whole Second Corps then gave way in despair. Randolph Barton of the brigade staff later wrote: "I remember quite well the bad impression made upon me when, in assisting to rally the men, I found officers, whom I had never seen flinch before, walking to the rear with their swords under their arms as if they had had enough." An Iowa soldier who took part in the Federal onslaught noted in his diary: "As the enemy passed through Winchester the women tried to rally them but so bad were they demoralized that they did not heed their entreaties but dashed on, saying that the Yankees were murdering all of them." [23]

The remnants of the Stonewall Brigade suffered severely, and the Second Virginia lost its prized battle flag in the engagement.[24] A Rebel artilleryman wrote in his diary afterwards that the Stonewall Brigade, the first unit Wesley Merritt's Federal cavalry struck, was to blame for the collapse of the Confederate line. "Alas!" he added, "There is very little left of that once splendid body of men & one has not the heart to blame this poor remnant for its bad conduct this afternoon." [25]

Winchester was abandoned late that afternoon. The Valley pike became jammed with wagons, ambulances, and dusty soldiers, and the thronging crowd moving southward. All the while, embittered Confederate troops held General Early solely responsible for their misfortunes. "The corps never had any confidence in him afterwards," Casler tersely commented, "and he could never do much with them." [26]

"Old Jube" frantically took up a battle position at Fisher's Hill and awaited Sheridan's corps. On September 22 the Federals struck and again turned Early's left. At that moment, John Opie wrote, "many an old soldier prayed for one hour of Stonewall Jackson." [27] Again the Confederates retreated up the Valley, this time to Woodstock and thence to New Market, where Early left the Valley pike and moved to Jackson's old camping grounds at the

---

23. Barton, *Recollections*, 65–66; Diary of Michael Cook, 28th Iowa Infantry, in possession of Mrs. Scott Hall, Alameda, N. M., entry of September 19, 1864.
24. *Official Records*, XLIII, Pt. 1, p. 185.
25. Diary of Henry R. Berkeley, Alderman Library, University of Virginia, entry of September 22, 1864.
26. Casler, *Stonewall Brigade*, 360.   27. Opie, *Rebel Cavalryman*, 252.

base of the Blue Ridge. Sheridan turned back northward and continued a systematic destruction of the Valley. Early's corps pursued him warily, but never attacked. By the middle of October the Federals were encamped confidently along Cedar Creek near the foot of the Massanutten Mountains. After personally reconnoitering the Yankee position from atop the hills, General John B. Gordon suggested an immediate assault. He received permission from a careworn Early to take three divisions around the mountains and strike the unsuspecting Federals in flank and rear.

The Stonewall Brigade—what was now left of it, and now under junior officers—was a part of that slashing attack at dawn on October 19. Scores of Federals were surprised and captured, and Gordon's onslaught sent other Yankees racing down the Valley pike in a rout one Confederate said "had not been seen since the famous battle of Bull Run." [28] But the victory was short-lived. To the amazement and disgust of the troops, Early vacillated between attacking and retiring until he stood immobile and did nothing, thus permitting the Federals to reform for a counterattack. Moreover, hungry Confederates ignored their officers and gorged themselves from wagons full of food. The Rebels were in as disorganized a condition as was possible when Sheridan struck back, and, Lieutenant Barton wrote, "want of discipline and undue discretion on Early's part, suddenly converted the success into a disastrous defeat." [29] Casualties in killed and wounded were slight. The heavy losses in Early's corps were prisoners—men too full of food to run or too despondent from setbacks to continue the struggle.

The battle at Cedar Creek ended the Second Valley Campaign, a period one brigade officer described as marked by nothing but "defeat and disaster." [30] Another Rebel stated it more bluntly: "When Jackson's old legions were destroyed, the end was near." [31] On December 6 the men of the Stonewall Brigade left the Valley for the last time. Only a fragment boarded the trains for the Peters-

---

28. *Southern Historical Society Papers*, III (1877), 120.
29. Barton, *Recollections*, 68.
30. Caption of Events card, 5th Virginia, Company H, September–October, 1864, War Records Group 109, National Archives.
31. Hunter, *Johnny Reb and Billy Yank*, 649.

burg defenses, where the troops arrived on the ninth. The Valley regiments were assigned positions on the Confederate right at Hatcher's Run; winter quarters were hastily built and the men spent Christmas "fighting famine from within and Grant from without." [32]

Pessimism prevailed in the ranks of the Old Brigade. Families of Valley soldiers were now inside the Federal lines; the Valley itself was a vast desert of destruction; hunger and cold plagued the Petersburg defenders. Moreover, as Randolph Barton stated, "the locusts of Egypt seemed small in number compared to the ever-enlarging Yankee army." Throughout the last months of 1864, he wrote, "we drilled, reorganized, preached, prayed, sang and played cards, and so whiled away the gloomy days waiting for the bloody springtime." [33]

By the middle of January, 1865, the Valley brigade was suffering terribly. Most of the men were half naked; food was almost as scarce as gold; and exposure each day took a heavy toll of life. The Staunton *Vindicator* made an urgent appeal for citizens to alleviate the unit's straitened conditions:

They are in need of clothes to keep them warm. They do not complain but we understand they suffer for many comforts. The men composing this Brigade are from our own midst—our own friends and relatives— and can be supplied with many things needful to them by us. If our people will but make the effort it need not be more than a few days before these gallant men, who participated in the glory and will share the fame of the immortal Jackson, may be made comfortable for the winter.[34]

General Lee, in forwarding to Colonel Terry a hundred dollars which an anonymous donor had sent to ease the unit's "suffering," wrote sympathetically:

From its conduct and association this brigade has acquired the affection of the whole Country, & stands high in the esteem of the army. I should very much regret it should suffer for anything that could be legitimately provided. I hadn't heard that it was in want & had hoped it had not

---

32. Gordon, *Reminiscences*, 378.
33. Barton, *Recollections*, 73. See also Casler, *Stonewall Brigade*, 455–56.
34. Staunton *Vindicator*, January 20, 1865.

been called on to undergo more than what all must suffer in a cause such as we are engaged in. I know that more will be cheerfully borne by it in accomplishing our purpose. I would however be glad if you would inform me if any suffering exists that I can relieve.[35]

On February 6 the Old Brigade fought a heavy skirmish with a portion of the Federal army at Hatcher's Run.[36] The action was indecisive, but it had a marked effect on morale. A stream of brigade members, fatigued in mind and spirit, began trickling into the Federal lines to surrender.[37] Those who remained continued strong in spirit, and in the closing months of the war, for the first time since Chancellorsville, they evidenced a resurgence of pride. General Terry limped back to the head of the brigade after a recuperative period in Wytheville. On February 16 members of the Fifth Virginia drew up a petition and circulated it among the remnants of the Valley brigade. The document was a plea to President Davis to designate the five Virginia regiments as an independent unit. Aware that their numbers were too small to permit them independence in the line, the men asked that they be reorganized into a cavalry company or, better still, into a single regiment to be known as the Stonewall Regiment. Thus they would retain their independence and perpetuate the fame they had won under Jackson.[38]

Apparently the petition received little attention, but an appeal to the Valley for relief from physical misery brought a generous response from loyal citizens in the form of food, clothing, and money. The Natural Bridge Ladies' Society, for example, contributed a total of four thousand dollars.[39]

Near the end of February the 1,293 men in Terry's brigade were transferred to the line facing the Crater; customary truces with pickets were quickly established.[40] Yet, to many, "March came in

35. Robert E. Lee to William Terry, January 16, 1865, letter in Confederate Museum.
36. See *Official Records*, XLVI, Pt. 1, pp. 391–92; *Confederate Veteran*, XXV (1917), 119.
37. See *Official Records*, XLVI, Pt. 2, pp. 636, 808, Pt. 3, p. 90.
38. Staunton *Vindicator*, March 31, 1865.
39. Lexington *Gazette*, February 22, 1865.
40. *Official Records*, XLVI, Pt. 1, p. 389; Barton, *Recollections*, 77–78.

gloomy and melancholy, and brought with it a dreadful certainty of disaster and defeat." [41]

The proximity of the picket lines farther to the north was a major reason for the last assault by the Army of Northern Virginia. Other factors influenced Lee to attack Fort Stedman, one of Grant's strongholds in the Union siege lines. If the charge were sudden it had more chance of success; also, if the Confederates could break the line, they would be in a position to veer right and left and sever Grant's communication lines with City Point while at the same time rolling up the Federals' right.

At 4 A.M. on a cold and gloomy March 25 the Stonewall Brigade and other units of Gordon's division stole from their lines and crept across the plateau toward the Yankee position. Axemen rushed forward and cleared away *chevaux-de-frise*, whereupon shouting Confederates surged through the broken line. Surprise was complete. Scores of Federals were captured while rolling out of their blankets. Gordon's men penetrated farther—and then everything seemed to go wrong. The guides directing the advance appeared uncertain of their destinations.[42] And, instead of fanning out right and left, the Rebels stopped in their advanced position and thus became subjected to a withering fire in front and on both flanks. As Gordon's men tried to get back across the field to the safety of their lines, Federal cannon raked the clearing with canister. An already scarred Colonel Terry was knocked down by a concussion and again was borne home to recuperate. The Fifth Regiment lost its colors. "Grant bombarded us a good deal that day," Randolph Barton added, "and then we settled down into the usual routine of the siege." [43]

On April 1 Grant cracked the Confederate lines at Five Forks. The ragged Confederates shivering in the damp earthworks farther up the line did not have to be told what this meant. The army moved out of the trenches the following morning and marched slowly through the desolate streets of Petersburg. The columns

41. McDonald, *Diary*, 248.
42. W. Gordon McCabe, in *Southern Historical Society Papers*, II (1876), 300, stated that the guides ran away.
43. Barton, *Recollections*, 78–79; *Official Records*, XLVI, Pt. 1, pp. 335, 342, 382.

were unusually quiet. Every man seemed to know that Richmond was doomed, and each man perhaps wondered what misfortune would next befall him and his comrades. Rumors flitted through the ranks that the army was headed for Danville and a rendezvous with Johnston's Army of Tennessee, moving up through North Carolina. On the other hand, many of the men were too numb from fatigue, hunger, and despair to think coherently. As Lieutenant Barton wrote:

> I recall few incidents of great interest on the retreat. I know the weather was in keeping with our spirits; that we were most scantily fed; that I checked my hunger for sometime with parched corn; that we trudged through mud and rain, from time to time repelling the enemy and that we had little sleep or rest. The Federal cavalry general J. Irvin Gregg was captured and made to ride at the head of the brigade —so that if his cavalry did attack the flank of the retreating column, he stood a good chance of being shot by his own men.[44]

Gordon's division formed the rear of Lee's army. Twice on Thursday, April 6, it repulsed attacks, and in one of the engagements the Twenty-seventh Virginia lost its colors. From Amelia Court House westward, General Ewell later wrote, Gordon's men were "constantly fighting." [45]

At three o'clock on the Sabbath morning of April 9, Gordon's force set out on the Appomattox road to drive back Federal cavalry from the escape route. The graycoats plodded along until they saw Sheridan's mounted cavalry astride their path. Gordon quickly massed his lines for one last assault. Ragged, dirty, and hungry, with no hope of victory and little hope of escape, the Confederates closed their lines obediently and gathered around tattered colors that hung limply in the still morning air. Slowly and silently the gray line started forward. No enthusiastic Rebel yell filled the air, no spasmodic firing of skirmishers broke out, no quick and confident steps were taken. Rather, the men moved toward Sheridan as soldiers too weary to fight but too dedicated to stop.

As the Confederates moved onward, Sheridan suddenly drew

44. Barton, *Recollections*, 81.
45. *Official Records*, XLVI, Pt. 1, p. 1259; *Southern Historical Society Papers*, XIII (1885), 250.

back his horsemen—who turned out to be little more than a screen. Before them the Rebels beheld massed ranks of blue infantry lined up on every hill and supported by row after row of gleaming cannon. The appearance of this mighty horde instinctively caused the hollow-cheeked Confederates to stop. In bewilderment Gordon's fragments stared at the overwhelming force; then slowly and sullenly they began to retrace their steps to the Appomattox works. Their feet seemed to drag, and their shoulders slumped. Reality could no longer be clouded by hopes. They were surrounded; they were beaten. A member of the Second Virginia wrote with heavy heart: "We could not even find courage in despair. All was lost, and the future seemed without aim or object. Death and the grave alone appeared inviting." [46]

As the remnant of the once-proud Stonewall Brigade slumped to the ground, Lee greeted his old adversary General Grant at the McLean House. During the truce, Gordon and Sheridan were conversing about the war when firing erupted down the Confederate line. Sheridan hotly demanded to know what Rebel unit was violating the truce, and Gordon reassured him that it could only be a brigade unaware of the armistice. A Federal officer was directed to ride down and stop the firing. To insure that the bluecoat himself was not shot by a trigger-happy Rebel, Gordon sent one of the members of the Stonewall Brigade as an escort.[47]

A few hours later, choking with emotion, Gordon faced his assembled troops and said, "Fellow soldiers, our hearts are as heavy as the murky clouds above us; yet we must not despair. Our duties in the field and camp are ended." Lee had surrendered his army.[48]

Wednesday, April 12, was a chilly, overcast day, but for the first time since Saturday it was not raining. Early that morning the men formed into marching columns. A total of 210 men comprised the five regiments of the Stonewall Brigade. Captain Joseph J. Jenkins commanded the Second; Captain Hamilton D. Lee, the Fourth; Captain Peter E. Wilson, the Fifth; Captain Franklin C. Wilson, the Twenty-seventh; and Captain Henry A. Herrell, the Thirty-

46. Baylor, *Bull Run to Bull Run*, 328.   47. Gordon, *Reminiscences*, 441.
48. *Southern Historical Society Papers*, XIII (1880), 39.

third.[49] In a gesture denoting their record and sacrifices, the proud remains of Jackson's old brigade took the lead of Gordon's division and moved slowly across the Appomattox River toward Federal troops waiting on the opposite ridge. With no straggling or faltering, the Confederates shuffled up the muddy road. A few regiments proudly displayed their battle flags; others bore bare standards, for many of the men had torn the flags to pieces or hidden them rather than surrender colors under which they had fought for four years.

The ragged Rebels filed past the First Division of the V Corps, standing at attention on each side of the road. A command rang out from a Federal officer. Instantly, hundreds of Springfields snapped from their position on the ground to a presentation of arms. The Confederates were aroused from their lethargy. Seeing this display of respect, they held their heads high and improved their march. When the lead columns reached the extreme left of the Federal line, they stopped, faced south, and fixed bayonets. A terse order broke the silence. Briskly, 210 men of the Stonewall Brigade moved four paces across the road, stacked their rifles, removed their cartridge boxes, and hung them over their tarnished rifle barrels. Color-bearers then stepped forward and stacked their revered standards in similar fashion.

The task was done; the war was over. Singly and in groups the Valley men turned and walked slowly through pine woods glistening from spring rains. What lay ahead, no one knew. What lay behind was a four-year chronicle of courage, devotion, and achievement that won for the Stonewall Brigade everlasting fame. These thoughts filled the minds of the men as they bade each other farewell and started up the muddy roads. Perhaps somewhere in the woods a mockingbird gave its lonely call and, heartened by that familiar whistle, footsteps quickened toward the Valley of Virginia—and peace.

---

49. *Official Records*, XLVI, Pt. 1, p. 1271.

CHAPTER XIX

EPILOGUE

The little white Presbyterian church in Lexington was crammed for Sunday morning services April 16, 1865. Bereaved families sat with a sprinkling of battered soldiers who had made their way home from Appomattox. In pews where Stonewall Jackson had once worshipped, the congregation wept openly as the pastor, his own voice trembling with emotion, opened the Bible and began to read: "Although the fig tree shall not blossom, neither fruit be in the vine; the labor of the olive shall fail, and the fields shall yield no meat; the flock shall be cut off from the fold, and there shall be no herd in the stall, yet will I rejoice in the Lord . . ." [1]

In the following weeks other Valley soldiers returned to similar, inauspicious homecomings. Except for a lame attempt by Wash-

---

1. Allan, A *March Past*, 186–87.

ington authorities to implicate members of the Stonewall Brigade
in the Lincoln assassination plot, the veterans were left alone to
reconstruct farms and small businesses, and to recall the days of
death and glory.[2] Sitting on benches in town squares, or struggling
behind mule and plow in an effort to carve anew fields destroyed by
war, the survivors of the Stonewall Brigade proudly remembered
First Manassas, the Valley Campaign, the Seven Days, Second
Manassas and Sharpsburg, Chancellorsville and Gettysburg, the
Wilderness and Spotsylvania, and even the pride of leading Lee's
army on the last march.

Nor could these veterans ever forget the eight men who had commanded the brigade. Only three survived the war. As Kyd Douglas
later wrote: "After General Jackson's promotion, no general of
that brigade ever lived long enough to secure further promotion;
none ever escaped wounds or death long enough to be made a Major
General."[3] Jackson, of course, fell at Chancellorsville. The case
of his successor, Dick Garnett, was equally tragic. After his removal
from command following Kernstown, Garnett labored four months
to have a court-martial refute Jackson's charges that stretched from
neglect of duty to unauthorized absence from command.[4] Just as
the court-martial convened, pressing military matters forced its
adjournment. Garnett, humiliated and hurt, was transferred to
General George Pickett's command, where, according to one officer,
"he was ever thereafter anxious to expose himself, even unneces-
sarily, and to wipe out effectually by some great distinction in
action, what he felt to be an unmerited slur upon his military
reputation."[5] Valorous service in Longstreet's First Corps cul-
minated on the third day's fighting at Gettysburg. Garnett left
a sick-bed and, bundled in an overcoat that sultry day, led his 1,727

---

2. For the full details of the Radical plot to involve the Stonewall Brigade in Lincoln's assassination, see Douglas, *I Rode with Stonewall*, 340–46.
3. *Ibid.*, 126.
4. See Richard B. Garnett to R. M. T. Hunter, April, 1862, Richard B. Garnett
Court Martial Papers, Confederate Museum. The first charge—that he neglected to
place his brigade properly in position—was the one of seven specifications Garnett
seemed least disposed to refute. The specific charges are listed in Freeman, *Lee's
Lieutenants*, I, 318.
5. Harrison, *Pickett's Men*, 20.

Virginians across the field in one of the most famous charges in military history. Only 300 of his men survived the assault; Garnett's body, riddled with bullets, was found twenty-five yards from the Federal lines.[6]

Winder was almost cut in two at Cedar Run, and his successor, Will Baylor, was killed in the closing moments of Second Manassas. Although never officially appointed to command the Stonewall Brigade, Andrew Grigsby ever remained one of its proudest members. He survived the war, lived in Lexington for thirty years, and, emaciated but erect, never missed a veterans' convention or informal get-together. After a five-day siege with pneumonia, the old warrior died December 23, 1895. As was his wish, he was buried on Christmas Day in Goss Cemetery near Stony Point (just north of Charlottesville).

"Stonewall Jim" Walker also survived the war, though his shattered left arm hung limply at his side. Six weeks after being wounded at Spotsylvania, he had returned to duty and seemed content to command the railroad defenses south and southwest of Richmond. And two months before Appomattox, he had, much to his delight, taken over the residue of Pegram's division, which contained his old Thirteenth Virginia.[7] He returned to Pulaski after Lee's surrender, resumed his law practice, and put in a crop of corn with two mules he "confiscated" from the army. In 1868 Walker ran for lieutenant governor of Virginia but was disqualified in the midst of the campaign by Federal orders. Ten years later, however, he was elected lieutenant governor and served under Governor Frederick W. M. Holliday, a former colonel of the Thirty-third Virginia. He moved to Wytheville with his wife and six children in 1880. Following defeat in his bid for state attorney general in 1882, he bolted his party and became a Republican "protectionist." Walker enjoyed two short terms in Congress before being defeated for re-election in 1898 by Judge William F. Rhea of Bristol. Walker contested the election and in the winter of 1899, while taking depositions in Bristol, became involved in a heated argument with Rhea's attorney, William Hamilton. An exchange of gun-

---

6. *Official Records,* XIX, Pt. 1, p. 841; Evans (ed.), *Confederate Military History,* III, 598.
7. *Official Records,* XL, Pt. 2, p. 700.

shots ensued. Walker, who fired first, missed; Hamilton shot.twice, striking Walker both times and partially paralyzing his one good arm.[8]

The crippled campaigner then retired from public office; his remaining years, though physically confining, were relatively happy. As the sole surviving commander of the Stonewall Brigade, he revelled in many pleasant visits from aged Valley warriors that he had led at Gettysburg and in the Wilderness. On October 20, 1901, after a month's illness, he died and was buried at a well-attended service in Wytheville Cemetery.

The last commander of the Old Brigade, William Terry, was at his Wytheville home recuperating from wounds received at Fort Stedman when news of Lee's surrender reached him. Terry promptly mounted his horse and was preparing to join Joseph Johnston's army in North Carolina when the earnest entreaties of family and friends deterred him. Like Walker, his neighbor, Terry resumed his law practice and entered public life. He was also disqualified in 1868 from running for office; yet when the restrictions were eventually lifted, he won a congressional seat handily and served two terms before retiring to the serenity of his farm. On September 5, 1888, he drowned while attempting to ford a swollen stream near his home.[9]

The years passed, each one trimming the number of survivors of the Stonewall Brigade. Yet those who remained ever epitomized the sentiments of a poem written—ironically—by a Federal soldier who greatly admired Jackson:

> And oft in dreams his fierce brigade
> Shall see the form they followed far—
> Still leading in the farthest van—
> A landmark in the cloud of war.
> And oft when white-haired grandsires tell
> Of bloody struggles past and gone,
> The children at their knees shall hear
> How Jackson led his columns on! [10]

---

8. Unidentified newspaper clipping, Walker's personal file, National Archives.
9. *Confederate Veteran*, XI (1903), 70.
10. Douglas, *I Rode with Stonewall*, 232.

There were moments, too, that swelled the hearts of those remaining Valley fighters. In October, 1891, a small group of veterans met in Staunton and set up a permanent Stonewall Brigade Association, with H. J. Williams, former colonel of the Fifth Virginia, as first president. However, sparsity of numbers and the continual knell of death cut short this organization's existence.[11] On May 10, 1913, the Virginia Military Institute held a memorial service in which two of the original guns in the Rockbridge Artillery—both of which had been donated to the academy in 1850 by President Zachary Taylor—were retired as monuments. Colonel William T. Poague, one of the battery's most beloved commanders, led the procession and directed the final salvo of the guns.[12]

Yet the final muster for the Stonewall Brigade actually came in July, 1891, when an impressive statue of Jackson was dedicated over Old Jack's grave in Lexington. A handful of gray-haired veterans, stoop-shouldered and slow of foot, gathered with thirty thousand people to pay a final tribute to the General. The soldiers were dressed in faded and tattered gray uniforms, and white whiskers covered most of their faces, but their devotion remained ever as strong. On the night before the ceremony a chill came in the air. The survivors of the Stonewall Brigade had been the center of attention throughout the day, and sympathetic townspeople were anxious that they should have warm and suitable accommodations for the night. But a diligent search of homes, hotel and dining rooms did not yield a soldier.

Frantically, program chairmen and local citizens combed the entire city; near midnight the Stonewall Brigade was found. There in the moonlight the old men sat huddled in blankets and overcoats around Jackson's statue in the cemetery. The citizens urged the men to get up from the damp ground and partake of the hospitality already arranged for them. No one stirred until one man finally arose. Speaking for the others, he said simply, "Thank ye, sirs, but we've slept around him many a night on the battlefield, and we want to bivouac once more with Old Jack." And bivouac they did.[13]

The next day was July 21—the thirtieth anniversary of that

11. See *Confederate Veteran*, IX (1901), 461.
12. *Ibid.*, XXI (1913), 478.   13. Allan, *A March Past*, 153–54.

memorable battle on Henry House Hill where Jackson and his brigade received their prized nickname. The procession started on schedule. Leading the Men of Manassas was "Stonewall Jim" Walker, "everywhere recognized" and "repeatedly cheered." Behind him came the remnants of the Second Virginia, Berkeley and Jefferson County men headed by venerable John Q. A. Nadenbousch. Adjutant William Wade followed with a small party of Fourth Regiment veterans from the upper Valley. A large contingent of the Fifth Virginia marched behind the soldier-like form of Colonel H. J. Williams, and several prominent Rockbridge County citizens were recognized in the ranks of the Twenty-seventh Virginia, led that day by Captain Frank Wilson. The no more than half-dozen veterans who formed the residue of the Thirty-third Virginia gave mute evidence of their wartime casualties. At the head of the Stonewall Brigade proudly strutted Sergeant R. S. McCartney, a color-bearer of the Twenty-seventh Virginia, who carried a brand-new Confederate battle flag especially made for the occasion.[14]

When the graveside ceremonies ended and the statue of Jackson stood gleaming in the afternoon sun, the Stonewall Brigade fell into ranks for the last time. Slowly, and painfully for some, the old soldiers marched irregularly up the gravel path to the cemetery gate. Just as they reached the exit, one of the Valley veterans stepped from the ranks. For a few moments he gazed at the hills and rolling fields that long ago he had fought to defend. Then his eyes fell on Jackson's grave. He removed his hat, waved it in the air, and, with a choking voice, shouted: "Goodbye, old man, goodbye! We've done all we can for you!" [15]

---

14. Undated newspaper clipping, Stonewall Jackson Memorial Association Records, University of Virginia.
15. Douglas, *I Rode with Stonewall*, 238.

APPENDIX

COMPANIES IN
THE STONEWALL BRIGADE

Listed below by regiment and letter are the forty-nine companies that composed the Stonewall Brigade. After each company is its nickname, place of organization, and first captain. Unless otherwise stated, the company came from within the present boundaries of Virginia.

SECOND REGIMENT

Company A—"Jefferson Guards"; Jefferson County, West Virginia; John W. Rowan.

Company B—"Hamtranck Guards"; Shepherdstown, West Virginia; Vincent M. Butler.

Company C—"Nelson Guards"; Berryville; William N. Nelson.

Company D—"Berkeley Border Guards"; Berkeley, West Virginia; J. Q. A. Nadenbousch.

Company E—"Hedgesville Blues"; Martinsburg, West Virginia; Raleigh T. Colston.

Company F—"Winchester Rifles"; Winchester; William T. Clark.

Company G—"Botts Greys"; Charlestown, West Vriginia; Lawson Botts.

Company H—"Letcher Riflemen"; Duffields community; J. H. L. Hunter.

Company I—"Clarke Riflemen"; Clarke County; Strother H. Bowen.

Company K—"Floyd Guards"; Floyd County; George W. Chambers.

FOURTH REGIMENT

Company A—"Wythe Grays"; Wytheville; William Terry.

Company B—"Fort Lewis Volunteers"; Big Spring area; David Edmondson.

Company C—"Pulaski Guards"; Pulaski County; James A. Walker.

Company D—"Smythe Blues"; Marion; Albert G. Pendleton.

Company E—"Montgomery Highlanders"; Blacksburg; Charles A. Ronald.

Company F—"Grayson Daredevils"; Elk Creek community; Peyton H. Hall.

Company G—"Montgomery Fencibles"; Montgomery County; Robert C. Trigg.

Company H—"Rockbridge Grays"; Buffalo Forge and Lexington; James G. Updike.

Company I—"Liberty Hall Volunteers"; Lexington; James J. White.

Company K—"Montgomery Mountain Boys"; Montgomery County; Robert G. Newlee.

FIFTH REGIMENT

Company A—"Marion Rifles"; Winchester; J. H. S. Funk.

Company B—"Rockbridge Rifles"; Rockbridge County; Samuel H. Letcher.

Company C—"Mountain Guards"; Staunton; Robert G. Doyle.

Company D—"Southern Guards"; Staunton; H. J. Williams.

Company E—"Augusta Greys"; Greenville community; Lycurgus Grills.

Company F—"West View Infantry"; Augusta County; St. Francis C. Roberts.

Company G—"Staunton Rifles"; Staunton; Adam A. Herman.

Company H—"Augusta Rifles"; Augusta County; George L. Andrews.

Company I—"Ready Rifles"; Sangerville Community; Oswald F. Grenman.

Company K—"Continental Morgan Guards"; Frederick County; John Avis.

Company L—"West Augusta Guards"; Staunton; William S. H. Baylor.

TWENTY-SEVENTH REGIMENT

Company A—"Allegheny Light Infantry"; Covington; Thompson McAllister. Later transferred to artillery and known as "Carpenter's Battery."

Company B—"Virginia Riflemen"; Allegheny County; Henry H. Robertson.

Company C—"Allegheny Rifles"; Clifton Forge; Lewis P. Holloway.

Company D—"Monroe Guards"; Staunton and Charlottesville; Hugh S. Giffany.

Company E—"Greenbrier Rifles"; Lewisburg, West Virginia; Philip F. Frazer.

Company G—"Shriver Grays"; Wheeling, West Virginia; Daniel M. Shriver.

Company H—"Rockbridge Rifles"; originally Company B, 5th Regiment. The "Rifles" were consolidated with two companies known as the "Old Dominion Guards" to strengthen the complement of the 27th Regiment.

THIRTY-THIRD REGIMENT

Company A—"Potomac Guards"; Hampshire County, West Virginia; P. T. Grace.

Company B—"Independent Greys"; Shenandoah County; Emanuel Crabill.

Company C—"Page Greys"; Woodstock; John Gatewood.

Company D—"Mountain Rangers"; Winchester; Frederick W. M. Holliday.

Company E—"Emerald Guards"; New Market; Marion N. Sibert.

Company F—"Mount Jackson Rifles"; Mount Jackson area; George W. Allen.

Company G—"Brook Company"; Mount Jackson area; George Crabill.

Company H—"Shenandoah Riflemen"; Page County; William D. Riffeter.

Company I—"Rockingham Confederates"; Rockingham County; John R. Jones.

Company K—"Hardy Grays"; Hardy County, West Virginia; Abram Spengler.

!!!

SOURCES

MANUSCRIPTS

William Allen Papers. Southern Historical Collection, University of North Carolina Library.

Barton Family Papers. In the possession of Lewis Barton, Winchester, Va.

George R. Bedinger Letters. Caroline D. Dandridge Papers, Duke University Library.

Henry R. Berkeley Diary. Alderman Library, University of Virginia.

Charles C. Burks Autograph Book–Journal. In the possession of Mrs. A. D. Depriest, Buena Vista, Va.

Joseph Carpenter Letter. In the possession of Joe Carpenter, Covington, Va.

History of Carpenter's Battery. Typescript in the possession of the author.

Jim P. Charlton Letters. In the possession of Mrs. Richard B. Lee, Roanoke, Va.

Julia Chase Diary. Typescript in Handley Library, Winchester, Va.

Raleigh E. Colston Papers. Southern Historical Collection, University of North Carolina Library.

Michael Cook Diary. In the possession of Mrs. Scott Hall, Alameda, N. M.

Robert L. Dabney Papers. Virginia Archives.

John Warwick Daniel Papers. Alderman Library, University of Virginia.

J. S. Dozle, "Reminiscences of the Wilderness." Manuscript in Jedediah Hotchkiss Papers, Library of Congress.

Journal of Clement D. Fishburne. University of Virginia.

"Recollections of A. M. Garber." Typescript in Jedediah Hotchkiss Papers, Library of Congress.

John Garibaldi Letters. Stonewall Jackson Memorial Association, Lexington, Va.

Richard B. Garnett Court Martial Papers. Confederate Museum, Richmond, Va.

Richard B. Garnett Papers. Virginia Archives.

Frederick W. M. Holliday Papers. Duke University Library.

Jedediah Hotchkiss Papers. Library of Congress.

Thomas J. Jackson Commissariat Papers. Duke University Library.

Thomas J. Jackson Papers. Confederate Museum.

Thomas J. Jackson Papers. Virginia Archives.

Thomas J. Jackson Papers. Virginia Military Institute.

James A. Kibler Letters. Virginia Archives.

James H. Langhorne Letters. Virginia Historical Society.

Robert E. Lee Letter. Confederate Museum.

Robert E. Lee Papers. Library of Congress.

McAllister Family Records. In the possession of W. Hugh McAllister heirs, Covington, Va.

Thompson McAllister Papers. Duke University Library.

David McCauley Letters. Southern Historical Collection, University of North Carolina Library.

Hunter McGuire Papers. Confederate Museum.

Joseph McMurran Diary. Virginia Archives.

William W. Moss Papers. University of Virginia.

Muster Rolls of the 2nd, 4th, 5th, 27th, and 33rd Virginia Infantry, and the Rockbridge Artillery. War Records Group 109, National Archives.

Paxton Family Papers. University of Virginia.

Pendleton Family Papers. Southern Historical Collection, University of North Carolina Library.

William N. Pendleton Order Book and Letter Book. Confederate Museum.

Personal war files of Generals T. J. Jackson, R. B. Garnett, C. S. Winder, E. F. Paxton, J. A. Walker, William Terry, and Colonels W. S. H. Baylor and A. J. Grigsby. War Records Group 109, National Archives.

Records of the 2nd, 4th, 5th, 27th, and 33rd Virginia Infantry, and the Rockbridge Artillery and Carpenter's Battery. Virginia Archives.

Regimental Returns and Captions of Events for the 2nd, 4th, 5th, 27th, and 33rd Virginia Infantry, and the Rockbridge Artillery and Carpenter's Battery. War Records Group 109, National Archives.

William Cabell Rives Papers. Library of Congress.

Stonewall Jackson Memorial Association Records. University of Virginia.

C. B. Strickler Diary. University of Virginia.

Charles E. Taylor Letter. In the possession of Ted Blackburn, Xenia, Ohio.

Andrew W. Varner Autograph Book–Journal. Alderman Library, University of Virginia.

J. Addison Waddell Diary. Jedediah Hotchkiss Papers, Library of Congress.

J. C. Wade Letter. Virginia Historical Society.

R. W. Waldrop Letters. Southern Historical Collection, University of North Carolina Library.

PERSONAL REMINISCENCES AND UNIT HISTORIES

*Additional memoirs will also be found in works listed under
Periodicals*

Allan, Elizabeth R. P. *A March Past*, edited by Janet A. Bryan. Richmond, 1938.

Avirett, James B. *The Memoirs of General Turner Ashby and His Compeers*. Baltimore, 1867.

Bane, Charles H. *History of the Philadelphia Brigade*. Philadelphia, 1876.

Barton, Randolph. *Recollections; 1861–1865*. Baltimore, 1913.

Baylor, George. *Bull Run to Bull Run: or, Four Years in the Army of Northern Virginia*. Richmond, 1900.

Bennett, William W. *A Narrative of the Great Revival Which Prevailed in the Southern Armies*. Philadelphia, 1877.

Blackford, L. Minor, ed. *Mine Eyes Have Seen the Glory*. Cambridge, 1954.

Booth, George W. *Personal Reminiscences of a Maryland Soldier in the War between the States, 1861–1865*. Baltimore, 1898.

Bosang, James N. *Memoirs of a Pulaski Veteran of the Stonewall Brigade*. [Radford, Va., 1912].

Bryant, E. E. *History of the Third Regiment of Wisconsin Veteran Volunteers*. Madison, 1891.

Caldwell, J. F. J. *The History of a Brigade of South Carolinians Known First as "Gregg's" and Subsequently as "McGowan's" Brigade*. Philadelphia, 1866.

Casler, John O. *Four Years in the Stonewall Brigade*. Guthrie, Okla., 1893.

Cooke, John Esten. *Wearing of the Gray*. New York, 1867.

Dabney, Robert L. *True Courage: A Discourse Commemorative of Lieut. Gen. T. J. Jackson*. Richmond, 1863.

DeFontaine, F. G. *Army Letters of Personnae, 1861–1865*. Columbia, 1897.

Douglas, Henry Kyd. *I Rode with Stonewall*. Chapel Hill, 1940.

Dunlop, W. S. *Lee's Sharpshooters*. Little Rock, 1899.

Early, Jubal A. *Autobiographical Sketch and Narrative of the War between the States*. Philadelphia, 1912.

Fonerden, Clarence A. *A Brief History of the Military Career of Carpenter's Battery*. New Market, Va., 1911.

Fremantle, Arthur J. L. *Three Months in the Southern States*. New York, 1864.

Gibbon, John. *Personal Recollections of the Civil War*. New York, 1928.

Gill, John. *Reminiscences of Four Years as a Private Soldier in the Confederate Army*. Baltimore, 1904.

Goldsborough, W. W. *The Maryland Line in the Confederate States Army*. Baltimore, 1869.

Gordon, John B. *Reminiscences of the Civil War*. New York, 1903.

Graybill, John H. *Diary of a Soldier of the Stonewall Brigade*. Woodstock, Va., n.d.

Harrison, Walter. *Pickett's Men: A Fragment of War History*. New York, 1870.

Haskell, John. *The Haskell Memoirs*, edited by Gilbert E. Govan and James Livingood. New York, 1960.

Howard, McHenry. *Recollections of a Maryland Confederate Soldier and Staff Officer under Johnston, Jackson and Lee*. Baltimore, Md., 1913.

Humphreys, David. *Heroes and Spies of the Civil War*. New York, 1903.

Jackson, Mary Anna. *Memoirs of "Stonewall" Jackson*. Louisville, 1895.

Johnson, R. U., and Buel, C. C., eds. *Battles and Leaders of the Civil War*. 4 vols. New York, 1884–87.

Jones, J. William. *Christ in the Camp, or Religion in Lee's Army*. Richmond, 1887.

LaBree, Ben, ed. *Camp Fires of the Confederacy*. Louisville, 1898.

Longstreet, James. *From Manassas to Appomattox*, edited by James I. Robertson, Jr. Bloomington, Ind., 1960.

McDonald, Cornelia A. *A Diary with Reminiscences of the War and*

Refugee Life in the Shenandoah Valley, 1860–1865, edited by Hunter McDonald. Nashville, 1934.

McGuire, Judith W. *Diary of a Refugee.* Richmond, 1889.

McKim, Randolph. *A Soldier's Recollections.* New York, 1910.

Moore, Edward A. *The Story of a Cannoneer under Stonewall Jackson.* New York, 1907.

Muffly, J. W., ed. *The Story of Our Regiment* [148th Pennsylvania]. Des Moines, 1904.

Neese, George M. *Three Years in the Confederate Horse Artillery.* New York, 1911.

Oates, William C. *The War between the Union and the Confederacy.* New York, 1905.

Opie, John N. *A Rebel Cavalryman with Lee, Jackson and Stuart.* Chicago, 1899.

Owen, William M. *In Camp and Battle with the Washington Artillery.* Boston, 1885.

Page, R. C. M. *Sketch of Page's Battery, or Morris Artillery, Second Corps, Army of Northern Virginia.* New York, 1885.

Poague, William T. *Gunner with Stonewall,* edited by Monroe Cockrell. Jackson, Tenn., 1957.

Quint, A. H. *The Record of the Second Massachusetts Infantry, 1861–65.* Boston, 1867.

Robson, John S. *How a One-legged Rebel Lives.* Richmond, 1876.

Sketches of War History, 1861–1865. Papers Read before the Ohio Commandery . . . 6 vols. Cincinnati, 1888–1919.

Taylor, Richard. *Destruction and Reconstruction.* New York, 1879.

Williams, Alpheus S. *From the Cannon's Mouth,* edited by Milo M. Quaife. Detroit, 1959.

Wood, George L. *The Seventh* [Ohio] *Regiment: A Record.* New York, 1865.

Worsham, John O. *One of Jackson's Foot Cavalry.* New York, 1912.

OTHER PRIMARY SOURCES

Blackford, Susan P., ed. *Letters from Lee's Army.* New York, 1947.

Carpenter, Mary E. H., comp. *History of the Carpenters of "Fort Carpenter," 1746–1949.* Lynchburg, Va., n.d.

Daniel, Edward M., ed. *Speeches and Orations of John Warwick Daniel.* Lynchburg, Va., 1911.

Gardiner, M. H. and A. H. *Chronicles of Old Berkeley.* Durham, N.C., 1938.

Hotchkiss, Jed, and Allen, William. *The Battlefields of Virginia: Chancellorsville.* New York, 1867.

Hunter, Alexander. *Johnny Reb and Billy Yank.* New York, 1905.

Jones, J. William, comp. *Army of Northern Virginia Memorial Volume.* Richmond, 1880.

Lee, Susan P., ed. *Memoirs of William Nelson Pendleton.* Philadelphia, 1893.

McAllister, J. Gray, ed. *McAllister Family Records.* Easton, Pa., 1912.

———. *Sketch of Captain Thompson McAllister, Co. A, 27th Virginia Regiment.* Petersburg, 1896.

McGuire, Hunter, and Christian, George L. *The Confederate Cause and Conduct in the War between the States.* Richmond, 1907.

Moffett, Mary C., ed. *Letters of General James Conner, C.S.A.* Columbia, 1933.

Paxton, John G., ed. *Elisha Franklin Paxton: Memoir and Memorials.* New York, 1907.

Slaughter, Philip. *A Sketch of the Life of Randolph Fairfax.* Baltimore, 1878.

U.S. War Department, comp. *War of the Rebellion: A Compilation of the Official Records of the Union and Confederate Armies.* 128 vols. Washington, 1880–1901.

Waddell, J. Addison. *Annals of Augusta County.* Staunton, 1902.

White, William S. *Sketches of the Life of Captain Hugh A. White, of the Stonewall Brigade.* Columbia, 1864.

BIOGRAPHICAL WORKS

Allan, Elizabeth P. *The Life and Letters of Margaret Junkin Preston.* Boston, 1903.

Arnold, Thomas J. *Early Life and Letters of General Thomas J. Jackson.* New York, 1916.

Ashby, Thomas A. *A Life of Turner Ashby.* New York, 1914.

Bean, W. G. *Stonewall's Man: Sandie Pendleton.* Chapel Hill, 1959.

Chew, Roger P. *Stonewall Jackson.* Lexington, Va., 1912.

Cook, Roy Bird. *The Family and Early Life of Stonewall Jackson.* Charlestown, W. Va., 1948.

Cooke, John Esten. *The Life of Stonewall Jackson.* New York, 1866.

———. *Stonewall Jackson and the Old Stonewall Brigade,* edited by Richard Harwell. Charlottesville, Va., 1954.

Cullum, George W. *Biographical Register of the Officers and Graduates of the U.S. Military Academy . . . to 1890.* 4 vols. Boston, 1891.

Dabney, Robert L. *Life and Campaigns of Lieut.-Gen. Thomas J. Jackson.* New York, 1866.

Daly, Louise H. *Alexander Cheves Haskell: The Portrait of a Man.* Norwood, Mass., 1934.

Eliot, Ellsworth, Jr. *West Point in the Confederacy*. New York, 1941.
Freeman, Douglas Southall. *R. E. Lee: A Biography*. 4 vols. New York, 1934–35.
Hamlin, Percy G. *Old Bald Head*. Strasburg, Va., 1940.
Henderson, G. F. R. *Stonewall Jackson and the American Civil War*. 2 vols. New York, 1905.
Hull, Susan R., comp. *Boy Soldiers of the Confederacy*. New York, 1905.
Johnson, John L. *The University Memorial*. Baltimore, 1871.
Johnson, Thomas C. *The Life and Letters of Robert Lewis Dabney*. Richmond, 1903.
McCabe, James D., Jr. *Life and Campaigns of General Robert E. Lee*. New York, 1866.
Riley, Elihu. *Stonewall Jackson*. Annapolis, 1920.
Sigaud, Louis A. *Belle Boyd, Confederate Spy*. Richmond, 1944.
Smith, Tunstall. *James McHenry Howard, A Memoir*. Baltimore, 1916.
——, ed. *Richard Snowden Andrews: A Memoir*. Baltimore, 1910.
Thomas, Clarence. *General Turner Ashby*. Winchester, 1907.
Vandiver, Frank E. *Mighty Stonewall*. New York, 1957.
Walker, Charles D. *Memorial, Virginia Military Institute*. Philadelphia, 1875.
White, Henry A. *Stonewall Jackson*. New York, 1909.

PERIODICALS

Annals of Iowa, 1915–21, 1 vol.
Charlestown *Spirit of Jefferson*, 1904, 1913.
Civil War History, 1955–61, 7 vols.
Confederate Veteran, 1893–1932, 40 vols.
Harper's New Monthly Magazine, 1866–68, 3 vols.
Harper's Weekly, 1861–65.
The Land We Love, 1866–69, 6 vols.
Leesburg *Washingtonian*, 1865.
Lexington *Gazette*, 1861–65.
Maryland Historical Magazine, 1958, 1 vol.
Rebellion Record, 1862–71, 12 vols.
Richmond *Enquirer*, 1862–65.
Richmond *Examiner*, 1861–65.
Richmond *Times-Dispatch*, 1904.
Richmond *Whig*, 1861–65.
Southern Historical Society Papers, 1876–1959, 52 vols.
Southern Illustrated News, 1862–65.
Staunton *Daily News*, 1916.
Staunton *Spectator and General Advertiser*, 1861–65.

Staunton *Vindicator*, 1861–65.
Tyler's Quarterly Historical and Genealogical Magazine, 1928–29, 1 vol.
Virginia Magazine of History and Biography, 1951, 1961.
Winchester *Republican*, 1862.

GENERAL STUDIES

Allan, William. *Jackson's Valley Campaign*. Richmond, 1878.
Army Regulations, Adopted for the Use of the Confederate States. Atlanta, 1861.
Ashby, Thomas A. *The Valley Campaigns*. New York, 1914.
Bigelow, John. *The Campaign of Chancellorsville*. New Haven, 1910.
Brock, B. A., ed. *Hardesty's Historical and Geographical Encyclopedia: Special Virginia Edition*. New York, 1884.
Bushong, Millard K. *A History of Jefferson County, West Virginia*. Charlestown, W. Va., 1941.
Chew, Roger P. *Military Operations in Jefferson County, West Virginia*. [Charlestown, W. Va., 1911].
Clark, Walter, ed. *Histories of the Several Regiments and Battalions from North Carolina in the Great War, 1861–65*. 5 vols. Raleigh and Goldsboro, 1901.
Couper, William. *One Hundred Years at V.M.I.* 4 vols. Richmond, 1939.
Dowdey, Clifford. *The Land They Fought For*. New York, 1955.
Esposito, Vincent, ed. *Atlas to Accompany Steele's American Campaigns*. West Point, N.Y., 1956.
Evans, Clement A., ed. *Confederate Military History*. 13 vols. Atlanta, 1899.
Fleming, Walter L., ed. *The South in the Building of the Nation*. 13 vols. Richmond, 1909.
Flournoy, Mary. *Sidelights on Southern History*. Richmond, 1939.
Fox, William. *Regimental Losses in the American Civil War, 1861–1865*. Albany, N.Y., 1889.
Freeman, Douglas Southall. *Lee's Lieutenants: A Study in Command*. 3 vols. New York, 1942–44.
Gilham, William. *Manual of Instruction for the Volunteers and Militia of the Confederate States*. Richmond, 1862.
Green, Louisa M., ed. *True Stories of Old Winchester and the Valley*. Winchester, 1931.
Grimsley, Daniel A. *Battles in Culpeper County, Virginia, 1861–1865, and Other Articles*. Culpeper, 1900.
Hendricks, Sam H. *Memorial to Confederate Soldiers, Elmwood Cemetery*. Shepherdstown, W. Va., 1937.

Henry, Robert Selph. *The Story of the Confederacy*. Indianapolis, 1931.

Hungerford, Edward. *The Story of the Baltimore and Ohio Railroad, 1827–1897*, 2 vols. New York, 1928.

Johnston, R. M. *Bull Run, Its Strategy and Tactics*. Boston, 1913.

Livermore, Thomas L. *Numbers and Losses in the Civil War in America, 1861–65*. Boston, 1901.

Lonn, Ella. *Desertion during the Civil War*. New York, 1928.

———. *Foreigners in the Confederacy*. Chapel Hill, 1940.

Lossing, Benjamin J., *Lossing's Pictorial Field Book of the Great Civil War*. 6 parts. Philadelphia, 1886–89.

Miller, Francis T., ed. *The Photographic History of the Civil War*. 10 vols. New York, 1911.

Morton, Frederic. *The Story of Winchester in Virginia*. Strasburg, Va., 1925.

Morton, Oren F. *A History of Rockbridge County, Virginia*. Staunton, 1920.

Munford, Beverly B. *Virginia's Attitude toward Slavery and Secession*. Richmond, 1909.

Pitts, Charles F. *Chaplains in Gray*. Nashville, 1957.

Shanks, Henry T. *The Secession Movement in Virginia, 1847–1861*. Richmond, 1934.

Strickler, Harry M. *A Short History of Page County, Virginia*. Richmond, 1952.

U.S. Army, *American Military History, 1607–1953*. Washington, 1956.

U.S. War Department, comp. *Atlas to Accompany the Official Records of the Union and Confederate Armies*. New York, 1958.

———, comp. *List of Field Officers, Regiments, and Battalions in the Confederate States Army*. Washington, n.d.

Wayland, John W. *A History of Rockingham County, Virginia*. Dayton, Va., 1912.

———. *A History of Shenandoah County, Virginia*. Strasburg, Va., 1927.

———. *Stonewall Jackson's Way*. Staunton, 1956.

———. *Virginia Valley Records*. Strasburg, Va., 1930.

Wiley, Bell Irvin. *The Life of Johnny Reb*. Indianapolis, 1943.

Williams, Kenneth P. *Lincoln Finds A General*. 5 vols. New York, 1949–59.

Wise, Jennings C. *The Long Arm of Lee*. 2 vols. Lynchburg, Va., 1915.

———. *The Military History of the Virginia Military Institute from 1839 to 1865*. Lynchburg, Va., 1915.

Wright, Marcus J. *General Officers of the Confederate Army . . .* New York, 1911.

INDEX

NOTE: Unless otherwise stated, all places mentioned are in Virginia.

Alburtis, Ephraim G., 39
Allegheny County, 250
"Allegheny Light Infantry," 250
"Allegheny Rifles," 21, 250
Allen, George W., 251
Allen, James W., 4, 18, 32, 54, 73, 83, 94, 101, 106, 109–10, 119 and n.
Amelia Court House, 239
Anderson, George H., 187
Andrews, George L. (C.S.A.), 250
Andrews, George L. (U.S.A.), 95 n.
Antietam Creek, Md.: battle of, 155–61
Appomattox, 12, 17, 239–42, 244
Ashby, Turner, 58, 61, 70–71, 82 and n., 86, 89, 100, 102–103
Augusta County, 11, 139, 196, 250
"Augusta Greys," 250
"Augusta Rifles," 250
Avis, John, 19, 250

Baldwin, John (soldier), 151
Baldwin, John B. (attorney), 196
Baltimore & Ohio R. R., 27, 29
Banks, Nathaniel P., 36 n., 58, 65, 68–69, 77, 84, 85, 89, 91–93, 97–100
Barton, David (son), 98
Barton, David W. (father), 21
Barton, Marshall, 98
Barton, Randolph: quoted, 172, 184 n., 185, 212, 215, 234–36, 238–39; mentioned, 187
Bath, W. Va., 58, 61, 65
Baylor, William S. H.: background of, 139–40; death of, 150, 244; mentioned, 5, 6, 17, 19 n., 83, 85, 94, 98, 119 n., 122, 130, 138, 141, 144, 148–49, 164, 228, 250
Beall, John Yates, 16 n.
Bealton Station, 210

Beauregard, P. G. T., 36, 39, 43, 80 n.
Bedinger, George R.: quoted, 174, 176–77, 190; mentioned, 193 n., 206
Bee, Bernard E., 37, 39
Benjamin, Judah P., 50 n., 67
"Berkeley Border Guards," 249
Berkeley County, 5, 247, 249
Berryville, 169, 249
Big Spring, 249
"Black Hat Brigade," 146 n.
Blackford, Launcelot, 135
Blacksburg, 249
"Bloody Angle." *See* Spotsylvania, battle of
Boonsboro, Md., 230
Botts, Lawson, 16, 19 n., 73 n., 127 n., 146 and n., 249
"Botts Greys," 16, 249
Bowen, Strother H., 249
Boyd, Belle, 19
Branch, Lawrence O., 134
Brandy Station, 210
Bristoe, 143–44, 210
"Brook Company," 251
Brown, John, 4, 5, 139, 196, 228
Buffalo Gorge, 249
Bull Run. *See* Manassas
Bunker Hill, 28, 161, 170
Burks, Charles C., 192 n.
Burks, Jesse S., 69, 71–72, 75
Burnside, Ambrose E., 171, 174
Butler, Vincent M., 248

Caddall, John, 21
Cadwallader, George, 32
Camp Allen, 169
Camp Baylor, 170–71
Camp Buchanan, 70
Camp Harman, 45, 47
Camp Maggot, 45
Camp Paxton, 194, 198
Camp Stearns, 28
Camp Stephenson, 52
Camp Stonewall Jackson, 215
Camp Winder, 175, 180, 183
Camp Zollicoffer, 67, 170
Carpenter, John, 22, 129
Carpenter, Joseph, 22, 71, 109, 113,

120–21, 129. *See also* Virginia Units: Carpenter's Battery
Carrington, James M., 106
Casler, John O.: quoted, 77 n., 89, 114, 142, 147, 179, 184, 190, 192, 201, 217 n., 225, 229
Cavins, Elijah H. C., 75
Cedar Creek. *See* Slaughter Mountain, battle of
Centreville, 35, 45
Chambers, George W., 249
Chancellorsville: battle of, 182–89; mentioned, 12, 172, 192, 195, 196 n., 207 n., 218, 228, 237, 243
Chantilly, 153
Charlestown, W. Va., 5, 9, 11, 16, 33, 99–100, 249
Charlottesville, 85, 214, 229, 244, 250
Charlton, Jim P.: quoted, 177, 211–12
Chew, R. Preston, 56
Clark, William T., 249
Clarke County, 249
"Clarke Riflemen," 249
Clifton Forge, 250
Colston, Raleigh T.: death of, 213–14; mentioned, 19 and n., 73, 113, 119, 134, 148, 150, 156 n., 193 n., 249
Colston, William, 73 and n.
Connecticut Infantry: 5th—135; 18th—200 n.
Conrad, Holmes, Jr., 43
Conrad, Tucker, 43
Conrad's Store, 83
Conscription, 82, 83, 88
"Continental Morgan Guards," 19, 250
Corbin, Roberta, 176
Covington, 113, 250
Cowardice, 6, 18, 32, 37, 44, 111, 121–22
Crabill, Emanuel, 251
Crabill, George, 251
Cross Keys, 105–106, 108, 111
Culp, Wesley, 203, 207
Culpeper, 127, 198, 211 n.
Cumberland, Md., 55, 64
Cummings, Arthur C., 38, 40 and n., 76, 83–84
Curtis, Finley: quoted, 185, 188

Dabney, Robert L., 18, 20, 115, 116 n., 143 n., 167
Dam No. 5, pp. 55–58, 59
Daniel, John W., 21
Danville, 239
Darkesville, 32, 208
Davis, Jefferson, 67, 80, 88, 163, 179, 193, 237
Dead, robbing of the, 120, 184 n.
Desertion, 141, 179, 211
Doles, George, 217, 222
Doubleday, Abner, 157 n., 205
Douglas, H. Kyd: mentioned, 18, 48, 189, 191, 192 n., 199; quoted, 83, 136, 160, 185, 187 n., 243
Doyle, Robert G., 250
Dozle, J. S.: quoted, 219 n., 221, 224–25
Duffields, 249

Early, Jubal A.: mentioned, 128, 130, 134, 159, 164, 196–97, 202, 218, 229–35; criticized, 234
Echols, John, 18, 72, 73
Edmondson, David, 249
Edmondson, James K., 19 n., 168, 173 n., 186
Elk Creek, 249
"Emerald Guards," 13, 174, 201, 251
Ewell, Richard S.: mentioned, 83, 84, 89, 95, 103, 105, 107–108, 112, 116, 127–28, 142–44, 147, 197–99, 201, 203 n., 208, 218, 221, 239; described, 195
Executions, 141, 179, 211

Fairfax, Randolph, 97, 121, 136 n., 174
Fairfax Court House, 47, 50–51
Falling Waters, W. Va., 30–32, 208
Fayetteville, Pa., 202
Fishburne, Clement D., 45–46, 70
Fisher's Hill, battle of, 234
Five Forks, battle of, 238
Flagg, George, 26
Fletcher, Louis J., 13
Floyd County, 249
"Floyd Guards," 249
"Fort Lewis Volunteers," 249

Fort Stedman, battle of, 238, 245
Fort Sumter, S.C., 4, 80 n.
Franklin, W. Va., 86
Fraternization, 46, 75, 123, 190, 207 n., 237
Frazer, Philip F., 193 n., 220, 250
Frazier, James, 42, 53
Frederick, Md., 65, 68, 154 n., 202, 230
Frederick County, 21, 250
Fredericksburg: mentioned, 18, 68, 168, 212; battle of, 171–74, 180, 228
Fremantle, Arthur J. L., 202
Frémont, John C., 84, 100–101, 105, 107–108
French, William, 213, 215 n.
"French furloughs," 46–47, 170
Front Royal, 92, 100, 198–99
Fulkerson, Samuel V., 69, 71–72
Fulton, John H., 21
Funk, John H. S., 19 n., 184–85, 187–88, 193 n., 205, 210–11, 214, 250

Gaines' Mill, 116–20, 197
Gardner, Robert D., 19 n., 122, 127 n., 156 n., 168, 174, 228
Garibaldi, John: quoted, 170–71, 178, 182, 200, 209–12, 215–16, 218
Garnett, James M., 151, 153
Garnett, Richard B.: background of, 54–55; mentioned, 60, 64–65, 68–69, 72–74, 80–81, 111; relieved from command, 78; death of, 208, 243–44; praised, 243
Garnett, Robert S., 54
Gatewood, John, 251
Geary, John W., 206
Germans, 12–13
Gettysburg, Pa.: mentioned, 12, 120 n., 202, 228, 243, 245; battle of, 203–208
Giffany, Hugh S., 250
Golladay, Jacob B., 156 n.
Gordon, John B., 218, 224, 228, 230–31, 235, 238–41
Gordonsville, 102, 114, 125–26, 138, 140–41, 172
Grace, P. T., 251

Grant, Ulysses S., 217–18, 223, 227, 229, 232, 236, 238, 240
"Grayson Daredevils," 17, 249
Green, T. C., 45
"Greenbrier Rifles," 250
Greenville, 250
Gregg, J. Irvin, 239
Gregg, Maxcy, 172–73
Grenman, Oswald F., 250
Griffin, Charles, 40–41
Grigsby, Andrew J.: mentioned, 20, 82, 83, 88, 94, 95, 111, 122–23, 132, 146–47, 150, 155, 158, 160; biographical data on, 162–65; death of, 244
Grills, Lycurgus, 250
Groveton, battle of, 145–48
Guiney's Station, 172, 175, 189–90, 192
Gwynn, Bronson, 43

Hagerstown, Md., 201, 208
Hall, John, 220
Hall, Peyton H., 249
Halltown, 100, 155
Hamilton, William, 244–45
Hamilton's Crossing, 172, 174, 183, 190, 193–94
Hampshire County, W. Va., 251
"Hamtranck Guards," 248
Hancock, W. Va., 58, 61, 65
Hardy County, W. Va., 251
"Hardy Grays," 18, 251
Harman, John A., 82, 164
Harman, William, 42, 74, 75, 82, 83
Harper, Kenton, 29, 38, 139–40
Harpers Ferry, W. Va.: 1861 capture of, 3–6; mentioned, 7, 8, 17, 19, 26–28, 48, 68, 99–100, 139–40, 159, 192, 199, 228; 1862 capture of, 154–56
Harrison, Peyton, 43
Harrisonburg, 11, 78, 84, 89, 105
Harrison's Landing, 123
Hatcher's Run, 236–37
Hawks, Wells J., 18
Hay, William, 19
Haynes, Charles L., 127 n.
Hays, Harry, 110, 220, 225
"Hedgesville Blues," 249
Hendricks, James, 142

Herman, Adam A., 250
Herrell, Henry A., 240
Heth, Henry, 211
Hill, A. Powell, 116–18, 120, 133–34, 148, 161, 164, 172, 191, 197, 211
Hill, D. Harvey, 116–19 and n., 121, 159
Holliday, Frederick W. M., 20, 56, 135, 244, 251
Holloway, Lewis P., 250
Hooker, Joseph, 12, 157 n., 159, 177, 183–84, 188
Hopkins, Abner C., 20, 103, 149
Hotchkiss, Jedediah, 101 and n., 165 n.
Howard, J. McHenry: mentioned, 101, 102, 127, 129–30, 164 n.; quoted, 106, 118–19, 125
Hunter, David, 229–30
Hunter, James H. L., 249
Hunter, Robert W., 18

Imboden, John D., 37
"Independent Greys," 251
Indiana Infantry: 13th—72 n.; 14th—72 n., 75; 19th—146 n.
Irishmen, 13, 56, 174 n., 201
Iron Brigade, 146

Jackson, Thomas J.: descriptions of, 7–8, 23–25, 40, 47, 62, 69, 89, 100, 118; discipline of, 8–9, 26, 29, 46–47, 52–53, 68, 78, 81, 88, 126, 141, 179; mentioned, 12–19 *passim*, 28, 36, 37–40, 54 and n., 56–64 *passim*, 69–73, 76, 83–95 *passim*, 101–17 *passim*, 122, 127–28, 131, 133 n., 138–48 *passim*, 153–67 *passim*, 172, 180, 183–84, 187, 197, 220, 228, 234–35, 237, 241; religion of, 20, 171, 178, 180–81, 195, 212, 242; soldiers' love for, 23–26, 53, 67, 96, 98, 124, 142–43, 190–92, 230, 245–47; nicknames for, 25; praises Stonewall Brigade, 27, 33, 44 and n., 48–50, 60, 66, 136, 178 n., 189; quoted, 39–40, 41, 65, 74, 75, 82, 87, 90, 96, 99, 106–107, 112, 115–16, 120, 130, 134, 143, 146, 149–52, 156, 176, 179; criticized, 66–

67, 77, 81, 101 n., 163, 196; wounded, 185, 189; death of, 190, 194, 198, 243; funeral of, 192–93; 1891 memorial service to, 246–47
Jefferson County, W. Va., 247, 248
"Jefferson Guards," 248
Jeffersonton, 141–42
Jenkins, Joseph J., 240
Johnson, Edward: mentioned, 84, 85, 198–200, 202–208, 213–214, 221–22, 226; description of, 195; captured, 224
Johnston, Joseph E., 27, 28, 32–35; 36 n., 50 n., 68, 70, 80, 239, 245
Jones, Frank B., 47, 119 and n.
Jones, J. B., 233
Jones, John M., 158, 204–205, 226
Jones, John R., 18, 251
Junkin, George, 166

Kearneysville, 169
Kernstown: mentioned, 11, 18, 52, 78, 82, 111, 151; battle of, 70–77
King, Leicester, 110
Kurtz, George W., 19 and n.

Langhorne, James H., 53, 62
Lee, Edwin G., 17–18, 127 n., 132–33, 168, 174
Lee, Hamilton D., 240
Lee, Robert E.: mentioned, 6, 18, 24, 113, 115–18, 142, 151, 155, 160–61, 171, 179–80, 191–92, 197 n., 198, 208, 213, 215, 226–30, 233, 238–40, 243–44; criticized, 196; affection for Stonewall Brigade, 216, 236–37
Lee, Robert E., Jr., 19, 109 n., 160
Lee, William Fitzhugh, 19
Leesburg, 153
Letcher, John, 4–5, 67, 162
Letcher, Samuel H., 20, 250
"Letcher Riflemen," 249
Lewisburg, W. Va., 250
Lexington, 5, 7, 8, 11, 30, 33, 66, 74, 165–66, 187 n., 191, 230, 233, 242, 244, 246–47, 249
"Liberty Hall Volunteers," 16, 53, 149, 205, 232–33, 249

Lincoln, Abraham, 68, 77, 166, 243
Longstreet, James, 37, 117, 148, 151, 154 n., 156, 171, 202, 204, 208, 243
Loring, William W., 57–58, 61, 64–67, 69
Louisa Court House, 229
Louisiana Infantry: *7th*—110–11
Luray, 89
Lynchburg, 229

McAllister, Thompson, 13, 250
McCartney, R. S., 247
McCausland, John, 13, 18, 230–31
McClellan, George B., 68, 77, 113, 115, 123, 157, 204
McDonald, Cornelia: quoted, 4, 5, 34, 97, 161, 201, 233
McDowell, battle of, 85–86, 88, 195
McGowan, Samuel, 186
McGuire, Hunter, 13, 18, 19, 152, 189 n.
McLaughlin, William, 13
McMullen, William, 31
McMurran, Joseph, 221, 229, 232
Madison Court House, 126, 128, 172
Maine Artillery: *2nd Btty.*—129 n.
Malvern Hill, battle of, 120–22
Manassas: Second Battle of, 11, 148–52, 162, 228, 243–44; First Battle of, 13, 14 n., 19, 37–48, 125, 139, 167, 189, 235, 243, 246–47; mentioned, 35–36, 51–52, 68, 70, 80, 143–45
Marion, 11, 12, 249
"Marion Rifles," 250
Martinsburg, W. Va., 5, 28–29, 33, 56, 58, 99, 154, 156 n., 169, 199, 208, 249
Maryland Infantry: *1st* (CSA)—207; *5th* (USA)—200 n.
Massachusetts Infantry: *2nd*—95 n.
Meade, George G., 204, 213, 215
Meade, Richard K., 18
Mechanicsville, 115–16, 124, 229
Mechum's River Station, 85
Mennonites, 104
Mercer, Douglas, 86
Michigan Infantry: *1st*—41
Middletown, 92, 102

Milroy, Robert H., 86, 198–200
Mine Run, 20, 211 n., 213–15, 218
Minor, Launcelot, 21, 101
Monocacy River, Md., battle of, 231–32
"Monroe Guards," 250
Montgomery County, 249
"Montgomery Fencibles," 20, 52, 249
"Montgomery Highlanders," 249
"Montgomery Mountain Boys," 249
Moore, Albert L., 15
Moore, Edward A.: quoted, 93, 109, 144–45, 160–61; mentioned, 129, 141 n.
Moss Neck, 174–75, 178
Mount Jackson, 69, 77–78, 82, 251
"Mount Jackson Rifles," 251
Mount Meridian, 106, 113
Mount Solon, 89
"Mountain Guards," 250
"Mountain Rangers," 251
Music, 34, 153–54, 174, 177, 201

Nadenbousch, John Q. A., 19 n., 168, 203, 219, 247, 249
Neff, John, 82, 94, 95–96, 107, 108 n., 112, 117, 147
Negroes, 14
Nelson, William (artillerist), 38
Nelson, William N. (infantryman), 249
"Nelson Guards," 249
"New Centreville," 52, 54
New Market, 13, 33, 56, 89, 234, 251
New York Infantry: 28th—135
Newlee, Robert G., 249
Newton, James W., 199 n.
Newtown, 69, 76, 92–93, 101–102
Nicholls, Francis T., 204–205
North Carolina Infantry: 1st—225

O'Brien, John, 94
Ohio Infantry: 5th—72 n., 75, 110; 7th —110; 8th—72 n.; 62nd—72 n.; 67th —72 n., 75; 122nd—200 n.; 123rd— 200 n.
"Old Dominion Guards," 251
Orange & Alexandria R. R., 143, 210
Orange Court House, 140, 172, 210
Otey, Mercer, 141 n.

Page County, 251
"Page Greys," 251
Patriotism, Southern, 10, 26, 183
Patterson, Robert, 28–29, 31–33, 36 n.
Paxton, E. Franklin: mentioned, 17, 42, 163–64, 174–75, 177, 179–80, 184– 86, 195; quoted, 58, 63, 65, 69, 76, 90, 125, 172–73, 178, 183; background of, 165–67; personal traits of, 180–81; death of, 187
Pegram, John, 224, 245
Pender, W. Dorsey, 151
Pendleton, Albert G., 249
Pendleton, Alexander Sandie: mentioned, 19, 196; quoted, 132 n., 157, 171, 176, 217
Pendleton, William Nelson, 11, 17, 20, 29–32, 33, 38–39, 68, 171 n.
Pennsylvania Infantry: 11th—31; 46th —135; 84th—72 n., 75; 87th—200 n.; 148th—225 n.
Petersburg, siege of, 235–38
Picket duty, 170, 176, 190, 210–12, 238
Pickett, George E., 208, 243
Piedmont, 36
Pisgah Church, 140, 215
Poague, William T.: mentioned, 56, 92, 95, 99, 106–12 passim, 120, 122 n., 129, 134 n., 144, 146, 149, 155–57, 160, 246; quoted, 66, 76, 116, 124
Pope, John, 126–27, 142, 144, 148–51
Port Republic, 105–106, 108–13
Porter, David D., 19
Porter, FitzJohn, 116, 118
"Potomac Guards," 251
Potomac River, 3, 26, 28, 55–57, 61, 64, 66, 91, 97, 153–55, 160–61, 201, 208, 230
Presbyterians, 13, 20, 163, 165, 242
Preston, James T. L., 14 n., 32, 54, 166
Pulaski, 11, 245
Pulaski County, 21, 196, 249
"Pulaski Guards," 14, 19, 197, 249
Punishments, 126, 179–80

Ramseur, S. Dodson, 186 n., 217, 23
Randolph, William F., 206, 218–19

Rapidan River, 127, 141, 210, 213, 215, 217

"Ready Rifles," 250

"Rebel yell," 42

Reynolds, John F., 120 and n.

Richmond, 8, 13, 18, 19, 54, 67, 69, 77, 80, 82 n., 85, 89, 113–14, 119 n., 123–24, 163, 186, 191–92, 227, 229–30, 239, 245

Richmond, Fredericksburg & Potomac R. R., 172, 175

Ricketts, James B., 40–42

Riffeter, William D., 251

Roberts, St. Francis C., 250

Robertson, Henry H., 56, 250

Rockbridge County, 162, 165, 170, 247, 250

"Rockbridge Grays," 249

"Rockbridge Rifles," 166, 250–51

"Rockingham Confederates," 251

Rockingham County, 83, 251

Romney, W. Va., 1862 campaign of, 58–67

Ronald, Charles A., 19 n., 83, 87–88, 94, 109, 127, 131–32, 134–35, 137 n., 158, 168, 249

Rowan, John W., 19 n., 248

Rude's Hill, 82

Sangerville, 250

Sawyers, John S., 161

Sayers, Samuel Rush, 19–20

Scantlon, David, 14

Scotch-Irish, 13, 195–96

Sedgwick, John, 213, 219

Sharpsburg, Md., battle of, 18, 155–61, 167, 197, 201, 204, 243

Shelters, 170, 172, 175–76, 215–16

Shenandoah County, 251

"Shenandoah Riflemen," 251

Shenandoah Valley. *See* Valley of Virginia

Shepherdstown, W. Va., 154, 169, 201, 248

Sheridan, Philip H., 18, 233–35, 239–40

Shields, James, 69–72, 76, 100–101, 103, 106–108

Shriver, Daniel M., 19 n., 250

"Shriver Grays," 250

Sibert, Marion N., 13, 251

Slaughter Mountain, battle of, 22, 127–36, 138, 141, 146, 164, 167, 174, 197, 219, 244

Small, J. N., 203

Smith, James Power, 19

"Smythe Blues," 249

South Carolina Infantry: *6th*—80; *12th*—154 n.

Spengler, Abram, 18, 214 n., 251

Spotsylvania, battle of, 12, 221–27, 243–44

Stafford, Leroy A., 216–17, 219, 231

Starke, William E., 148, 158

Staunton, 5, 11, 16, 19, 33, 74, 84, 85, 86, 88–89, 104–105, 139, 196, 236, 246, 250

"Staunton Rifles," 250

Stephenson's Depot: mentioned, 52, 98; 1863 battle of, 199–200

Steuart, George H., 199–200, 204–205, 213, 222, 225 n., 226

Stickley, E. A., quoted, 149–51, 157

Stonewall Brigade: organization of, 6–9; religion in, 8, 16, 25, 27, 47, 68, 70, 88, 171, 178, 180–81, 186, 190, 194, 212, 229; reputation of, 9; nicknames of regiments in, 11; membership of, 12–22; ceases to exist officially, 12, 226; misconduct in, 26, 46–47, 53–54, 78, 81–82, 88, 126, 156, 172 n.; camp life of, 26–28, 45–46, 57, 59, 63, 67, 105, 116, 170–71, 236; praised, 27, 28 n., 33, 44 and n., 48–50, 52, 60, 66, 77, 136, 147, 152, 174, 178 and n., 189, 191, 200, 236; morale in, 27, 46, 47, 64, 68, 76, 82, 113, 125, 155, 161, 170–71, 174, 177–79, 182–83, 190, 211–12, 232, 235–38; marches of, 28, 35–36, 58–60, 70, 83, 85, 89–90, 101–102, 115; first battle of, 30–32; origin of name "Stonewall," 39 and n.; sickness in, 52–53, 65, 170; rations of, 58–60, 159–60, 177, 198, 215; straggling in, 70, 156, 172 n.; criticized, 134 n., 201, 234; recreation of, 177–78, 216–

Stonewall Brigade: recreation of (*Cont.*) 17; official nickname of, 193; described, 202; pride of, 233, 237; survivors of, 242–47. *See also* desertion, fraternization, shelters
Stonewall Brigade Band, 47, 153–54
Strasburg, 5, 52, 69–70, 91–92, 100–103
Stuart, James E. B., 29, 32, 40, 148, 186–87, 208

Taliaferro, William B., 64–65, 82 n., 106, 112, 132 n., 136, 147, 172, 180
Taylor, George W., 144
Taylor, Richard, 89, 94–96, 105, 108, 110, 112, 114
Terrell, Oliver H. P., 126
Terry, William: mentioned, 17, 19 n., 20, 186 n., 193 n., 219, 223–25, 229, 237, 249; praised, 206, 228, 231; wounded, 214, 225, 233, 238; biographical data on, 227–28; death of, 245
Timberlake, David, 21
Trigg, Robert C., 249
Trimble, Isaac R., 144, 197
Tyler, D. Gardiner, 21
Tyler, Erastus D., 108, 110, 112

U. S. Military Academy, 7, 54, 79, 162, 164–65
Updike, James G., 249

Valley of Virginia: described, 4–5; 1862 campaign of, 12, 84–113, 243; 1864 campaign of, 229–35
Vass, L. C., 194
Virginia Central R. R., 85, 105
Virginia Military Institute, 7, 9, 18 n., 19, 166, 196, 204, 246
"Virginia Riflemen," 250
Virginia Units—ARTILLERY: *Rockbridge Artillery*—11, 13, 14, 17–19, 21, 27, 30–33, 38–39, 45–46, 56, 62–63, 66, 70, 74, 77, 92–101 *passim*, 106–14 *passim*, 120–21, 122 n., 129–30, 135, 137 n., 144–49 *passim*, 155–57, 160–61, 167, 174, 195, 230, 246; *Carpenter's Battery*—13, 71, 95, 99–100, 107, 109–11, 120, 122 n., 129, 144, 146, 155, 157, 250; INFANTRY: *2nd*—11–20 *passim*, 22, 26–28 and n., 30, 32, 33, 38–48 *passim*, 51, 54, 72–73, 76, 83, 92, 94, 97, 100–103, 106–109, 113, 116–19 and n., 121, 127 n., 131–32, 134–35, 142, 148–49, 156 n., 168–69, 173, 175, 186–89, 193 n., 199, 202–207, 213, 218–19, 221–22, 225, 227 n., 234, 240, 247–49; *4th*—11, 14, 16–21 *passim*, 30, 32–33, 38, 41–44, 47, 51–54, 62, 67, 72–73, 76, 83, 85, 87, 92, 94, 107–10, 116–17, 121–22, 124, 131–33, 135, 152, 156 n., 158, 166–76 *passim*, 186–87, 189, 192 n., 193 n., 197, 205, 210, 214, 219–25 *passim*, 227 n., 228–29, 232–33, 240, 247, 249; *5th*—11, 12, 16–21 *passim*, 24–33 *passim*, 38, 42–43, 47–48, 51–53, 61, 71, 74–76, 82–83, 85, 92, 94, 97–100, 107–108, 110–11, 116–19 and n., 121–22, 127 n., 130–32, 135, 138–41, 154, 156 n., 158, 168–69, 173, 175, 186–87, 189, 193 n., 199, 205–10 *passim*, 214, 219–21, 225, 227 n., 232, 237–38, 240, 246–47, 250–51; *27th*—11, 13, 18, 20–21, 27, 30, 33, 38, 41–42, 44, 51, 56, 71–73, 76–77, 82–83, 88, 92–95, 107–108, 110–11, 116–17, 122, 127 n., 131–36, 147, 156 n., 161–69 *passim*, 173, 175, 178, 182, 184 n., 186, 189–94 *passim*, 198, 200, 203, 205–207, 218–21, 225, 227 n., 239–40, 247, 250–51; *33rd*—11, 13, 18–19, 27, 33, 37–43 *passim*, 51, 56, 59, 72–73, 76, 82, 83, 92–95, 98, 108 and n., 109, 112, 116–18, 120–23, 127 n., 128, 131–35, 147, 150–51, 156 n., 168, 173–76, 185–93 *passim*, 201, 205–206, 216, 219, 221–22, 225–26, 227 n., 233, 240–41, 244, 247, 251; *36th*—18; *21st*—71–72, 225 n.; *23rd*—71, 227 n.; *37th*—71–72, 227 n.; *Irish Bttn.*—72; *42nd*—74–75, 227 n.; *10th*—141, 227 n.;

13th—197, 244; 25th—227 n.; 44th
—227 n.; 48th—227 n., 50th—227 n.
Virginia, University of, 17, 139, 165,
228

Walker, James A.: mentioned, 17, 19
and n., 20, 199–200, 203–207, 210,
214–23, 226, 244, 249; biographical
data on, 195–98; praised, 197, 212–
13, 247; criticized, 211; wounded,
225; death of, 245
Washington, D.C.: mentioned, 55,
142–43; 1864 raid on, 230–33
Washington College, 16, 139, 165–66
Waters, James H., 18
Welsh, John: quoted, 177–79, 184 n.,
190, 198, 200; mentioned, 207, 211
"West Augusta Guards," 5, 16–17, 139,
250
"West View Infantry," 250
West Virginia Infantry: 12th—200 n.
Weyer's Cave, 113
Wheeling, W. Va., 250
White, Elizabeth H., 165
White, Hugh A., 47, 67, 68, 149–50
White, James J., 16, 249
White, William S., 8, 48 n.
White Oak Swamp, 120
Wilderness, battle of the, 9, 218–20,
223, 243, 245
Williams, A. Seth, 65, 136 n., 159
Williams, H. J., 19 n., 127 n., 154, 156
n., 158–59, 168, 199, 246–47, 250

Williamsport, Md., 29–30, 100, 154,
230
Wilson, Franklin C., 156 n.
Wilson, Peter E., 240
Winchester: mentioned, 4, 5, 11, 12,
19 n., 21, 28–29, 32–35, 48–57 *passim*, 65–70, 73, 91–93, 99–102, 161,
169, 171, 201, 213, 230, 233, 249,
251; 1862 battle of, 94–98, 140; 1863
battle of, 198–99; 1864 battle of,
233–34
"Winchester Rifles," 249
Winder, Charles S.: biographical data
on, 79–81, 102; praised, 80, 88–89,
136–37; discipline of, 82, 87–88, 122,
126; relations with Jackson, 82 n., 86–
87, 115–16, 126 n.; mentioned, 92–
101 *passim*, 104–108, 110–12, 117–
23 *passim*, 128–29, 138, 165, 228;
disliked, 126; illness of, 127; death of,
129–30, 132 n., 244
Winter quarters, 59, 63, 67, 175–76,
215–16
Wisconsin Infantry: 1st—31; 2nd—146
n.; 6th—146 n.; 7th—146 n.
Wooding, Harry, 146
Woodstock, 234, 251
Wounded, 161, 190
Wright, John, 15
Wright, Samuel, 39
"Wythe Grays," 20, 21, 228, 249
Wytheville, 11, 20, 228, 237, 244–45,
249